Charles Campbell's involvement with the field of corrections began with employment as a probation & parole officer in Virginia more than fifty years ago. He had service at seven different federal prisons and was later appointed Director of Corrections in Alaska. Mr. Campbell has served as a consultant to state and federal courts and to state prison systems. He has done numerous studies and toured places of confinement throughout the United States, England and in the Czech Republic.

The distinguished American criminologist, Esther Heffernan, has been a frequent advisor to state and federal correctional agencies.

The *Defense* shortly before she burned off the Woolrich docks in 1857.

# THE INTOLERABLE HULKS

## BRITISH SHIPBOARD CONFINEMENT 1776-1857

CHARLES CAMPBELL

*The Intolerable Hulks: British Shipboard Confinement 1776–1857*

Third Edition

International Standard Book Number: 1-58736-068-3
Library of Congress Control Number: 2001094482

First and second editions published in 1993 and 1994 by Heritage Books Inc., Bowie, Maryland.
Copyright © 1993, 1994 Charles Campbell

Third edition (2001) published by Fenestra Books™
610 East Delano Street, Suite 104
Tucson, Arizona 85705, U.S.A.
www.fenestrabooks.com

Cover design by Annie Kincheloe

*Simultaneously printed in the United Kingdom and the United States of America*

*To Mason Holley*

# CONTENTS

# LIST OF ILLUSTRATIONS

# FOREWORD

Charles Campbell begins his narrative history of the English prison hulks with the haunting vision provided by Dickens in *Great Expectations,* of Pip's encounter with Magwitch in a graveyard on the edges of a lonely marsh, a fugitive from a "black Hulk lying out a little way from the mud of the shore, like a wicked Noah's ark." Campbell regrets that Dickens did not provide us with a glimpse of life in the "wicked Noah's ark" as he had brought hundreds of thousands of his readers into the grim workhouses and crowded debtors' prisons that were a constant reminder of the realities of life for England's poor and dispossessed. But the hulks, in use as a "temporary expedient" for over eighty years, remained without their spokesperson— as hidden in the history of prisons as they were from their contemporaries.

More than a hundred and fifty years later, Campbell has given us that glimpse. But *The Intolerable Hulks* provides us with much more than a glimpse of the hulks that lay in the harbors of England, Bermuda and Australia, filled with men whose lives, as prisoners, were at the mercy of decisions made by other men. The research is a carefully wrought case study of those decisions and their consequences for thousands of men and women — both the kept and the keepers.

This study is of unique value because Campbell brings to his research the curiosity and care of an historian as he reconstructs the social and political context within which the hulks played their role in England's massive system of prisoner transportation, and at the same time, demonstrates a special understanding of the events he chronicles, which comes from his own life-long involvement with prisons, prisoners, prison administrators and politicians.

In a sense, what Campbell has provided is the dual vision of a man who has, in his own life, experienced the realities that the documents reveal of the development and daily life of the hulks. As he examines the reports of prison inspectors in response to Parliamentary inquiries into conditions of the hulks, he can, with some irony, as a former federal prison warden, comment on the ways in which an administrator will tidy up conditions before the arrival of the investigating official. Having served more than once as a court-appointed overseer of prisons, he can recount with enormous authority the vicissitudes of an outsider attempting change in an entrenched system. In his chapter on the fiasco that was the Millbank Penitentiary experiment, Campbell describes the devastating consequences when "experts" and "benevolent" reformers, armed with the certitudes of science, used stone, as well as codes of punishment and discipline, to construct an establishment where both bodies and minds were destroyed. Reflectively, he notes that living with the unintended consequences of good plans gone awry did not cease with the coming of the twentieth century.

In his exploration of the fate of the boys committed to the hulks, one clearly sees that his early experiences in the 1950s as a caseworker at the Natural Bridge Camp and the old National Training School for Boys have made him particularly sensitive to the vulnerable position of young boys in prison.

Throughout the book Campbell describes the policies and financial considerations that permitted the unsupervised crowding of prisoners together below decks at night after their labors ashore throughout the day, leaving the weak and inexperienced at the mercy of the predatory. His observations reflect his years of experience in prisoner classification and inmate management, dealing personally with the complex relationships that arise among the diverse persons who must be worked with in prison. His careful examination of issues of health, and the "invalid" hulks, should be viewed in the context of his years as associate director of a prison medical facility.

As his title, *The Intolerable Hulks,* clearly reveals, there is no question about Campbell's condemnation of the conditions on the hulks and of the men who were responsible. But his condemnation is tempered by a sympathy for administrators who were so often caught in circumstances over which they had no control. His sympathy flows easily from his experiences as head of a state prison system, where he faced the realities of tight budgets, personnel and policies inherited from previous administrations, and a legislature and general public disinterested in, even hostile to, changes that might entail the "coddling" of criminals. The keystone of the eighteenth century British system — the principal of *less-eligibility* — that the misery of those in prison should always be greater than that of the working poor, lest the poor be tempted to "evil ways," has not lost its adherents in the present day.

As one reads these pages, it is not only late eighteenth and early nineteenth-century penal history that comes alive, but also the haunting realization that the past is the present. Precisely the same short-sighted responses to political decisions motivated by fiscal exigencies that brought the prison hulks into being continue today. Consider the significance of the hulks having been recently reincarnated in the United States. New York City officials, facing ever-increasing numbers of prisoners "captured" in the war on drugs, purchased and fitted out two deactivated troop barges used in the Falklands war, as twentieth-century American counterparts of England's hulks. They have been replaced now with a more impressive vessel, a floating, and entirely seaworthy state-of-the-art prison, built at a Louisiana shipyard and tied up at an East Bronx pier.

Foucault, in his insightful study of the development of the "carceral system" in France, remarks that he is not writing a history of the past "in terms of the present," but "writing the history of the present." Campbell's work reveals how familiar the past becomes, because we are living it in the present.[†]

Esther Heffernan
Edgewood College
Madison, Wisconsin

---

[†] Foucault, Michel (1979) *Discipline and Punish: The Birth of the Prison.* New York: Vintage.

# AUTHOR'S NOTE

For their help and cooperation, and for their early confidence in this book, I must express my thanks to Laird Towle, Karen Akermann and others at Heritage Books, Inc. of Bowie, Maryland, original publishers of The Intolerable Hulks.

During the writing and preparation of the manuscript Paula Sampson-Mckenzie, Ed Schoenfeld, Kristi Allen and, most particularly, Betsy Longenbaugh, gave me invaluable help. I owe them my thanks. I am indebted as well to John Longenbaugh, Esther Heffernan and to my late distinguished friend, Paul Keve, each of whom read the original manuscript and offered many valuable suggestions. My thanks also to historian Dan Byrnes of Tamworth, New South Wales, who provided a number of useful insights from an Australian perspective. Annie Kincheloe designed the cover for the first and subsequent editions of this book, and used her remarkable computer-graphics skills to provide other significant help with this and earlier editions.

Julian Watson, of the Borough of Greenwich library system, is a local historian who has extensive knowledge of the history of the Thames River basin and of sources of information for that history. There is no way I could overstate the value of the help he gave to me during my research for the first edition. He continued to provide encouragement and invaluable help during preparation of an edition for the English market.

Ellen Campbell, to whom I have been married for fifty-three years, read, or had read to her, the entirety of the original manuscript—but in various bits and portions imposed on her by me all during the time of its writing. Her criticism was invariably insightful, sometimes unmerciful, but always offered with a lot of love. I could not have done this book, or very much of anything else, without her.

Charles Campbell
Juneau, Alaska
August 2001

# INTRODUCTION

For his opening scene in *Great Expectations,* Dickens created a lonely little churchyard on the edge of a great, ghostly marsh. Readers of Dickens will recall young Pip's harrowing encounter there with an escaped convict. It was "on a memorable raw afternoon toward evening." The escapee, "startled up from among the graves . . . was a fearful man, all in coarse grey, with a great iron on his leg." He snarled at Pip, "Keep still you little devil or I'll cut your throat." But while successfully terrorizing the child Pip into doing his bidding, it was the convict, Magwitch, who was most beset by terror, as well as an obsession for vengeance toward another escapee who was skulking on the marshes that night.

After capture of the two convicts, Dickens has young Pip see by the light of the search party's torches "the black Hulk lying out a little way from the mud of the shore, like a wicked Noah's ark, cribbed and barred and moored by massive rusty chains, the prison ship seemed to [Pip's] young eyes to be ironed like the prisoners." Regrettably, we are denied a Dickensian description of conditions aboard the hulk from which Magwitch and his hated cohort escaped, nor is the ship identified. According to Dickens' biographers, the little churchyard in this unforgettable scene was inspired by the churchyard at Cooling, a remote Kentish hamlet that lies between the Medway and the Thames, a region known since antiquity as the Hundred of Hoo. Prison hulks were never stationed in that vicinity, however, and Cooling is not close to waters that would have provided a suitable hulk anchorage. Except for his wanting Pip's village to be "as the river wound, twenty miles of the sea," it would have well suited the novelist's purposes to situate the churchyard on the northern fringe of the Essex marshes that lay along the Thames, across from the town of Woolwich, a place where there were hulks as well as desolate marshlands.

If Pip was ten at the time of his encounter with the convict, a reasonable conjecture is that the year was 1841, a time when more than three thousand civilian prisoners were confined aboard nine hulks anchored in English waters, and three others in Bermuda. The English hulk stations were at Portsmouth, Deptford and off the Royal Arsenal docks at Woolwich.

Magwitch and the other convict would have escaped from the *Warrior* or the dilapidated old *Justitia,* unofficial flagship of the hulk fleet. Normally both ships would have been anchored off the south shore but either might have been towed by longboats to the Essex side, to be closer to a dredging task, or perhaps for reasons of sanitation. Or the hulk might have been stationed temporarily on the north side of the Thames because of unrest and escape plotting among the convicts. Escapes to the more populous Woolwich waterfront were more common than to the north shore. There was fear of the Essex marshes, long thought to be the source of pestilence and mysterious death.

In 1775 the War of American Independence ended Great Britain's century-and-a-half-old practice of regularly transporting criminal offenders to the North American colonies. William Eden, the Home Office secretary to whose lot it fell to deal with the resulting crisis, estimated that alternative accommodations would be needed each year for about a thousand convicts, far more than could be crammed into the already overcrowded gaols and bridewells of England. A decision was taken to retain in English waters certain of the ships engaged in the convict transportation, and to utilize them there as places of confinement. The arrangement was viewed as a temporary expedient, and thus it was first authorized by Parliament for only two years. It was an arrangement that had no defenders. Conservatives condemned it because of the likelihood of its exacerbating the criminality of offenders. Liberals agreed and furthermore deplored its inhumanity. But in spite of these constantly renewed expressions of chagrin from all quarters, it was an arrangement that endured for eighty years.

The Essex marshes have long since been enveloped by the metropolis, but before this century they lay desolate and foreboding along the north shore of the Thames. The Woolwich Warren was a labyrinth of workshops, warehouses, barracks, foundries, firing ranges and mountainous stacks of oak, teak and pine, spread along the Woolwich shore across the river from the marshes. A few miles upstream lay the Tower Hamlets, and the worst of London's 18th and 19th century slums. The Warren had been the site of naval ship building since about 1500. The Royal Arsenal was not officially established there until 1805, but the Warren had been the home of a bustling military arms works for more than a century before that time. An adequate river harbor was essential to the projects that were carried forward on Woolwich Warren.

In about 1775 it became apparent that major dredging needed to be done in order to overcome a drift of the channel toward the center of the river. Labor for this project, as well as for the development of the arsenal and arsenal docks, was provided by convicts housed aboard the *Censor* and the *Justitia* (an earlier *Justitia* than the ship we have assigned to Dickens' story.) These were the first of the English prison hulks, discounting several months confinement of convicts aboard two naval vessels in 1775 and brief initial use of the merchantman, *Tayloe*.

During the early decades of the hulk establishment, England was engaged in the Napoleonic conflicts, as well as protracted military action in North America. Indefinite custody was needed for several thousand prisoners-of-war. For this purpose, perhaps forty ships of the British Navy were converted for use as prison hulks. One was established at Gibraltar, others at Bermuda, at Antiqua, and off Brooklyn in Wallabout Bay. In view of the well-documented difficulties associated with shipboard confinement under the most favorable of circumstances, together with the British Navy's then-draconian approach to shipboard discipline, credence can be given to reports describing conditions of confinement aboard the prisoner-of-war hulks as worse than appalling.

Conditions aboard the civilian hulks, some of them no more than a half-day's carriage ride from Parliamentary scrutiny, were exceedingly bad, but perhaps less egregious than those that prevailed on the Navy's prison ships. The record concerning the civilian hulks, in fact, might not be quite the chronicle of unrelieved horror as has come to be assumed. The pages that follow will shed some light on this proposition.

No attempt will be made here to deal with the Navy's prisoner-of-war hulks. They deserve a separate examination. The author's interest is in the background of English and American criminal justice practices. This book will limit itself to a recounting of Great Britain's experience with the use of the hulks for civilian prisoners, from the time of their establishment until the *Defense* hulk burned off Woolwich Warren in 1857, bringing this unhappy epoch to a close.

# I

# HOW THE NEED AROSE

Before the beginning of the 18th century, the stability of English society had become dependent on transportation of its excess population to the new world. The practice of transporting prisoners dated from the reign of James I. For most of two centuries, hundreds of destitute British subjects volunteered each year for terms of indenture in exchange for passage to America; these in addition to the transported convicts.[1]

By the end of the 17th century, the roads and wooded tracks that traversed the English countryside—for centuries the domain of merchants, traveling gentry and contingents of men-at-arms—were becoming inhabited by forlorn bands of displaced peasants. They were the victims of a change that was occurring in Britain from an agricultural to a mercantile economy. Countless poor people were finding themselves no longer needed for the traditional occupations of the manor. Over the years they had become accustomed to bearing an assigned burden of deprivation and a resulting predictable measure of misery, but now the lot of England's poor had become one of unstable destitution.

The flow was toward the cities, most especially London. Thieves' rookeries burst their seams into slums, which threatened to envelop the metropolis with debauchery and crime. Weekly hangings in London and similar grisly celebrations held elsewhere around England were hardly enough. The appalling death among prisoners from disease at Newgate, Marshalsea, Fleet and gaols throughout provincial England, provided a morbid kind of saving grace.

During the 18th century, the death penalty was prescribed for about 300 criminal offenses, ranging from murder to stealing anything valued at more than a shilling. Hangings were invariably well-attended public occasions, offering exhilarating diversion, primarily for that class of citizens from which most of the victims of the noose were drawn. Most London hangings were held at the place then called Tyburn, at the angle of Edgeware Road and Oxford Street (then Tyburn Road). Newgate Prison was almost two miles distant, at the site of present-day Old Bailey. The condemned was subject to an unseemly trek in an open cart through crowds of raucous spectators. If his crime had been especially odious, he might have been tied to the back railing of the cart, thus required to walk behind it, receiving lashes along the way. The crowd's behavior toward him depended on his status and reputation. If a daring highwayman or a clever swindler, known for victimizing gentry or rich merchants, he would be cheered and comforted with such exhortations as "Die game, Jack." But if a fallen foppish gentleman or a child molester, he would more likely be jeered and pelted with garbage.

For centuries, it hardly occurred to most Britons that public execution of criminals was other than necessary for the good order of society. Upper-class gentlemen, sometimes with their ladies, joined the boorish rabble in witnessing public hangings. Samuel Johnson approved the practice but had no stomach for viewing it. Boswell, on the other hand, seemed to have trained himself to enjoy the proceedings.[2]

While not at first questioning the necessity of hangings, John Howard and other reformers attacked the repugnant processions from Newgate to Tyburn as serving no purpose other than to titillate the bloodthirstiness of the crowds lining the roadway. In 1783 reformers succeeded in having the place of hangings in London changed to a location just outside the front gate of Newgate Prison.[3] Another eighty years passed before belief in the efficacy of public executions was sufficiently discredited to allow relocation of the gallows to a place of relative privacy inside the prison.[4] Those most adamantly opposed to this change were not conscientious adherents to the principle of deterrence, but denizens of the London slums who not only lost a cherished periodic diversion, but also were deprived of the means to fulfill their sober responsibility to see that the hangings were "done proper."

A blessed mitigation in severity of English criminal justice had been practiced from ancient times. It was the tradition that allowed accused criminals to "call for the book." When done, the accused was required only to read a passage from the Bible in order to escape hanging. The presumption was that the accused, if literate, was clergy and therefore not subject to punishment by civil authorities. In 1705 Parliament eliminated the requirement that the accused actually read from the scriptures. If the accused called for the book, he was assumed to be clergy (despite all evidence to the contrary) and excused after branding on the thumb to ensure that the clergy privilege would not be invoked again. Twenty-five offenses, however, were declared to be "non-clergyable." Regardless of station or declarations as to clergy, persons convicted of any of these crimes were hanged, unless reprieved by the Crown. It seems, therefore, that for a brief era early in the 18th century, there was a flicker of humanitarianism in British criminal justice. It did not long survive. Parliament tumbled over itself in adding offenses to the list of those that were "non-clergyable." Before the end of the century, the list of such offenses approached 200 in number.[5] Dozens of unfortunates at a time were carted off to Tyburn on Saturday mornings. The gibbeted remains of publicly slain law violators, some of them children, were displayed along the roads of England in grisly profusion.

This unhappy time corresponded with a profound lapse in moral standards throughout the country. There were contemptuous memories of the stringent pieties of Cromwell's rule. The Church was weakened to the point of ineptitude. Land-owning gentry began to amass great fortunes producing grain for distilling gin. Cheap gin replaced weak beer as the favored drink among London slum dwellers of all ages and poor people throughout England.[6] Crime and profligacy flourished as did a resurrection of savagery in English justice practices.

It can hardly be said that all vestiges of decency were obliterated. James Oglethorpe was one of those whose moral and religious convictions pushed against the tide. His limited, but not insignificant, prison reform efforts came during the worst of these times. Oglethorpe and John Wesley were kindred spirits, despite stresses in their relationship. At Oglethorpe's behest, John Wesley went on a mission in 1736 to the colony in Georgia that had been founded only three years earlier by Oglethorpe with a complement of salvaged debtors from the gaol in Fleet Street, London. Concurrently, work among prisoners became an important missionary activity with George Whitfield, Charles Wesley and others of the Wesley group at Oxford. John Wesley's sojourn in Georgia was miserable and unproductive except in molding his character. The results of his efforts during the decades that followed were profound. The Wesleyan revival found fertile ground throughout England. The all-but-comatose Church of England condemned the ardor of Wesley and his early Methodists, but in arousing itself to do so, somehow strengthened its own piety and social conscience.[7]

It was the stern, pious congregationalist High Sheriff of Bedfordshire, John Howard, who was most effective in exposing the wretchedness of British prisons, and who spent his life and fortune trying to improve conditions for people in confinement throughout the British Isles and Europe. Howard began his prison reform efforts in 1773, only two years before the transportation of convicts to America was ended by the outbreak of hostilities between the Colonies and Great Britain. The role he had in the development of the hulk establishment contains an interesting irony that will be examined in a later chapter.

Meanwhile, leaders in the Colonies are hardly to be blamed for their happiness over the termination of transportation of British convicts to their shores. Early in the 18th century, both Maryland and Virginia passed ordinances against the importation of convicted criminals. For a time, such laws had some force. England's habeas corpus laws made exile illegal. Therefore, transportation was accomplished by pardoning convicts on condition of transportation and indenture. The requirement that all pardons be granted by the Crown was gotten around by bureaucratic resourcefulness. The colonial ordinances interfered with this device, but only until 1717, when Parliament passed a law authorizing the sentencing of convicted law violators to transportation and indentured servitude for terms of seven years, fourteen years, or for life. This act of Parliament swept aside the colonial statutes and thus the English courts were able to continue unabated their sentencing of hundreds of convicts each year to terms of transportation in Maryland and Virginia.[8]

In addition to giving the courts an alternative to hanging persons convicted of "nonclergyable" offenses, the 1717 legislation made transportation a legal penalty for many minor offenses. The effect was that minor offenses, while remaining "clergyable" with respect to hanging, became "nonclergyable" with respect to transportation. And thus, in addition to thousands of more serious offenders, innumerable petty violators were sent to the Colonies rather than being let off with a flogging or a day or two in the pillory.

There were no prison settlements in the North American Colonies such as those established after 1788 in Australia. Transportees were released after dockside auctions to the dubious custody of the highest bidding plantation proprietors. And when it came to be seen that innumerable pickpockets, prostitutes, thieves and assorted brigands from all over England were proliferating in the lanes and villages of the Tidewater and Piedmont counties of Maryland and Virginia, spilling over into Delaware and the Carolinas, the leaders of the Colonies were not pleased. As early as 1751 a caustic letter attributed to Benjamin Franklin, appeared in the *Pennsylvania Gazette*, suggesting that the Colonies should repay the kindness of Mother England by exporting rattlesnakes to the British Isles, and perhaps releasing them in St. James Park.[9] And in May of 1751 the *Virginia Gazette* lamented:

When we see our Papers fill'd continually with accounts of the most audacious Robberies, the most Cruel Murders, and infinite other Villainies perpetrated by Convicts transported from Europe, what a melancholy, what terrible Reflections it must occasion! What will become of our Posterity? Those are some of thy favors, Britain. Thou art called our Mother Country; but what good mother ever sent Thieves and Villains to accompany her children; to corrupt some with their infectious Vices and murder the rest? . . . In what can Britain show a more Sovereign contempt for us than by emptying their Jails into our Settlements; unless they will likewise empty their Jackes [chamberpots] on our tables![10]

Some of the chroniclers of the first families of Virginia and Maryland have down-played the significance of convict transportation during the colonial era by all but ignoring it. Walter Blumenthal scolds those who may have done so by asking:

Why should we blink at the fact that old England shunted over convicts and the gaol deportees, aggregating thousands and tens of thousands during the last century and a half . . . since as many were petty malefactors as were confirmed criminals and since many of both sexes suffered dragnet deportation for vagrancy, fraud, thievery, counterfeiting and other malefaction, why not state that the odium was due more to the wretched social conditions than to innate depravity? Rather than hush up these colonial origins of a scorned segment of those who peopled the middle seaboard—as is commonly done by regional historians who would paint the lily of local pride— were it not better to stress that most of those "jailbirds" in a new environment stood redeemed from their turpitude and, if not they, then their children?[11]

Beyond question, many of the convicts off loaded from British prisoner ships at Norfolk, Alexandria and Annapolis, were petty offenders, and among them there are sure to have been many God-fearing unfortunates who had committed crimes of desperate necessity. And yet, if the influence of environment is of any importance in the development of human character, we can be certain that the thousands of convicts transported to America before the traffic was terminated were not, on the whole, an admirable group (despite having obviously produced admirable progeny.)

Events at Concord and Bunker Hill in the late spring of 1775 had not the slightest effect on the inclination of England's criminal courts to sentence offenders to terms of transportation, never for less than seven years. The already overcrowded gaols of England were becoming jammed full. Filth, sickness, corruption, profligate exploitation of prisoners by other prisoners, the worst of all that John Howard was only beginning to call to the attention of the conscience of England, were flourishing. A few ships embarked for the West Indies and one or two for Nova Scotia, but the sudden loss of Maryland and Virginia as the main repositories for that non-absorbable surplus of undesirable people perpetually being produced by economic and social conditions in England, presented his Majesty's government with a problem for which no precedent was to be found.

When the American War of Independence broke out, the Earl of Suffolk was Minister of the Northern Department. He assigned to his distinguished Undersecretary, William Eden, the task of dealing with the crisis of prison overpopulation, which immediately loomed.

Eden was the brilliant author of *Principles of Penal Law*, having been influenced earlier by the writings of Cesare Beccaria, and by his study of the law under Blackstone.[12] He has been ridiculed for having suggested that some English criminals might be disposed of by exchanging them for worthy Christians held by the Barbary Pirates.[13] Such a preposterous notion was hardly characteristic of Eden. Apparently it was offhandedly put forward with a number of other ideas from other quarters, most of them similarly impractical, when the government was grappling with a precipitous rise in the prison population.

Had Eden not pressed hulks into emergency service, it is likely that prison conditions all over England would have deteriorated to a point worse than those that were soon enough to become prevalent. He did so by prevailing upon the Admiralty to take a hundred convicts aboard two ailing but commodious warships berthed at the Woolwich dock. This was a thumb-in-the-dike arrangement that would suffice, it was hoped, until a longer term "temporary expedient" could be worked out.[14]

By midwinter it was becoming apparent that confinement of prisoners aboard ship would entail many difficulties. Still, Eden saw no alternative to pressing ahead. He drafted two bills for introduction in the House of Commons. One of them was needed to regularize the already commenced practice of shipboard confinement in English waters, and authorize use of their labor on public works projects. Authority was sought to use the hulks as prisons for two years only. The temporary nature of the proposal was emphasized. The second bill called for the erection of a penitentiary to serve each of the criminal court jurisdictions in England.

Despite the obvious seriousness of the pending prison overpopulation crisis, passage of the hulk bill was by no means a certainty. George Johnstone, who had been a governor of West Florida for a time, argued against the bill, pointing out that the West Indies were still available as a place of destination for transported convicts.[15] There were arguments against Johnstone's idea based on the patent unfairness of rewarding those Colonies who had remained loyal to the Crown, by flooding them with convicts.[16] But the notion may have been finally put to rest by economic considerations. Contractors had been transporting convicts to Virginia and Maryland without cost to the Government, or with no more than a five-pounds-per-convict surcharge. Their profits came from the sale of the indentured services of the convicts to plantation proprietors. There was no significant demand for convict labor in Canada or Florida; there was an increasingly abundant source of slave labor in the West Indies. Settlement of New South Wales was ten years off, with no prospect of there ever being cheap transportation of convicts to that distant land.

In any case, there were objections to the hulk bill on various grounds. Throughout the winter of 1776-1777, citizens who lived near the shore of the Thames in Woolwich had complained about the noise, the untidiness and the lack of security of the Navy ships used then for confinement. There was indeed much public interest in the matter. Spring would bring boat tours on the Thames, enabling curiosity seekers to view the floating gaols close at hand.[17] We can be certain that neither the complaints of the Woolwich citizens, nor the severe privations suffered by the convicts, seen or imagined by gaping spectators that first winter, escaped the attention of either conservative or liberal opponents of the hulk bill in the House of Commons. There being nothing auspicious about the beginning of the scheme, interest in other alternatives remained alive. Stressing the urgency of the problem and the temporary nature of his proposed solution, Eden argued, "The fact is that our prisons are full and we have no way at present to dispose of the convicts but that what would be execrably bad; for all the proposals of Africa—desert islands—mines etc., mean nothing more than a more lingering method of inflicting capital punishment."[18]

Such advocates as Edmond Burke and Charles Bunbury overcame their misgivings and came forcefully to Eden's side. The hulk bill (16 Geo.III cap 43) was approved in May of 1776.

Parliament delayed for another three years before passing the penitentiary bill. It called for construction of separate penitentiaries for men and women in each of the home counties, and for implementation of a reformed and standardized approach to imprisonment. The assumption was that, after the effect of enlightenment was demonstrated in these seven jurisdictions, all of England would be moved toward prison reform. The bill, incidentally, included authorization for retention of the hulks for another five years.[19]

The provisions of this legislation were hammered out over many weeks and pushed through Parliament by men who, for the most part, were brilliant, enlightened and compassionate. What was the result? Implementation of the penitentiary construction provisions of the legislation was reduced and delayed. And then the most cherished notion of the reformers, penitential solitary confinement, proved to be hardly more than a sanitized form of inhumanity. The hulks were retained for eighty years.

Parliament delegated to the Justices of the Peace of Middlesex responsibility for negotiating an arrangement for provision and management of the hulk establishment at Woolwich. An inevitability of events led to the award of the contract to convict transporter, Duncan Campbell. Campbell had influential friends in the House of Commons who were aware of the reverses he was suffering due to the cessation of convict transportation to the North American Colonies. Indeed, after the death of his predecessor and former partner, John Stewart, in 1772, the Government had been willing to continue its contract with Campbell only on the condition he forego the five-pound-per-prisoner subsidy he and Stewart had previously enjoyed. Dockside sales of the convicts' services in Maryland and Virginia would have sufficed for good profits had it not been for a disastrous drop in the price of tobacco in England, causing Campbell significant losses on the cargo he had previously so profitably loaded on his ships for return voyages.[20]

Campbell was the last in a succession of London businessmen who, during the previous sixty years, had held contracts for transporting convicts to America, primarily from London and the home counties. The first of them was the somewhat disreputable Jonathan Forward. The last before Campbell was John Stewart, who acquired the contract in 1763 and took Campbell into partnership with him five years later. Not without some justification, Stewart considered himself several cuts above his predecessors so far as integrity and reliability were concerned, and certainly superior to the agents of the Government with whom he had to deal. He complained, in fact, that those involved in prisoner transportation were "the lowest and most corruptible class of public officers."[21]

To go along with his self-esteem, John Stewart enjoyed advantages during the nine years of his involvement with prisoner transportation certain to have given him handsome profits -- eight to twenty-five pounds per prisoner from the American plantation proprietors, the questionable five-pounds-per-prisoner subsidy from the Government, and a favorable tobacco market. Campbell had shared in this largesse of circumstances until Stewart's death in 1772. Thereafter, the days of highest profits did not return. While hardly destitute, Campbell was able to argue with some effect his hard luck in service of a needed cause, that of taking the last dozen or so shiploads of convicts to America. Given all of these circumstances, there was no serious competitor for the contract to supply and manage the hulks.[22]

Fittingly, the *Justitia*, flagship of the Stewart-Campbell fleet of convict transporters, became the first of the hulks under contract to the British government. In testimony before a committee of the House of Commons, Campbell referred to her as "an old Indiaman" of "about 260 tons."[23] According to the Public Record Office, however, she was registered in 1764 in London as a French prize of 305 tons.[24]

She sailed to America in 1765 with her first cargo of prisoners. Her master on that voyage, and on five subsequent voyages, was Colin Somerville. Under the command of Neil Gillis, she made her last voyage to America in 1772, four years before becoming a prison hulk.[25] The records give no account of voyages she may have made during the intervening four years. Perhaps she went to the breaking yard, and perhaps Campbell did after all acquire an "old Indiaman" for service as the first hulk. It is more likely he was simply not as familiar as he should have been with this particular piece of his capital equipment. It most probably had been acquired by his former partner, John Stewart. The term Indiaman was frequently used to describe ships built on order of, and suitable to, the demanding navigational needs of the East India Company. Campbell's contract called for provision of a 240-ton ship. His testimony before the committee that the *Justitia* was a ship of "about 260 tons" suggests, that while reasonably confident she exceeded the required weight, he simply did not know what her registered tonnage was. It is more than likely that fourteen trans-Atlantic crossings in seven years, by this aged vessel, added to her previous service with the French, which may have included voyages around the Horn of Africa, had by 1772 weakened the joints and planking of *Justitia's* hull to the point of questionable seaworthiness. Campbell had less arduous uses to which she may have been put after 1772 and until

1776 when she was seen to be so splendidly suitable for the confinement of convicts on the River Thames.

There were, in any event, not fewer than three *Justitias*. The last of them, moved over to Woolwich from Chatham in 1829, was perhaps the largest and most poorly supervised, and thus the most despicable of the hulks. Five hundred convicts were housed below decks with but a single warder on board, and he, judiciously, standing his watch topside. The least imagination as to the details of that scene is discomforting.[26]

The first *Justitia* never became a prison hulk, but as a convict transporter, contributed appropriately to the woeful heritage of hulks. She made her only two convict crossings before the middle of the 18th century. Her master during a 1753 voyage was the infamous Barnet Bond, who presided during that crossing over some of the most heartless atrocities committed against prisoners during the whole melancholy history of convict transportation.

Eden, Bunbury, Burke and others in the British criminal justice establishment were altogether sincere in their belief that the hulk arrangement would be needed only as a "temporary expedient." Although the outcome of the revolt in the North American Colonies could not be known, it was assumed that when the fighting stopped, transportation of convicts to Virginia and Maryland would be resumed. It was recognized that leading public opinion in America was opposed to an uncontrolled influx of convicts from Great Britain. But for those to whom commercial and agricultural development was important, the availability of convict labor was an advantage. Whatever outcome the fighting might produce, other than the expected capitulation of the colonial rebels, peace terms would surely be reached that would include an accommodation on the transportation question. Instead, it was the British who capitulated. The peace treaty of 1783 contained no provision for convict transportation, but there was no prohibition either, and so England, with gaols and hulks now breaking their seams with prisoners, would try again.

The *Swift*, under the command of Captain Pamp, sailed from London in August of 1783 with 143 convicts on board. Nova Scotia was the intended destination. Not far out from port the convicts repaid the Captain for certain kindnesses by taking control of his ship. Before she was recaptured, forty-eight of the convicts had escaped in longboats to the south shore of England, frightening the country people thereabout, who failed to realize that most of these fellows would want nothing more than a piece of bread, a dram of rum and directions to London Road. In October, the *Swift* tried again, this time sailing for Baltimore, hoping for a friendly reception. Records indicating that eighty-seven convicts were disembarked in Maryland contain discrepancies. In any case, the outcome of this voyage is sure to have provided encouragement to those who hoped for a resumption of regular convict transportation.

The next effort, however, was enough of a fiasco to convince Great Britain that the solution to her problem of excess numbers of convicted criminals did not lie in America. Through the enterprise of one George More, another ship, the *Mercury*, was readied for a voyage to Savannah in March of the following year. One-hundred-eighty convicts were on board when she embarked. Once again the convicts were able to take the ship. More than a hundred of them escaped before a storm drove the *Mercury* into port at Torbay. Most were recaptured; the ship was repaired and dispatched toward America once more, this time with orders for Baltimore. George More had become more sanguine about prospects for a reception there, perhaps because of the experience of the *Swift* during the previous autumn. The record is confused as to whether she ever reached her first intended destination. In any event, the convicts were not allowed ashore in Maryland. The *Mercury*, now at loose ends, sailed for Honduras. There, for the third time in less than a year, the convicts took charge of things, this time escaping to uncertain fates on the Central American mainland.[27]

In 1788 the Continental Congress finally decided on the wisdom of passing an unappealable resolution prohibiting importation of convicts from Europe. It was with a certain sadness that the British criminal justice establishment accepted the demise of the seemingly splendid arrangement that, for 150 years, had allowed regular shipments of English criminals to North America. The abortive voyage of the *Mercury* was England's last effort.

## II

# MR. HOWARD'S SCRUTINY

Humanitarianism was hardly a prominent feature of 18th century England. For that matter, not much grief was displayed over the plight of unfortunates during most of the 19th century. That John Howard was invited periodically to expound his views on the need for improving conditions of confinement for English prisoners, before committees of both houses of Parliament, attests more to certain of his remarkable personal traits than to any great measure of compassion abounding in that body or in that society.[1]

Most of the meager sentiment for prison reform that arose during the 17th century was a result of mounting chagrin over the debauchery and filth that so characterized Newgate Prison and, to a similar extent, other gaols throughout England. To be sure, there was concern about the corruption of children and others, such as debtors, who were viewed as not so remote from virtue as the typical gaol occupant was presumed to be. There was some concern, moreover, about the physical suffering of prisoners.

John Howard was unique. From early life he was possessed of restless curiosity as to why conditions of life for common people couldn't be made less miserable, and an unwillingness to accept illogic on the grounds of its having been traditionally practiced. Howard was born sometime around 1726 of well-to-do middle-class parents. Though persistently in poor health, he traveled widely in Europe as a young man, to some extent overcoming his lack of a first-class education. In February 1773, John Howard was appointed High Sheriff of Bedfordshire. The expectation of him in that honored position was that he arrange appropriate pomp for commencement of the Assizes term in his jurisdiction, participating periodically in this and other ceremonials, while trusting the day-to-day administration of his office to the undersheriff. Instead, Howard initiated his duties with a close inspection of the Bedfordshire gaol. To say the least, he was dissatisfied. Among the many outrages he observed was the practice of requiring prisoners, acquitted of guilt, to pay certain fees to the gaoler before they

The hulk *Tayloe* anchored off Woolwich,
where prisoners are working on shore, 1777

Prison ship at Deptford, about 1826

could be released. The result was that innocent people sometimes remained in confinement indefinitely.

Howard's first travels were to neighboring county gaols in search of precedents for reform. Before his death of a fever in Russia in January 1790, he had traveled perhaps 50,000 miles across Great Britain and Europe; he had visited virtually every gaol in the British Isles, the major ones not less than five times. He had touched the conscience of Parliament and had produced a watershed body of writings on the need for reforms in gaols, prisons and houses of public relief. He was devout; he was indefatigable, and he was remarkably reasonable, while passionate in his desire to bring about reforms. But he did not always keep matters in good perspective, and he was subject to being turned aside by those who knew how to play on his prejudices.

Between 1776 and 1788, Howard visited the hulks at Woolwich at least seven times. He made several trips to those at Plymouth and Portsmouth during the same period. At times he appears to have been astonishingly tolerant with respect to the hulks. In any case, it was his expression of concern that caused the formation of a special committee of the House of Commons, chaired by Sir Charles Bunbury, to inquire into the management of hulks within a year after their first use. The Bunbury Committee gave general oversight to the hulk establishment for several years. The first inquiry was thorough. Thereafter, the attention given was perfunctory. It is probable that Sir Charles and his colleagues all had concerns of higher priority during these days of warfare and economic crises. A close look at the record of John Howard's visits and observations suggests that pragmatism governed his forbearance. Rather than launch an all-out assault on the hulk system, he chose to chide and commend where appropriate, hoping that the best of a bad situation could be achieved in the use of the hulks until a better long-term alternative became available. Howard joined Bentham, Blackstone, Eden and others in urging construction of penitentiary houses where all of England's convicted felons could be humanely confined, but he was a realist, seeing no alternative to the use of the hulks until that solution could be reached.

As a young man, Howard, with his fellow passengers on an English vessel, was taken prisoner by a French privateer, and thus he experienced the privations of imprisonment for a number of months. Further, before his first visit to the hulks at Woolwich, he had spent three years visiting virtually every gaol in the realm and many places of confinement on the Continent. He therefore is sure to have judged conditions of confinement aboard the hulks from a different perspective than that possessed by most critics. He had by no means become calloused, however, and was anything but an easy guest. The House of Commons journal account of Howard's appearance before the Bunbury Committee in 1778 provides insight into his manner of approach.

On the occasion of his first visit to the hulks, a Sunday in October 1776, all convicts of the *Justitia* were mustered on deck for his inspection. "he took two walks round them and looked in the faces of every individual person, and saw by their sickly looks, that some mismanagement was among them." John Howard knew several of the prisoners, having previously encountered them during gaol inspections. One whom he knew was obviously ill. Reporting on Howard's testimony before the Committee, the House of Commons journal continues:

> ...he touched his pulse and asked how he did? He said he was ready to sink into the earth—that the conductor swore an oath, and said that the convict had the venereal disease—the conductor was an inspector of convicts, one of the head officers as the witness supposes. The witness then said, 'some care ought to be taken of this man.' The witness then asked the man if he had it? And he said no; the witness then turned to the conductor and the conductor said nothing; the witness found afterward by inquiry that no care had been taken of this man; the witness then asked the conductor how he could tell such a falsity? And he said nothing.

With respect to the food served to the convicts, Howard testified that he asked the captain for a sample of the bread, that he "was brought down some good, wholesome brown biscuit." He was soon to learn, however, that much of the bread being served the convicts was mostly crumbs and was "moldy and green on both sides." Howard challenged the captain on this score and was not especially reassured when told that "they would soon be out of the moldy batch."[2]

Among other causes for concern Howard found during his October 1776 visit to the Woolwich hulks, was the failure of the captains to have "divine services" regularly conducted. It is conceivable, if not probable, that had they taken pains to avoid this deficiency, and had they greeted Howard on board with evidence of an emphasis on religion, avoiding as best they could an appearance of insincerity, the captains would have been credited by their prestigious visitor with some measure of Christian charity and thus less in need of close inspection.

Howard's next visit to the hulks was on January 26, 1778. He spent much of that day on the Woolwich Warren observing convicts at work on Royal Arsenal projects. He was not impressed by the industry of the convicts, but observed in his testimony that the midwinter day on which he visited was probably not a time to make a fair assessment of their work. Further, he complained, as he had before, about the heavy chains worn on the legs of the convicts employed on the Warren. Howard persisted in his argument about the leg chains until, eventually, lighter shackles were put into general use. This change enabled the men to work much more efficiently without any serious loss of security. It is significant that Howard at no time based his argument for lighter shackles on a concern for the comfort of the convicts.

It is clear that John Howard was not immune from the tendency to view the results of his own efforts in the best possible light. After a visit to the Woolwich hulks in November 1779, he made the following observations in his second edition of *The State of Prisons*:

> In my first edition I passed some censures on the management of convicts committed to hard labour on the Thames; and in a subsequent visit I was still more convinced of the faults I had observed. The effects of these became so alarming as to attract the notice of Parliament. A public inquiry was instituted, by which it appeared, that from August 1776, when the convicts were first put on board the *Justitia*, to March 26, 1778, out of 632 prisoners who had been received, 176 had died. It is with pleasure that I can give an account, which will show in a striking light the beneficial effects of this Parliamentary inquiry as to the health of the prisoners, and the obligations the public were under to the committee appointed on this occasion,and particularly to its chairman, Sir Charles Bunbury.

Howard could hardly have expected here less than a good deal of reflected approbation. His account continues:

> At my visit, November 16, 1779, there were at Woolwich, for the reception of convicts, an old Indiaman, called the *Justitia*; and a frigate, the *Censor*. In the former were 256 and in the latter, 250 ... Another called the *Reception*, was empty: in this, convicts were examined by the surgeon, and continued three days before they were sent either to the hulks or to the hospital ship.

The prisoners on board the *Justitia* looked healthy and well: the decks were clean. They had bedding; their provisions were good of the sort; and there were not any (as at my former visits) without shoes and stockings. I found the *Censor,* below decks, cleaner than the *Justitia*; yet on carefully viewing the convicts, they had not so healthy and contented an aspect as those in the other; and a much greater proportion of this ship's company was sent to the hospital. This created in me a suspicion that something was wrong. I examined all their provisions, bedding etc., and found that they were the same as on board the *Justitia*. It would be highly proper that a table of their stated allowance should be hung up, and scales, weights and measures assigned them, to check the pursers who give out their provisions. In the hospital ship on the two decks (one of which is for recovering patients) were 25 cradles, but smaller than those in the Royal Hospitals at Haflar and Plymouth where all lie single. Of the few who were very sick, I found their irons were off. The cleanliness and quietness of the hospital did honor to the conductor. It is to be wished that the patients had better nourishment, as that in many cases would be more salutary than medical prescriptions.

There were about 150 at work in the Warren in 1779; most of them clothed in a brown uniform. I observed that the situation of these unhappy people was altered for the better. Yet their bread allowance of one pound a day was too little, especially for those who worked, although they had an extra allowance of beer.

At my visit, December 27, 1782, the *Censor* and the *Reception* were laid up here. [There] were on board the *Justitia* 180 convicts and in the hospital ship, 24. Of these, 116 were employed in removing ballast, planking, etc., onshore and 36 were heaving ballast in the lighters.† The hospital ship was very clean; the other not dirty. Some alteration is made in the bread allowance. The mess of six men is now seven pounds. The diet table is hung in the cabin of the *Justitia*. I could wish it were for the inspection of the convicts, and that scales and weights were provided for them. There should be to each bed in winter an additional blanket.

October 19, 1783, there were on board the *Justitia* 172 and in the hospital ship 22. The men in the *Justitia* looked well, which I doubt

---

† In his use of the word "ballast" here, Howard isreferring to sand and gravel dredged from the bottom of the Thames.

not was in great measure owing to their being employed, and also restrained from spirituous and other strong liquors. Of late, but few of them have died: this shows that their situation is better with respect to health; but the association of so many criminals is utterly destructive to morals.

Here, John Howard's account records the weekly food allowance for each mess of six men:

| | |
|---|---|
| Breakfast | Everyday; a pint of barley or rice made into three quarts of soup. |
| Dinner | Sunday, six pounds of salt pork or seven pounds of beef with five quarts of beer.<br>Monday, Wednesday, Friday, six pounds of bullocks head. |
| Supper | Sunday, Monday, Wednesday, Friday, A pint of pease and barley made into three quarts of soup.<br>Tuesday, Thursday, Saturday, A pint of oatmeal made into burgou.[†] |

Howard clearly preferred to report optimistically on the results of his efforts, but it is equally clear that he was able to maintain essential honesty and that he had not the slightest reluctance to confront authorities when he saw the need to do so. He had no compunctions about embarrassing gaolers and hulk captains by chiding them unmercifully, sometimes in the presence of prisoners (a practice not recommended by the author). But unlike many latter-day prison reformers, he was careful to give hulk and gaol keepers credit for improvements. He was at times accused of being easily hoodwinked. A letter, written after Howard's death by a prison keeper in Bodmin to James Neild, illustrates the point. Neild was an early 19th-century prison reform advocate who made a commendable, but not especially successful, effort to claim the mantle of John Howard:

Sir,                                         Portsea, Feb. 24. 1802
Yesterday I brought from Bodmin and Launceston Gaol eleven Male Convicts, and put them on board the La Fortunee Hulk, in Langston Harbour. I inquired after ten others, which I put there the 14th of

---

† "Burgou", a thick-oatmeal porridge, is spelled variously burgoe and burgoo in other sources.

September, 1800. Six of them are dead, and the other four look very poorly. Upwards of one hundred and twenty died in 1801; and forty since this year began. I inquired of several of the Convicts, as to the treatment they received: they say they have chiefly died for the want of provision; they have not sufficient food to live on; indeed, they now say these that are here are half-starved. It appears to me, that want of food is the chief cause of so many deaths; for, were they carried off by any putrid or infectious distemper, would it not affect the Officers on board? These appear in perfect health, while the Convict looks pale and half-starved. I have often reported to sundry Gentlemen these many years past, but the evil is not remedied. It will be a humane act, would any Gentleman of Note examine the Convicts in person, by having them before him, separate from the presence of the Overseers, etc. The late worthy Mr. Howard was deceived when he visited; the Overseers, etc. being present, the Convicts were afraid to complain.

> I am, Sir, Your very obedient servant,
> JAMES CHAPPLE
> Keeper of New Prisons, Bodmin
> To James Neild, Esq. Chelsea[3]

Aside from revealing qualities of compassion and concern on James Chapple's part, uncharacteristic of his station and his time, the letter suggests an awareness, shared by others, that for all his efforts and his acclaim, John Howard did not leave places of confinement in England greatly improved over the way he found them. He did succeed in improving conditions of confinement, mainly through innumerable small persuasions, but these improvements were, in fact, modest.

Of more importance, John Howard provided inspiration for prison reformers who were to follow him. James Neild was one of them. Elizabeth Gurney Fry was by all odds the most effective of them. Like Howard, she was motivated by her religious zeal. She demonstrated early in her life that she considered compassion for unfortunate people to be first among the fruits of the Spirit. Her earliest work was with the women prisoners of Newgate, which place she had visited when a very young woman. Had she known about Mary Langridge, Sarah Morris, Maria McIntyre and Ann Roberts, four women placed on board the *Northhampton* hulk at Deptford in 1814, before their departure for New South Wales, she is likely to have visited them.[4] Three years later she formed an association for furtherance of reform efforts aimed toward improving gaol conditions for women. By that time, undaunted by the demands of her large family and the recalcitrance of the system, she had become a seasoned reformer, one who had captured the attention of Parliament like no one since Howard. When she was past sixty she was still traveling and visiting places of confinement throughout Great Britain and Europe, and maintaining a vigorous correspondence with prison authorities and others in positions of influence over prison management.[5]

Elizabeth Fry got results. Reforms that came as a result of her efforts were hardly dramatic, but they were more substantial than were the specific achievements of John Howard. It was, in any case, Howard who led the way. He is sure to have inspired Elizabeth Fry and the lesser reformers who followed. The greatest significance of his prodigious effort was that it instilled in the minds of those who governed Great Britain, and other literate people throughout the western world, a slow-burning awareness of the desperate need for reforms. The inertia blocking the reforms he sought was not overcome during his lifetime, nor in the lifetime of Elizabeth Fry. Indeed the ponderous presence of that inertia remains today.

So what of John Howard and the hulks? Had he launched an all-out assault on the hulk system in his writings and in his testimony before committees of Parliament, it is unlikely that the hulks would have continued as a part of England's prison system for eighty years; they may not have survived the 18th century. But what would have replaced them? As likely as not, any alternative that might have been improvised during those times would have been more lamentable than the hulks at their worst.

# MR. CAMPBELL'S ENTERPRISE

As a young man, Duncan Campbell, the son of a Scottish clergyman, had served as a midshipman in the Royal Navy. The shipping business, rather than the Navy, was to be his career, one that he pursued with much vigor and shrewdness. The profitable arrangement he had enjoyed with John Stewart in the convict transport trade was but one of his many business interests, all of them profitable, all of them connected with trans-Atlantic shipping. Campbell maintained a splendid residence at Blackheath, the substantial town just inland from the Thames River port of Woolwich. He golfed on the Heath with his cronies and served as a Captain of the Blackheath Golf Society, which over subsequent years has become the prestigious Royal Blackheath Golf Club. Members of the Society met during the winter months as the Knuckle Club, most probably a secret masonic lodge. It seems likely, however, that members of the Knuckle Club spent more time discussing business than posturing through secret rituals. The club had among its membership other shipping men whose business interests, like Duncan Campbell's, had been seriously hurt by the Crown's failure to advantageously settle the troubles in America. They were among the group that formed the *Committee for the Merchants Having Traded to North America*. Their goal was to convince the government that some redress was due them because of their loss of business.

Campbell became manager of the hulks at Woolwich almost by default. He wanted the contract but there is no reason to assume that he was elated by this turn of events. His Jamaican sugar trade remained of more interest to him even during his twenty-two-year tenure as manager of the hulks. His wife's father had substantial sugar plantation holdings in Jamaica. Duncan Campbell eventually came into possession of these properties. He also had a house at the Adelphi and a country place in Kent. The picture that has been drawn of Duncan Campbell as a sadistic taskmaster, preoccupied with flogging and half-starving the hapless hulk convicts over the course of twenty-five years, is hardly accurate. His culpability lies in his having been a hard-driving man of business who was not quite willing to give his attention to efficient, humane management of the hulks. For most of Campbell's tenure, the kind and relatively competent Stewart Erskine served him as deputy and senior hulk captain at Woolwich. Unfortunately, most of hulk employees were of lesser quality. Campbell has also been wrongly accused of crooked practices as supplier of stores and victuals for the First Fleet to Botany Bay. He was, however, never involved in that enterprise, other than to make convicts available at Portsmouth for the voyage.[1]

Under the terms of his first contract as manager and supplier for the hulks, Duncan Campbell was to receive an annual payment of thirty-two pounds for each of 120 prisoners. The contract became effective in August 1776. Eighty-four convicts were on board his merchantman, *Justitia*, by October. Shortly thereafter sixty-four more were received from Maidstone and other gaols. It is unlikely Campbell would have agreed to accept these additional prisoners had not deaths among the first group from gaol fever and other causes reduced their number. He would not have provisioned for more than 120.[2] In March 1777 he was offered an amendment to his contract whereby he was to provide another ship and confine 120 more prisoners, with a reduction of the per capita payment to twenty-eight pounds.

From among his ships in the Jamaica trade, Campbell selected the *Tayloe*, a vessel of 160 tons, to serve as sister hulk to the *Justitia* at Woolwich. On March 28, 1777, he wrote to Richard Ackerman, gaoler at Newgate, advising him that the *Tayloe* was ready[3]. A similar notification was sent to at least one other provincial gaoler in April, probably because of some special influence applied on that gaoler's behalf. For the next two years the pleas of gaolers outside London went unheeded, but thereafter, a reasonable representation of prisoners from all over England was put aboard the hulks. This change was undoubtedly due to the influence of provincial members of Parliament with the Home Office. Furthermore, Campbell and his hulk captains are likely to have been more than agreeable when they came to realize that prisoners from the outlying counties were less prone to attempt escape and more inclined to be good workers on the Royal Arsenal projects at Woolwich than those from London. After 1788, when transportation to Australia was initiated, all offenders convicted and sentenced to transportation in England, and some in Scotland, were sent to the hulks to await passage. Prisoners from the outlying counties were held over at Newgate or other London-area gaols on those occasions when the hulks were crowded beyond capacity.

Convicts at work on the Woolwich Warren

We cannot be certain as to the number of convicts finally placed aboard the *Tayloe* during her short career as a prison hulk. Most likely the anticipated complement of 120 was quickly reached. For the remainder of the year Campbell's correspondence with gaolers throughout England was devoted to insisting that they hold on to their prisoners, rather than sending them to the overcrowded hulks, giving vague assurances all the while that "further provision" for additional prisoners would soon be made. During this period he was almost certainly in full compliance with the terms of his contracts, calling for his housing 240 convicts. Indeed, with Newgate being overcrowded and reduced in capacity because of reconstruction,[4] it is likely the Court of King's Bench sent prisoners to the hulks without asking Duncan Campbell's leave. Most of the provincial gaolers would have doubtless been more than willing to have their problems, arising from overcrowding, compared with those of Duncan Campbell's hulks on the River Thames.

In any case, the spring and summer of 1777 was for Campbell a difficult time, to say the least. Housing prisoners on shipboard under a government contract was, for him, a secondary business enterprise. His primary interest was his lucrative trade with the Jamaican sugar merchants. It is apparent that he was not pleased about the need to withdraw the *Tayloe* from his Jamaica trade to use for housing prisoners at Woolwich. Illness and death among the convicts were cause for concern. Escapes and disturbances were especially upsetting to him. His letter dispatched in April 1777 to his trusted colleague, the master of the *Justitia,* is hardly one written by a happy man:

Captain Stewart Erskine:
Mincing Lane                                                    17 April 1777

I this moment received your very disagreeable account. I am afraid there has been some neglect somewhere. Pray what officer was in charge of this lighter? Surely she was not entrusted without one, and without a proper number of people to guard them. I hope for your sake and mine these men had chains on. If not I am sure you are much to blame after what has already happened. Send me the particulars of this escape with all possible expedition, and make the needful inquiry yourself.

Duncan Campbell

P.S. Send the names of those that escaped.[5]

This letter indicates that eight months after he had begun to house prisoners on the hulks under contract with the government, Campbell had not established specific requirements with respect to the reporting of escapes. It is also clear from his correspondence (perhaps ten letters about other business matters to every one concerning the hulks) that the Jamaica trade continued to be his principal interest.

Duncan Campbell was a resourceful man. Convicts aboard the *Tayloe* had hardly enough time to learn their mess mates' names before being rousted on deck for transfer to his new acquisition, the *Censor*. This ship was undoubtedly a great bargain as she was a decommissioned British Navy frigate, somewhat larger than the *Tayloe*, a vessel for which others would not have had much use. It is probable that she was saved from the breaking yard and made available to Campbell through the good offices of William Eden. Campbell had earlier asked the Undersecretary for his assistance in an unsuccessful effort to obtain the *Crescent*, a French prize that had been declared unseaworthy.

The *Censor* took the *Tayloe's* prisoners aboard in August of 1777 at the height of an epidemic of gaol fever, coming then to be known more often as hulk fever. A disturbance among the prisoners occurred at about the same time. There was disease and unrest among the convicts on board *Justitia* as well, but the *Censor* was the scene of the more serious trouble.

Duncan Campbell knew very well that gaols all over England were overcrowded. His contract for maintenance of the hulks at Woolwich became effective almost eleven years before any significant transportation of convicts to foreign shores was resumed. He also knew that whatever success the penitentiary bill might eventually have, years would pass before additional on-shore places of confinement would be constructed. His contacts with economic interests in America and his past involvement with convict transportation seem to have given him a more realistic view than that held by most members of the Government, as to the chances of convicts being accepted again someday in Maryland or Virginia. The initial below-decks arrangement on the *Justitia* suggests that Duncan Campbell anticipated the day when a far greater number of convicts than 120 would be placed aboard that vessel, and other ships of similar size. By crowding the prisoners, he was able to accommodate all of that number, after a fashion, on a lower deck, leaving space above and in the stern for housing his officers. Plenty of space, moreover, was allowed for the ship's master's rooms, for storage of supplies and equipment, and for general utility. The forecastle of the ship was given over to use as a hospital, probably because the bad smells and infectious vapors that emanated from the sick were more likely to be wafted away on the breeze from that above-deck location.

It is probable that strap iron bars were bolted across all portholes and bays large enough for a man to exit, and that hasps and padlocks were installed on the hatch covers. Little more was considered necessary for security as the prisoners were in irons, and guards, armed with drawn cutlasses, patrolled the upper deck. Nevertheless, during the years that followed, there were to be many escapes from the hulks and from hulk work parties ashore.

In testimony before a committee of Parliament, Campbell described the *Justitia* as having first been fitted out with two tiers of beds for convicts. He boasted of having provided them with more standing up space than had been customary on convict transportation ships. It was soon apparent, however, that the side-to-side sleeping space allotted to each prisoner was inadequate. Campbell's own officers recommended an increase in bed width from eighteen to twenty-four inches. Furthermore, the tiered bunk arrangement proved to be unsatisfactory. The tiered bunks were removed from the *Justitia* and replaced by low wooden platforms, six feet long and four feet wide, each accommodating two men. A single straw pad and a blanket were provided for each platform, and thus shared by two prisoners. The more fortunate were those who had an extra blanket or quilt provided by family or friends. It is certain to have been bitterly cold aboard the hulks on midwinter nights. We can be sure that the weaker convicts who were provided with extra blankets by family did not remain in possession of them for very long.

Campbell insisted that the convicts' bedding was frequently aired, but at the same time, testified that the straw pads were nailed to the sleeping platforms to prevent their being thrown about by the prisoners. During the day, the sleeping platforms, with pads attached, were stacked along the sides and bulkheads, as was a vermin-infested collection of folded and wadded bedding. The arrangement on the whole was certain to have been more comfortable for rats, lice and roaches than for the convicts. To make things worse, from the standpoint of sanitation, food apportioned to messes of six men each, was taken below decks and eaten there. The sleeping platforms, standing on their sides, were used as dining tables.

When the *Censor* was fitted out in April 1777, hammocks were installed instead of wooden platforms. Campbell ordered this departure on the recommendation of Mr. Solander, a botanist member of the Royal Society, an acquaintance certainly, if not a friend, of Duncan Campbell. He was one of those who visited the hulks and took obvious pains to give more reassuring reports than were deserved. Another was Sir Herbert Mackworth, a member of Parliament, who, after nibbling a sample of convict rations, judged them to be "very good for a poor man to eat."

In any case, the undoubtedly well-meant recommendations regarding hammocks for the *Censor*, did not have a good result. They indeed would have promoted improved cleanliness, as they could have been taken on deck for regular airing and brushing in accordance with practice aboard naval and merchant vessels. Unfortunately, it soon became apparent that trying to sleep in a hammock while draped and riveted in heavy chains was very difficult. The record reports only that complaints by the convicts resulted in replacement of the hammocks with the tried and true wooden platforms. Since the cost of providing 120 to 150 hammocks is not something Duncan Campbell would have written off lightly, we can be certain that dissatisfaction on the part of the convicts was severe. Moreover, Campbell was probably concerned about the requirement that he have a contingent of convicts adequately rested and fit for work ashore each day.

The necessity to have convicts available for work on the Warren undoubtedly resulted in their having better fare than would otherwise have been the case. Food was issued to each mess in bulk, to be shared by six men. Typical of his business ingenuity, Campbell learned that the best source of meat for the prisoners was the slaughtering yards on Tower Hill, three miles upstream from Woolwich. The heads of butchered cattle were available there at minimal cost, thus "ox cheeks" became the primary meat staple aboard the hulks.[6] The prisoners complained that they were often "kept too long and stinking," but they were served five days a week. Servings of the stringy and unpalatable meat from the ox cheeks were supplemented on Sundays with salt pork. There were two or three "burgoe days" each week on which two pounds of cheese and an extra portion of oatmeal porridge were issued to each mess, instead of the ox cheeks. Campbell testified that he adjusted the diet of the prisoners according to what seemed proper, insisting that the food he served was no worse than that served on naval vessels (hardly a standard of which to be proud). He also invoked comparison with the Navy in defending his practice of taking water from the Thames (upstream from the hulks, we would hope) and using filtering stones to "purify" it. If Campbell's testimony was reasonably accurate in this respect, it is probable that the convicts on the hulks at Woolwich drank water similar in quality to that then available to most of the inhabitants of London, not an unqualified endorsement of its purity. We can, in any case, assume the river was a source of periodic attacks of dysentery and typhus, but the convicts suffered from such an array of ailments during those first twenty years, it is not possible to lay any specific measure of blame on impure drinking water.

At times a modest ration of "small beer" was given to the convicts. Those who worked on the Warren and on the dredging crews got as much as three-and-a-half pints extra on the days they worked. It may be that small beer, a weak, almost spiritless brewery byproduct, was more easily provided on the Warren than was drinking water. No ale or beer was given to the convicts. Wine was used for medicinal purposes only, by direction of the surgeons.

The quality of the food served to prisoners on the hulks throughout the history of their use, varied from time to time and station to station, but there was little significant improvement in the diet until 1847. From descriptions we have of the weekly mess allowances, the nearly total absence of vegetables and fruit is noteworthy. Not surprisingly, scurvy was a continuing problem, despite repeated warnings from visiting observers (more often than from hulk surgeons) about the lack of antiscorbutic food. John Howard had a special concern about the quality of the bread. Indeed, it was almost a preoccupation — perhaps because of his childhood grounding in the Holy Scriptures, which refer to bread more frequently than to vegetables. He seemed to think that if good bread was served in adequate quantity, the battle was all but won. Therefore, his was not the strongest voice in urging the diet improvement that was most urgently needed for the scurvy-ridden inhabitants of the hulks.

Duncan Campbell's opinion was that the second contingent of prisoners placed aboard the *Justitia* in October 1776 brought infectious diseases with them from Maidstone and the other gaols. He observed that "they began to droop and sicken very fast." From August 1776 until April 1778, at which time Campbell made a report in the form of testimony before a committee of the House of Commons, 632 prisoners were placed aboard the hulks. Of this number, 176 had died. The most serious loss of life occurred on the *Censor*, shortly after she was placed in service. For a period of several months, prisoners were dying there at three times the death rate of the *Justitia*. This fact suggests an epidemic which might very well have come aboard the *Censor* with the prisoners. And yet, there is no record of such a calamitous death rate during that period in any of the gaols of London. By late fall 1777, the worst of the virulence aboard the *Censor* had run its course, but frequent deaths among the prisoners on the hulks at Woolwich continued without much abatement.

During the first twenty years about 8,000 convicts were sent to the hulks. They died on board at a rate of almost one in four. Gaol fever came to be known during this period as hulk fever, a form of typhus that had flourished in the filthy, crowded conditions that had characterized confinement in Great Britain for centuries. Although there were undoubtedly devastating outbreaks of this disease, especially before the close of the 18th century, it did not continuously hold sway as the principal cause of death aboard the hulks. Data on the earliest period are not specific. Later records indicate that pulmonary tuberculosis became the leading cause of death, followed by other chest disorders, and then by a variety of causes. The fact of the matter is that most of the deaths aboard the hulks were caused by neglect. With adequate medical care, even of the quality available during the 18th and early 19th centuries, there is no reason deaths should have resulted from "nervous atrophy", "debility", "decay of nature" or "mortification," which is rather like saying death resulted from death.[7]

A serious affliction besetting early assignees to the hulks was depression. With respect to the prisoners received in 1776 and 1777, Campbell reported that "The universal depression of spirits was astounding, as they have a great dread of this punishment." One of the physicians he belatedly engaged to try and stem the epidemic of fatal illnesses during 1776 and 1777, described eight or ten convicts as having died "merely of lowness of spirit, without any fever or other disorder upon them."

Under his original contract, Campbell was not required to provide for the services of a physician. He was, however, expected to have a complement of able-bodied convict workers available for work on the dredging projects and at the Royal Arsenal. The epidemic of gaol fever, which struck with such virulence during the earliest days of Campbell's management, prevented him from fulfilling this responsibility and forced him to give more attention to medical care.

A surgeon, identified in the House of Commons Journal only as Mr. Banks, was briefly engaged to give advice to Duncan Campbell on management of the hulk convicts. Like Solander and Mackworth, he was an advocate of hammocks for sleeping instead of wooden platforms. James Irwin and Dodo Eckens were artillery surgeons, recruited to give some assistance to sick prisoners during the worst of the epidemic. They also were inclined to help Duncan Campbell by putting the best face on matters in testimony before the Bunbury Committee. Eckens strongly supported Campbell's contention that the gaol fever on the hulks came from

Maidstone and the other county gaols. Irwin stamped his approval on the way health problems were being handled on the hulks, and joined Campbell and Eckens in placing blame for the epidemic on the gaols. The testimony of Irwin and Eckens seems to have been aimed more toward justifying Campbell's arrangements for the hulk prisoners than giving information that might lead to improvements. Both had worked with sick prisoners and given advice to Campbell and his overseers. They might well have wanted to give the impression that conditions had improved as a result of their help. In any case, the conditions of confinement were less than horrifying to them, given conditions for so many in England during the 18th century. These men had seen cholera epidemics sweep through the hovels of London's slums. They knew how life was in the almshouses and asylums for the insane. They were acquainted with the grim privations of naval service. Convicted felons were, after all, a wretched lot, hardly deserving more effort on their behalf than was being expended. This is the point of view the two doctors undoubtedly brought with them to the Bunbury Committee.

Irwin, Eckens, Solander and Mackworth may or may not have been cronies of Duncan Campbell, willing for his sake to palliate conditions they observed aboard the hulks. It is more significant that they were representatives of their age, who viewed misery as the inevitable lot of convicted criminals. They were men of affairs. In all likelihood they had visited Newgate and other gaols. The best conclusion to be drawn from their reaction is that they found conditions aboard the hulks to be not much different from other places of confinement. Reform-minded men like Romilly and Samuel Hoare were the exceptions. John Howard was unique in his time. The more characteristic 18th-century attitude toward criminals in confinement is seen in the comments of an observer, writing about boating on the Thames in 1802:

> On our way to the boat, we had a melancholy proof of the profligacy of the times by a sight of the multitude of convicts in chains, labouring in removing earth; eight are employed in drawing each cart. They were well clad and, by their appearance, seemed well fed; but in general the sense of shame is lost. If they had any at first, it soon is changed into hardened impudence by the depravity of their fellow prisoners.[8]

It was the testimony of John Howard, not that of the doctors, that influenced the Committee to urge use of a separate ship for a hospital. It can be safely assumed Campbell was able to pass along to the government the cost of providing the additional ship. We have no description of that first hospital ship, except that it was a small craft with "cradles" for twenty-five patients on each of two decks. The more seriously ill prisoners were housed on the lower deck. From them only were shackles removed. Recuperating patients, with shackles replaced, were assigned to beds on the upper deck. When John Howard visited the Woolwich hulks in November 1779, twenty men were hospitalized aboard this little vessel. He reported that "the cleanliness and quietness of the hospital did honor to the conductor" but observed that the patients should be better nourished "as that in many cases would be more salutary than medical prescriptions." Howard made four more visits to the Woolwich hulks, each time finding the hospital ship — perhaps a different one each time — to be in good order. It appears that Howard made no effort at surprise, and thus his visits to the gaols and hulks were, more often than not, anticipated. His prestige and influence exceeded that of almost anyone who visited the hulks. This fact undoubtedly resulted in his usually finding things in better shape than they otherwise would have been, and better than seen by other observers. Howard never saw the patient census on a hospital ship at Woolwich to be above thirty-six. It is sure to have occasionally been double that number. The sustained death rate of 25 to 30 percent is evidence that medical care of the prisoners continued to be appallingly deficient. Howard must have known this to be true, unless conditioning provided by his extensive exposure to poor conditions of imprisonment throughout Great Britain and Europe significantly skewed his judgement. In any event, Howard's influence undoubtedly staved off horrors worse than those that did occur. Moreover, as present-day prison administrators very well know, having to put things in good order from time to time, because of the expected visits of dignitaries, helps in the development of better operational habits. None of this is to suggest, however, that affairs aboard the English prison hulks were ever in very good order.

Given the appalling number of deaths among the prisoners on the hulks, the Bunbury Committee displayed curiously little concern about Duncan Campbell's arrangements for deceased prisoners. He was asked where the dead were buried. His reply was that a piece of ground had been made available on the Woolwich Warren "behind the butt." He may have been referring to an existing proof-butt, or one under construction by the convicts. Previously, the dead had been buried, in Campbell's words, "along the shore." He added that funerals were conducted by "an officer." The House of Commons Journal indicates no further pursuit of this matter by the Bunbury Committee, except for inclusion in its findings a recommendation that a clergyman should be provided to "hold Divine Services on Sundays and Great Festivals and to bury the dead."

Inquiries concerning the hulks conducted during subsequent years were impelled y circumstances to give closer attention to the cavalier manner in which the bodies of deceased convicts were handled. Meanwhile, we are haunted by melancholy images of those early shoreline burials so casually reported by Duncan Campbell. There must have been hundreds of them. Were they done openly and by daylight along the Thames shore, upstream or downstream from the Arsenal docks? Possibly, but it seems more likely that burial parties were sent after nightfall to isolated places along the marsh flats on the Essex side, to avoid the ire of the citizenry around Woolwich, and to reduce scrutiny by the heavy river traffic to and from the Woolwich Warren anchorage.

Duncan Campbell's contract for management of the hulks at Woolwich did not require that he provide chaplains. He attempted to assuage the feelings of those who expressed concern, especially John Howard, by dubious talk of prayers being conducted aboard the *Justitia* and the *Censor* twice weekly by his officers, despite the lack of reason to believe that there was significantly more piety among his officers than among the convicts. The Church of England appears not to have been overtaken by any burden of conscience about the men on the hulks. Neither did the Wesleyan revival, then fully flowering, reach out to them. Lady Huntington is reported to have sent an Anglican clergyman to the Woolwich hulks to conduct regular services for a short while, but he seems to have begged off sometime before the end of 1777. Despite the urging of John Howard and others, and the recommendations that resulted from the Bunbury Committee's inquiry, attention to the spiritual life of the convicts on the hulks continued to be sporadic at best, for all of the years of Duncan Campbell's contracts. Whether what followed was an improvement is questionable. As shall be seen, the Bishop of London and his colleagues in other dioceses did not always assign the best of their men to service aboard the hulks. There was, for example, the Reverend Mr. Samuel Watson, who served at Woolwich some years after the end of Duncan Campbell's administration. He is remembered as having elected to remain on board his ship during burials of cholera victims. He would stand solemnly at the bow, visible, though at a great distance, to those at the site of the burial. Then he would proceed with the reading of the service. At the moment of committal he would drop a handkerchief, as a signal to the officer in charge of the burial party to lower the remains into the ground. Whereupon Chaplain Watson would continue reading those comfortable words from the Book of Common Prayer.[9]

IV

# NEWGATE

Many, if not most, of the prisoners who went aboard the hulks during the eighty years of their use first spent time in confinement at Newgate Prison. The old gaol was one of Britain's most enduring public institutions. Records of a gaol at the old Roman gatehouse site date from the reign of Henry I.[1] In 1187 adjacent land was acquired for expansion of the ancient gatehouse dungeon.[†] Two centuries later a legacy from the estate of Dick Whittington provided funds for the remodeled structure known thereafter among London's slum dwellers as "Whit's Palace" or, eventually, as "the Whit."[2] After the great fire of 1666 devastated central London, a gaol of some description was put back together sufficiently well to last, with periodic make-do remodelings, for a hundred years.[3]

George Dance was admitted to the Royal Academy in 1768 and soon thereafter commissioned to design a new Newgate Prison.[4] Construction was begun in 1770, three years before John Howard began to make his pleas for more humane confinement of prisoners. Progress on construction was excruciatingly slow. Present-day prison administrators are all too aware of the difficulties that attend major remodeling or construction in a prison setting where prisoners must continue to be held. The project was still not completed in 1776 when all transportation of prisoners to the North American colonies was terminated—a time when allotments of space aboard the *Justitia* or the *Tayloe* offered the only relief for overcrowding at the much disrupted Newgate Prison. In the spring of 1779 the number of sentenced felons had been reduced to eighty-four—less than half the usual

---

† England's Newgate Prison acquired two namesakes in America. The first of them was Connecticut's notorious Newgate Prison, built atop an abandoned copper mine in Simsbury in 1773. It used the mine's shaft and tunnels for housing close-custody prisoners under inhumane conditions. By contrast, New York City's Newgate Prison, opened in 1790, was one of the more progressive prisons built during that era. See American Correctional Association, *The American Prison: From the Beginning, a Pictorial History*, (Laurel, Maryland: ACA Publications, 1983), 26-27, 33.

count—in order to facilitate a speed-up in construction.[5] The prison was required to maintain a fluctuating number of detainees and debtors but, nonetheless, the project moved apace. One year later the Gordon Riots erupted. Mob violence reigned in London for six days. Newgate was sacked and three-hundred prisoners were set free. It is probable that furnishings, scaffolding, and perhaps some of the ancient wooden flooring burned, while George Dances's elaborate new stonework, as well as the ancient stone foundation, escaped serious damage.[6]

As the militia got the disturbance under control, hundreds of rioters are certain to have been jammed into undamaged gaols and other compounds more distant from central London. Perhaps the unscheduled drop in Newgate's prisoner count occasioned by the Gordon Riots aided in a rapid cleanup and acceleration of the construction, even though it is reported that many escapees applied for readmission soon after the fire was out. In any event, the project was completed two years later, an imposing new edifice, built over and around the old gaol. It was George Dance's masterpiece — he had wanted to design a handsome building, but he also intended to achieve a mood of solemnity and foreboding. In this he succeeded brilliantly but, except for installation of more modern systems for drainage and ventilation, little or nothing was done to significantly improve conditions of confinement during the course of the twelve-year improvement project. Some of the most doleful reports of mistreatment, debauchery and misery at Newgate come from those years immediately following its 18th-century transformation.

Because of Britain's misguided convictions as to the efficacy of separate and silent confinement, numerous private cells were provided at Newgate by remodelings in 1858 and 1860, a classic example of the right thing done for the wrong reasons.[7] Before that time none of Newgate's numerous reincarnations had resulted in any change in the character and atmosphere of the prison's interior. It remained a dark, dismal labyrinth of wards, courts and corridors, housing a teeming contrariety of unfortunates. Savage, writing in *Newgate Calendar*, caught the spirit of the place: "Condemned felons surrounded by their admiring doxies, rummaged their befuddled brains for appropriate speeches to be made on the scaffold. Madmen tore about or wailed disconsolately in the corridors."[8]

After the end of 1776, perhaps half of Newgate's population were convicted felons awaiting transfer to the hulks and, after 1787, eventually to Australia. Among them were rapacious, hardened criminals, housed together with boys of twelve and thirteen, as well as a number of altogether

Newgate Prison, London, about 1850

terrified first-time situational offenders. Detainees awaiting trial were of a similar mix. There were also special state prisoners and the inevitable large complement of debtors. Classification was limited to a perfunctory effort to keep females separate from males, and debtors separate from prisoners accused or convicted of crime. The planned capacity of Newgate after the 1770-1782 reconstruction was 427, a meaningless figure, given the reliance on so many open wards, and the scarcity of beds.[9] There were, and had been for many years, a few individual cells for special prisoners and for those who were condemned to be hanged. John Howard concludes his description of these specialized compartments by telling us that "criminals who had affected an air of boldness during their trial and appeared quite unconcerned at the pronouncing of sentence upon them, were struck with horror and shed tears when brought to these darksome solitary abodes."[10]

The capacity of a particular ward had to be subjectively based on the level of misery observed to be bearable by the warder in charge. Such judgments are sure to have varied greatly, according to the individuals making them, and also according to the pressure of new commitments. Mayhew tells us that in 1787 Newgate housed a population of 140 debtors and 350 "criminals," a total of 490, not much higher than estimated capacity. One year later, however, the total count was 613. Rather than improvements being made after the turn of the century, the Newgate prisoner count is reported on at least one occasion in 1818 to have soared to 1,200.

Long after the British Parliament appeared to be genuinely moved by the pleas of John Howard for the elimination of inhumane and patently unreasonable practices in the administration of gaols, such practices continued. Accused prisoners underwent protracted confinement under miserable conditions, oftentimes when their most reprehensible crime was that of being poor. Prisoners with outside means and influential friends fared reasonably well, though not spared exposure to the choking stench for which Newgate had achieved centuries-long notoriety. Efforts to reduce the offensive smell by improving sanitation in the gaol were made from time to time, more in response to the complaints of neighboring free citizens than as a result of concerns about the welfare of the prisoners. Furthermore, when the frequent epidemics of gaol fever became especially virulent, anguished objections were expressed by and on behalf of those who had to be exposed to the convicts in regular sessions of the criminal court—judges, solicitors, witnesses and court officers. Thus, efforts to control the disease were made that most certainly would have been less resolute had the health of the prisoners been the main consideration. Though conditions in other gaols in London, and those in the counties, were similarly miserable, Newgate had a character all its own. Centuries-old traditions flourished, frequently at the expense of the weaker and less pecunious prisoners. The practice of the *garnish* persisted long after its having been eloquently condemned by John Howard. Self-appointed ward bosses among the prisoners saw to it that all newcomers paid a garnish fee or suffered the penalty, which might range from mere deprivation of decent food and bedding, to having to run a gauntlet of blows and kicks by other prisoners. Presumably, garnish monies were used to purchase candles, fuel and other things for betterment of the ward. We can be sure the extra funds, those remaining after the gaolers had their payments, were used as well to purchase beer, gin, extra food and other privileges for members of the prisoner power structure. Kangaroo courts were held to deal with violators of the prisoner code. The world of Newgate functioned more by subcultural ritual and practice than by rules of order. By day the prison swarmed with an assortment of seedy solicitors, bewildered wives, children and parents of prisoners. There were clerks and petty officials collecting the highest fees possible for copying documents and performing picayune bureaucratic services. Visitors, crossing a yard en route to some appointment, would often be beset by hordes of begging prisoners. Prostitutes plied their trade in the crannies and "associated rooms", and neighboring grog shop owners prospered from the brisk traffic in gin inside Newgate's walls.

As has been the case in prison systems everywhere in the western world during subsequent centuries, women suffered most from the mismanagement and the overcrowding that characterized Newgate. Accommodations for them were even poorer than those afforded the males. Sir Richard Philip, a City of London Sheriff, wrote a letter to the Livery of London after a visit to the gaol in 1808, observing that "When the female prisoners lie down on their floors at night, there must necessarily . . . be the same bodily contact and some arrangements of heads and legs as in the deck of a slave ship . . . twenty-five or thirty women, as it may be, in a row, having a breadth of eighteen inches by her length."[11] And among such shamefully treated females were little girls of eleven and twelve, victims of poverty and neglect, jammed in thigh to belly with disease-ridden veterans of London's whore rookeries, and hence apprenticed to them, while available to them for depraved diversion. Needless to say, detainees under flimsy accusation on minor charges were not separated from the most hardened among the convicted. Indeed, we can be certain the more hardened among this company suffered the least from deprivation.

Other London gaols fed prisoners onto the hulks, though not on such a regular basis as did Newgate, which held prisoners before and after their appearances at Old Bailey. Among the home county gaols was Horsemonger Lane, a facility built in Surrey at the urging of John Howard, dubiously characterized as presenting attractions rather than terrors (as if terrors were the more appropriate).[12]

Tothill Fields, an ancient gaol in Westminster that underwent a number of incarnations over the centuries, was less egregious than some of the other London-area gaols during the latter years of the 18th century.[13] It eventually became a house of correction for women and boys, but before that time had periodically dispatched chains of prisoners to the hulks. Clerkenwell, the house of detention for Middlesex, was built at about the time Duncan Campbell was first taking prisoners aboard the *Tayloe* and *Justitia* at Woolwich. Though this was the time of John Howard's greatest influence, his reform notions were not significantly reflected in Clerkenwell's design. Advantages the prisoners might have gained from its newness did not long survive, nor were they regained during a 19th century reconstruction.

Except for Newgate, Coldbath Fields was perhaps the most infamous of the London-area prisons. During the era of the hulks, it functioned as the house of correction for Middlesex.[14] This is the gaol whose dubious reputation inspired Coleridge to write:

> As he went through Coldbath Fields,
> he saw a solitary cell;
> And the devil was pleased,
> for it gave him a hint
> For improving his prisons in hell.

The Fleet Street gaol, notorious for having a character similar to Newgate's and no less imposing a place in history, had been used almost exclusively as a debtors prison for more than a century before establishment of the hulks. Presumably, transfer of prisoners from Fleet Street to the hulks was rarely seen.

Duncan Campbell's early correspondence indicates that the keepers of gaols at such places as Maidstone, Horsham and Cambridge were anxious for any accommodation the hulks would give them. It is unlikely they were given much relief until the hulk fleet was expanded to Plymouth,

Gosport and Portsmouth. The keepers of the gaols at Gloucester, Leicester, Lancaster, Chester and others of the more distant jurisdictions, pleaded with Campbell for permission to send prisoners down to Woolwich, but it is probable they were accommodated even less frequently. At the end of the first year of the era of the hulks in England, the fleet consisted of the *Justitia* and *Censor*, both moored at Woolwich, and therefore available primarily to London and home county prisoners. Ten years later, the hulk establishment had expanded to include the *Dunkirk* at Plymouth, the *Lion* at Gosport, and the *La Fortunee* and *Ceres* at Langstone Harbor near Portsmouth. In July 1788, the number of prisoners confined at these outlying ports totaled 1196. By then, presumably, gaol keepers from all parts of provincial England were able, from time to time, to transfer prisoners to these vessels. Meanwhile, the *Stanislaus* joined the *Justitia* and *Censor* at Woolwich where, in July 1788, a total of 741 prisoners were confined.[15]

We cannot know with certainty that conditions of confinement on the hulks at Woolwich (and later Deptford) which served London, were worse than those on hulks moored elsewhere. It is reasonable to conjecture, however, that those aspects of confinement affected by predatory behavior among the prisoners, were more lamentable aboard the *Justitia*, the *Censor*, the *Stanislaus* and the other hulks subsequently in London vicinity ports, than on the hulks serving the lesser towns and rural counties. There most certainly were many murderous rogues aboard the hulks moored at Plymouth, Langstone Harbour and other outlying ports, but with them were numerous less criminalistic rural fellows, and offenders from the towns, most of whom were probably well able to take care of themselves, while not particularly inclined to prey on the weaker prisoners. On the other hand, from the memoirs of James Hardy Vaux and other sources we know that a reign of fear and predaciousness often prevailed on the hulks that were populated mainly by Londoners. A Londoner confined to a Woolwich hulk toward the end of the 18th century might have hailed from one of the scattered enclaves of poverty in the west part of the city, such as the rookery of St. Giles. As a street urchin he might have turned cartwheels for an occasional penny among the crowds on Haymarket or the Strand, or mudlarked for scraps of coal below Vauxhall Bridge. It is more probable that his abode would have been in the East End, perhaps a back alley hovel in Spitalfield or Whitechapel. His character and standards would have been fashioned by those shabby, boisterous streets, where the women were typically gin sodden, the men typically prepared to steal anything of slightest worth at the slightest opportunity; all of them afflicted by despair but nonetheless determined in pursuit of their sleazy survival skills. They were Londoners whose progeny, still wretched after a hundred years, were described by Jack London as the *People of the Abyss*. About the city they knew Shelley wrote:

> Hell is a city much like London,
> A populous and smoky city.
> There are all sorts of people undone-
> And there is little or no fun done;
> Small justice shown and still less pity.

# V

## ON THE WARREN

By the time Howard made his last visit to the Woolwich hulk station in 1788, three principal ships and several smaller vessels were in use there for confinement and management of 741 prisoners. Of these, 265 were assigned to the *Justitia*, 248 to the *Censor* and 228 to the *Stanislaus*. Thirty-two were patients aboard the hospital ship and perhaps a dozen were being held for the five-day quarantine period aboard a small receiving vessel. There may have been a washing ship and there are sure to have been a number of ballast lighters (dredging boats) on which a few convicts were sometimes lodged. As a replacement for the *Ceres*, the *Stanislaus* had been in use at Woolwich for only two weeks on the occasion of Howard's final inspection. Presumably the *Ceres* was the most seaworthy of Duncan Campbell's ships at Woolwich. She had been selected for the considerable voyage to Portsmouth for service as a hulk there. The longer a hulk remained at one station, the less suitable she would become for passage under sail to another location. Masts and rigging were removed; ladders were nailed to the gunwales; tool shacks were built on the decks and innumerable rickety modifications were made, most probably in an unscheduled, haphazard way. Furthermore, there was no schedule of repair to the hulks, and they were frequently allowed to rest in the mud, baking in the sun at low tide. We can assume that certain ships were kept in a seaworthy state so they could be moved between stations as needed. It is also probable that, by makeshift patching, efforts were made to keep the hulls of all the hulks reasonably sound, as it was necessary periodically to tow them from place to place on station. In almost all cases, use as a hulk was the last purpose a vessel would serve. Therefore, it eventually became necessary over the eighty-year history of the hulks to tow each of them in turn to the breaking yard. There were exceptions. At least one of the hulks burned, and we can be sure that some of them became derelicts in place. There is no record of a hulk being lost at sea during a voyage to a different port. A complement of reasonably healthy convicts would have been retained on board during passage.[1] Correspondence between Duncan Campbell's clerk and masters of hulks at Woolwich and Langstone Harbour, throws light on some of the details of a ship transfer. On June 8, 1787, the clerk's letter was dispatched to Captain Hill, master of the *La Fortunee*, then anchored at Langstone Harbour, Portsmouth:

> "I am desired by Mr. Campbell to acquaint you that the Ceres, one of the Hulks at Woolwich, is ordered round to Langstone Harbour and that she will depart in about eight or ten days hence. The Ceres is to be moored head and stern to keep clear of the Fortunee and Mr. Campbell desires you will consult with and give the officers of the Dock yard every assistance in your power as to the laying of mooring lines for the ship."[2]

The letter further inquired as to how many of *La Fortunee's* water casks could be spared for the *Ceres*, and at what distance the *Ceres* could be moored from the *La Fortunee*. On June 13, 1787, a letter was sent from Campbell's office to the Duke of Richmond, commander of the Royal Arsenal, asking for arms for the extra guards that would be needed aboard the *Ceres* during her passage to Portsmouth. Ten muskets, four pair of pistols and "three or four blunderbusses" were requested.[3] Campbell wrote on June 16 to Captain Erskine at Woolwich, placing him in command of the *Ceres* during its passage to Portsmouth with 200 convicts aboard: "It must be needless for me to recommend care and attention in the management of the ship of convicts. Your own knowledge and experience in which I have highest confidence will lead you to take such measures as may be proper on that score." Captain Erskine was advised that the sloop of war *Bonnetta* would be in Gallion's Reach to accompany the *Ceres* during the passage. He was instructed to "bring up at Spithead & immediately acquaint Mr. Gilbert, the Master Attendant who will furnish you with a pilot to Langstone Harbour."[4]

A primary expectation of Duncan Campbell was that the hulk prisoners at Woolwich would be available to perform the arduous labor involved in dredging the channel. He was counted on to abate the increasingly troublesome problem caused by the shifting river bottom along Barking's Reach, just downstream from the Woolwich Warren docks. For this, Duncan Campbell acquired or had built several ballast lighters. (The need for the lighters was taken into account in Campbell's first contract, while the need for the services of physicians was not.) The ballast lighters were equipped with bucket and windlass machinery for raising silt and sand from the river bottom, and with platforms on which the prisoners could work. These vessels had load capacities up to twenty-seven tons. Cranking up the "ballast", stowing it, eventually rowing it to shore and unloading it, provided backbreaking work for the convicts, made no easier by the shackles all of them wore. None of the available accounts refer specifically to convicts sleeping aboard the ballast lighters. A description of the lighters provided in W.T. Vincent's *Records of Woolwich*, however, indicates sleeping arrangements for convicts were built into these work boats, as were little forecastle sleeping cabins for the overseers. It is reasonable to assume work crews did sleep aboard the ballast lighters on occasion. Dredging was often done considerable distances downstream from the waters off Woolwich Warren where the hulks were moored.[5]

*Scots Magazine*, May 1777, provides a description of convict labor during the first year of the hulk establishment:

Some are sent about a mile below Woolwich, in lighters, to raise ballast, and row it back to the embankment at Woolwich Warren, close to the end of the Tiger Walk; others are there employed in throwing it from the lighters; some wheel it to different parts to be sifted; others wheel it from the screen, and spread it for the embankment. A party is continually busied in turning round a machine for driving piles to secure the embankment from the rapidity of the tide. Carpenters &c. are employed in repairing the *Justitia* and *Tayloe* hulks, that lie hard by for the nightly reception of these objects, who have fetters on each leg, with a chain between that ties variously, some round their middle, others upright to the throat. Some are chained two and two, and others, whose crimes have been enormous, with heavy fetters. Six or seven men are continually walking about with them with drawn cutlasses, to prevent their escape, and likewise to prevent idleness. So far from being permitted to speak to any one, they hardly dare speak to each other; but what is most surprizing, is the revolution in manners: not an oath is to be heard, and each criminal performs the task assigned to him with industry, and without murmuring.[6]

Two years after first establishment of the hulks at Woolwich, Duncan Campbell had six ballast lighters, each suitable for a work crew of ten or twelve convicts, though sometimes accommodating more. He was given permission by the Trinity House Corporation to work downstream from Woolwich, not upstream. The record does not reflect to what extent

Campbell conferred with Trinity House as to the specific areas to be dredged. Aside from these general instructions, it appears that Campbell was at first left to his own devices.[†] The Board of Ordinance was not immediately receptive to employment of convicts on the Warren or on the waters off Woolwich, but this was to change. If for no other reason, use of convict labor was a major consideration when Parliament first authorized putting prisoners on hulks. The Board's first concession was granting permission to Campbell to lay ballast ashore on marshlands adjoining the Warren to the east. Soon after, as many as 250 convicts were ashore screening ballast for the Greenwich Hospital road. Others were soon engaged in building butts and embankments for arsenal use. One of the more ambitious projects was the construction of a 120-foot-long quay for use as a wharf at high tide. It was located downstream, at the east end of the Warren, actually outside the Warren boundaries. Campbell's views on location of the quay prevailed over original Ordinance Board plans, further evidence of his strong and persuasive nature. Moreover, it is apparent that the Board was becoming increasingly appreciative of the value of this new source of labor.

Another project undertaken by the hulk convicts was construction of a proof-butt just inland from the quay, to replace one located in the center of the Warren. The old proof-butt had been suitably located when built, but encroachment of new buildings on the Warren created safety problems, as the butt, a massive, elongated mound of dirt, was used for testing artillery shells. Campbell testified before the Bunbury Committee in 1778 that the new butt, then under construction, was to be 319 feet long and 28 feet high, a larger structure than had been anticipated by Arsenal authorities.[7] These projects were completed and were of significant benefit to the Arsenal, as were a number of other projects that followed. Their construction entailed movement of many thousands of tons of muck and gravel from the river bottom to the shore, then to the sites of the projects. There was an arrangement for payment by the Arsenal to the Treasury for convict labor, offsetting to some extent the cost of Campbell's contract.

During the summer months, convicts assigned to these projects, and others who worked on shore, labored from 7 a.m. until noon, then from 1 p.m. until 6 p.m. During winter, work began at 8:30 a.m.; the convicts worked without a lunch break until two or three in the afternoon, when the prisoners would return to the hulks for the rest of the day. Lack of early

---

[†] The Trinity House Corporation, an association of English mariners chartered in the 14th century to attend to navigation matters on the Thames. According to Byrnes, Duncan Campbell was an associate of Trinity House.

daylight and the effect of bitter weather on the poorly clad convicts forced the sharp curtailment of work during the winter months. Work hours were also affected by the status of projects and other considerations. Duncan Campbell testified in April 1778 that the convicts at Woolwich were then working on the ballast lighters three hours a day. In all seasons, rainy, misty weather was cause enough to keep the convict workers on board the hulks. Rain made dredging ballast and hauling it in carts and barrows difficult, to say the least. Firearms became less dependable and poor visibility increased chances of escape attempts.

All able-bodied adult convicts went to work ashore or to the ballast lighters on days when the weather was reasonable. Most of them were assigned to hard, dirty, sometimes dangerous work. Little attention was paid to safety precautions. Injuries were frequent. Relatively few of the convicts had trade skills. When identified, convict carpenters, metal smiths and masons were put to work in the Arsenal shops or elsewhere on the Warren. During Campbell's tenure the convicts received no pay. Those who worked on the Warren were given extra rations of small beer and an occasional "dram" on cold days or when they were "ill with colic."

At the time of the Bunbury Committee's second round of hearings, April 1779, Newgate was in the process of extensive new construction. For that reason the number of felons held there had been reduced to eighty-four from a more usual count of about two hundred. As a consequence, the hulks at Woolwich were filled to what was viewed as their absolute capacity. Two hundred and fifty were assigned to the 800-ton *Censor*, two hundred and sixty to the *Justitia*. Yet, as the years passed, means were to be devised whereby these ships and ships of similar size would have almost twice those numbers.

Most of the convicts who went aboard the hulks from Newgate and other gaols had sentences to transportation of not less than seven years, even though there had been a cessation of all convict transportation. New South Wales was not to be opened up for reception of convicts until 1788. In addition to the long-termers, many young, "robust" offenders, whose sentences required less than five years confinement, were committed to the hulks at Woolwich. As has always been the case, the younger, more energetic men, especially those with shorter sentences and less baleful future prospects, presented management problems, and because of their aggressiveness, were a source of added grief to the older prisoners. Moreover, with completion of some of the major work projects on the Warren, less work was available. Fewer hours were spent ashore and the resulting long

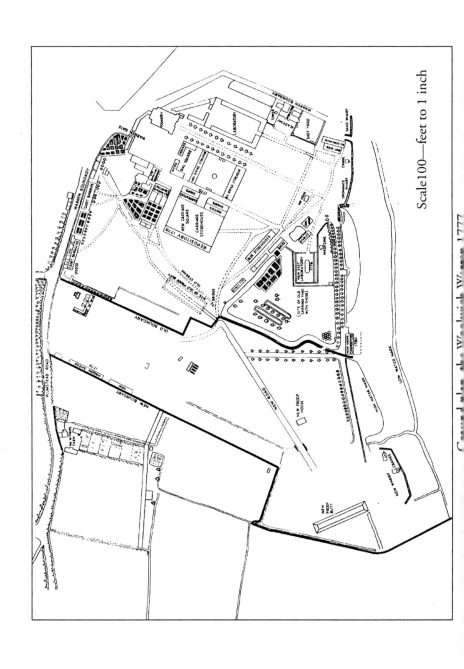

Ground plan the Woolwich Warren, 1777

Scale 100—feet to 1 inch

stretches of idleness below decks on the hulks had a poor effect on conditions of confinement for all, but especially for the more passive, nonaggressive men.

Invariably, many convicts were unable to work ashore due to illness or infirmity. At Woolwich, twenty to forty are likely to have been assigned to "cradles" aboard the hospital ship. There were others with serious disabilities. At least one blind prisoner was aboard the *Justitia* in 1778. And there were a number of exceedingly young prisoners, younger than those who tend to be most aggressive and troublesome in confinement. In April 1778, eight lads of fifteen were assigned to the hulks at Woolwich. Another eight were fourteen or younger. Various accounts indicate that boys as young as ten and eleven were sometimes confined on the hulks during the earlier years. They remained aboard as "cabin boys" (though with hardly the advantages or prospects that term usually implies) or as "swabbing boys", which means simply that they were not sent ashore to work but were assigned instead to various maintenance and cleanup jobs on the ships. Lack of physical stature alone seems to have settled the fate of these boy convicts with respect to the privilege of going ashore to work. Most of the jobs on the Warren were torturously strenuous but others were not. In any case, the boy convicts were denied the relief that a few hours on shore each week would have provided. Remaining on board during the working day was hardly a sought-after privilege. As exhausting and dangerous as the work on shore sometimes was, it provided minor rewards and gave respite from the cramped, fetid misery aboard. Those who were constantly under predatory threat from other prisoners were safe while ashore. Escape plotting and countless other kinds of scheming were undoubtedly done during the long hours of idleness below decks, but most escape attempts were from work parties ashore. Especially for the more sophisticated convicts, there were opportunities to "kite" letters, obtain contraband and engage in other schemes, as often as not involving free workers on the Warren.

It is not probable that the very young boys were victimized by predatory convicts, most of whom were undoubtedly in the age categories just beyond them, sixteen through twenty-five. Nor is it likely that they preyed on each other as often as they were to do after establishment of hulks for the boy convicts some years later. The record does not affirm this observation directly but parallels between late 18th-century imprisonment and the whole realm of imprisonment in Great Britain and America after two hundred years, are in many respects so striking as to give support to certain sub-cultural patterns among the prisoners aboard the hulks. The mixing of children with adults in confinement cannot be advocated, but some heterogeneity as to age usually works to reduce aggressiveness among youthful prisoners. In any case, there was no separation of convicts on the hulks for many years. Those who were but children were housed with the very oldest and the most dangerous and unpredictable as well as with the weakest and most vulnerable. Eventually a hulk for boy convicts was established. The results of this effort will be examined in a later chapter.

Life aboard the hulks was a protracted horror for some and nothing better than an ordeal for others. But for the more sophisticated and predatory, it offered opportunities for the kind of exploitation of the weak by the strong that has characterized prisons for centuries. There were no arrangements for supervision that would have prevented thefts, assaults or the commission of various other outrages. Officers who patrolled the upper decks had no inclination or ability to interfere in whatever happened below.

Duncan Campbell testified that among the convicts "the universal Depression of spirits was astounding." Others were struck by the same impression. There is evidence that the prospect of the hulks was dreaded beyond almost any other punishment. The opinion of an Irish prelate in the early 19th century was that many men of his country would have systematically committed crimes in order to deliberately exchange their lives of squalid poverty for transportation to the Australian colonies, had it not been for the year or two most of those then being sentenced to transportation were held on the hulks.[8]

For all but a few, whose special circumstances enabled them to gain certain comforting privileges, the prospect of a term aboard the hulks gave good cause for despair. Londoners would have tolerated hulk confinement somewhat better than those from the outlying towns and countryside. Most of the London convicts had been slum dwellers, accustomed to privation, stench and close proximity. A great number of them, moreover, had existed on the margins of life since infancy, having the psychological callouses that sociopathy provides. Life aboard the hulks was miserable for virtually all, an agony for many.

It would have been the fate of many a prisoner to have languished for weeks against the cold stones of a provincial gaol cell, waiting for the assizes term. For a routine first felony conviction, he would have been given a sentence of seven years transportation, then marched in chains or taken in a rough coach to Newgate where his education for the coming years of desolation would begin. He would be preoccupied there with fending off the depredations of vermin, disease and his predatory fellows. Huddled on the common-side felons ward, his fare at Newgate would be tepid barley soup, slopped out to prisoners who had no money to buy better. Perhaps he would learn for the first time that, rather than having the prospect of an imminent voyage to New South Wales, he would most likely go aboard a prison ship on the Thames for an indeterminate wait. He would hear baleful accounts of the miseries aboard the hulks but would perhaps be grateful that his wife, now destitute, just might have time to scrape together a few farthings to visit him before he was taken beyond hope of seeing her again. One morning, long before first light, he would be rousted up from his straw, shackled to a dozen or so other unfortunates, then marched through the misty pre-dawn London streets to Blackfriars Gate. Grim, wordless fellows, also wearing chains, would be at the oars of the longboats. Cutlass and pistol bearing guards would be stationed fore and aft. The longboats with their wretched passengers would slip away on an outgoing tide and enter Gallion's Reach an hour after sunrise. The silhouette of two dilapidated merchantmen would loom against the fog shrouds of the Woolwich Warren shore, but the longboats would tie up to a smaller vessel, anchored farther out. Our newcomer and his fellows would be cursed and prodded aboard, stripped, doused in a tub of lye water, given ragged "slop clothing" in place of their crusty gaol clothes. Then they would be reshackled and rowed to one of the two hulks. The more sickly and feverish prisoners would stay aboard the receiving ship, but our newcomer would soon be descending the ladder into the choking vapors of the lowest, darkest sub-deck of the ship. He would meet his mess mates there, having despair with him in common, but he would soon find that there was no comfort to be had from their company. Thus his long years of purgatory would begin, promising yet-unimagined misery, all of it sanctioned by the British Crown and by the peoples' advocates at Westminster. But then he would have brought these unhappy circumstances on himself, by stealing a pig or a watch or perhaps, more reprehensively, by taking a stick to an overly abusive rent collector.

In any event, there should be no wonder at the "universal Depression of spirits" among the convicts, observed by Duncan Campbell, or that some of them "appear(ed) to have died from the effects of their depression without any fever or disorder upon them."

Given the social standards of his time, it cannot be said that Duncan Campbell was an evil man. He was a shrewd, successful man of business, respected in his community. His ardor for profits undoubtedly shielded him from the possibility of developing any significant measure of compassion for the unfortunates under his care, and enabled him to rationalize the unavoidability of the agonies they suffered. They were, after all, of their own making — not his. This was the view of most law-abiding Britishers toward convicted criminals. (A similar point of view is far from extinct two centuries later in America or Great Britain.)

To Duncan Campbell, in any event, it soon became clear that the distress being suffered by the hulk convicts was, for many of them, simply more than they could bear. He and his officers could hardly fail to realize that for some of the prisoners, abject hopelessness was resulting in illness, inability to function, and even death. These circumstances were not having a good effect on Campbell's profit-and-loss picture.

Less than a year after first use of the hulks, commutations of sentence were granted to several worthy fellows who impressed Campbell as good candidates for employment in the hulk establishment. (He undoubtedly relied on Stewart Erskine's opinion.) The undersecretary who forwarded the pardons made it clear to Campbell that if the released men were not retained as guards on the hulks, they were to be sent to the navy.[9] Early in 1777 William Eden suggested to Campbell that he should recommend additional pardons, as a means of reducing the prisoner count at Woolwich. Eden had been receiving letters from various town councils around the kingdom, complaining about Campbell's continued refusal to accept their prisoners. In August 1777 Campbell responded to Eden, pointing out that he did indeed have too many prisoners. He furthermore told the undersecretary that his captains were having to deal with much convict unrest, referring to the "late malignant disorder" that had occurred, principally aboard the *Censor*.[10] These circumstances led to a positive response to the Under Secretary's suggestion. Recommendations for a number of pardons were prepared and forwarded.

Duncan Campbell may not have been especially troubled by the plight of the county authorities whose gaols were jammed beyond capacity, but he was surely not pleased that so many complaints about him were being sent to Under Secretary Eden, and to other members of Parliament as well. Campbell did not initiate the idea for pardons, but he knew that in the interest of good order on the hulks a reduction in the prisoner count would be desirable. Moreover, he was perceptive enough to know that the granting of pardons to some of the more deserving men would be beneficial in ameliorating the despair that lay so heavily on the convicts, threatening his ability to meet the labor demands at the Royal Arsenal and elsewhere on the Warren.

At the time of Campbell's testimony before the Bunbury Committee in April 1778, sixty convicts had been pardoned, and thirty others were to be recommended. His claim that only two of the sixty had gotten into further trouble is questionable, given the difficulties that pertain after two centuries, in establishing reliable recidivism data. But he may have been not far off the mark. Among the several hundred prisoners then in his custody aboard the hulks at Woolwich, are sure to have been many minor offenders who would have presented little or no risk to the community. Some of those pardoned faced the condition that they go to sea as ordinary seamen. Undoubtedly there were misgivings among these fellows. Samuel Johnson is remembered to have said, "No man will be a sailor who has contrivance enough to get himself into a gaol." These were times when press gangs were showing little discrimination in gathering up luckless idlers from the streets of England's major seaports, for service on ships of the Royal Navy.

These grants of pardon alleviated the disabling despair that had affected convicts aboard the hulks at Woolwich so profoundly during the earliest years of their use. It is not likely that the hopes of the more hardened criminals were raised by pardons granted to minor, first-time offenders, but then it is also unlikely that the problem of serious depression was much in evidence among these more serious criminals, most of whom were conditioned to miserable circumstances, and were accomplished at making life interesting for themselves in confinement, usually at the expense of their less criminalistic fellows.

# VI

# THE AUSTRALIAN CONNECTION

The embarkation of the First Fleet to Australia in May 1787 provided another amelioration of the despair that had been so alarmingly prevalent among convicts on the hulks. This prodigious event, coyly shrouded for decades by Australian historians, is now celebrated proudly by most citizens of that magnificent country. In any case, it was an event that is sure to have kindled hope in the hearts of some of the more wretched fellows who remained behind aboard the *La Fortunee*, the *Justitia* and their sisters moored at other hulk stations in the southeastern coastal waters of England. The hope of pardon, however faint, was viable for the less criminalistic convicts on the hulks; the hope of transportation to Australia was one in which long-term, serious offenders could indulge. During the earliest years of transportation to Australia, perverse and disreputable convicts enjoyed better chances for selection than did their docile fellows. It follows that among those who were transported may have been a larger proportion of spirited and resourceful men than among those left behind on the hulks. Moreover, due to the fear loosed in England by the Reign of Terror that was to run its bloody course in France during 1793, a significant number of altogether admirable individuals were convicted by British courts to long terms of transportation on charges of sedition. One of them was the Scottish patriot, Thomas Muir, who was given a fourteen-year sentence essentially because of his advocacy of constitutional reform. He managed to eventually quit his exile to New South Wales, but more than a smattering of his kind stayed on in Australia, lending character to the blend of persons who founded that nation.[1]

The six hundred male prisoners who embarked with the First Fleet from Portsmouth Harbour in 1787 had been collected from the Portsmouth and Woolwich hulks, from Newgate, and perhaps directly from the Clerk of the Arraign at the Old Bailey.[†] There were to be times in passage when these men surely cursed the day they were taken up from their miserable

---

† The central criminal court for London.

circumstances in English confinement and sent off on this wretched voyage. But as the years passed, the Australian colonies would offer far better prospects for many of them than they could have hoped for in England.

The era of the hulks lasted for eighty years. Except for the first eleven of those years, convicts were periodically collected from the hulks in England and transported to Australia. New South Wales accepted them until 1840. Convict voyages to Van Diemen's Land continued until 1852, and to Western Australia until 1867. In their respective ways, the First Families of Australia, like the First Families of Virginia and Maryland, are perhaps as proud and accomplished as any people on earth, notwithstanding the convict blood that undoubtedly flows through the redoubtable veins of many of them. The hulks are significant in the history of Virginia and Maryland, as they were the expedient adopted by the British when transportation to those colonies was terminated. They were significant in the history of Australia as many thousands of the men who became settlers of that continent before 1857 had been prisoners aboard the English hulks for months, if not years. Some 160,000 men and women, convicted of crimes in the British Isles, were transported to Australia before the era of convict transportation ended. By then the population of the Australian continent was ten times that number.[2] The influx of free settlers had been significant as, undoubtedly, had been the fertility of the several thousand women convicts, 250 of whom were among the first convicts transported to Botany Bay with the First Fleet.


Lord Ellenborough, Lord Chief Justice of England, saw fit to describe transportation for the convicts as "a summer's excursion in an easy migration to a happier and better climate." Needless to say, he had never undergone the experience.[3] Any convict from the hulks selected for transportation to Australia who expected a pleasant voyage and an idyllic life at the other end of the world, was doomed to crushing disillusionment. Being chosen to go out with the First Fleet was soon enough recognized as something other than a blessing. Some of the male convicts so honored were transferred from the ships in Portsmouth Harbour to the several First Fleet transports early in 1787, languishing there for four months before clearing English waters for Australia. During the weeks before embarkation, Arthur Phillip, who was to command the fleet and serve as the prison colony's first governor, wrote a number of urgent letters to Lord Sydney and to other Home and Colonial Office officials involved in planning the

Arthur Phillip, Commander of the First Fleet
and First Governor of New South Wales

voyage. He detailed the appalling inadequacy of supplies and warned against the consequences of overcrowding the small vessels that had been procured for the fleet.[†] Phillip's pleas had little effect.[4] His advice was eminently reasonable. Had a lesser number of convicts arrived at Port Jackson in good health, well supplied for the long and arduous task of establishing the colony, the aims of the authorities in England, so concerned about problems then besetting Great Britain's criminal justice system, would have been far better served.

It should be said, in any event, that very few if any of the convicts would have survived the eight months' voyage had some of the more extreme reports of their treatment been altogether accurate. But even by late-eighteenth century standards, horrifying circumstances did indeed pertain, especially on certain of the transports that followed the First Fleet. There were differences from ship to ship in the manner of handling the convicts during the voyage, depending on the inclination of the transport's master.[5]

There can be no doubt that the voyage to Botany Bay with the First Fleet was an agony. Perhaps it was no worse an experience for the transportees than many earlier convict voyages, but these first Australian settlers were at sea five times longer than the length of time then required for an Atlantic crossing. The First Fleet was in passage for seven months. Ports of call for resupply and repair were Tenerife, Rio de Janeiro and Cape Town. The convicts, battened down in the stifling below-decks "prisons," were more rebellious and more inclined to reckless demeanor while in port than during the long, miserable days at sea.

Troubles with the convicts would have been more difficult to control had not so many of them been sick. A tempting assumption is that the hulk overseers and gaolers were allowed to select the First Fleet transportees, and that they used the opportunity to rid themselves of troublesome prisoners, including some who were in poor health. It is more likely this kind of uncharitable strategy was employed in making selections for the Second Fleet. For the First Fleet, a formal selection procedure was established, which required the participation of officials at Old Bailey, the head keeper at Newgate and hulk manager Duncan Campbell.[6] This approach was moderately successful at best. It obviously did not result in selection of an entirely healthy contingent of prisoners. The physical

---

[†] The ships that comprised the first convict fleet to Australia were: *Alexander, Charlotte, Friendship, Lady Penrhyn, Prince of Wales* and *Scarborough.*

condition of the First Fleet's convicts was a simple reflection of the state of health of the nation's prison population. If there was a moderately workable procedure in 1787, it appears to have broken down completely before selections for the Second Fleet were made. Of the 1,006 convicts who in 1789 embarked on that disastrous excursion, 267 perished at sea of various diseases, another 150 not long after going ashore at Port Jackson.[7]

After the earlier voyages, the poor condition of the convicts who reached New South Wales was apparently called to the attention of the Home Office with sufficient force to cause some concern there. In 1795 Sir John Fitzpatrick, Inspector General of Health, was stationed at Portsmouth Harbour, where he inspected both ships and convicts bound for Australia. He was given authority to order substantial modification of the ships whenever he saw this as necessary to good health and hygiene. He was also authorized to order removed from ships the convicts he considered unfit as well as those who might be carrying infectious diseases.[8] The presence of one able and conscientious health official at one of the ports of embarkation was hardly enough to overcome the problem of unhealthy convicts being shipped out on unsanitary vessels, but Sir John's efforts are sure to have helped.

There were improvements after the voyages of the Second Fleet, and more markedly after the turn of the century, but convict voyages from England to Australia were never to be healthy or edifying experiences. The convicts were crowded below decks, having to endure the heat and stench of the ship's prison for many hours of each day. The more humane of the captains struck the irons of the convicts early in the voyage, but this occasioned extreme caution during the times they were brought on deck for airing. Indeed, if rumors of rebellion were heard, the convicts could expect to stay below decks, sometimes for days on end. Neither adequate clothing nor more than one thin blanket per convict was provided. Stifling heat had to be endured during passage through the tropics, followed by bitter cold when the ships reached the frigid waters of the Tasman Sea.

There was great contrast between the best and worst of the convict transports and the treatment of convicts aboard them. Literate, middle-class convicts were given such jobs as clerk to the captain or steward, and assigned to special quarters. Furthermore, many common prisoners made the voyage to Australia under reasonably tolerable circumstances. Others were unfortunate enough to go on board ships captained by the likes of Thomas Dennott, master of the *Britannia* on her passage from Plymouth to Port Jackson in 1796. Captain Dennott saw fit to reject the advice of his surgeon, a man whose compliance took easy precedence over his dedication to medicine. The convicts were kept chained below except for an occasional few minutes on deck in small groups. One man, suspected of plotting rebellion, was given three hundred lashes, rested for the night, then given five hundred more. Women convicts, their heads shaven, were neck yoked, caned on deck and heavily ironed. For her attempt to commit suicide, one Jenny Blacke had her head shaved and was personally caned on the face and shoulders by the captain. Several prisoners died of floggings, or of thirst during the protracted course of floggings.[9]

Though found culpable by a court of inquiry and dismissed from further service in convict transportation, Dennott was not prosecuted; another example of the lenient attitude so often shown during those days by the British government toward the misdeeds and failings of persons in authority.

It appears that the 1796 voyage of the *Britannia*, "the hell ship," may have helped break the back of the egregious character of convict transportation. There was significant improvement in the treatment of prisoners in transport after turn-of-the-century reforms. But then greed sometimes sufficed for sadism. In 1802 Richard Brooks, master of the *Atlas*, loaded his filthy ship to the gunwales with merchandise for private trading, cramming the shackled prisoners into whatever fetid crannies that remained.[10] The result in suffering and death among them could hardly have been more horrifying had his intent been less benign.

Aside from the agonies they so often suffered during safe transit, Australia-bound convicts shared with ship's company the perils of a voyage that included passage through some of the most dangerous waters on earth. Indeed, those perils would often beset them within sight of British shores. On August 31, 1833, at three o'clock in the afternoon, the *Amphitrite*, bound from Woolwich to Port Jackson, ran aground in heavy seas off the coast of France. On board were her crew of sixteen, 107 women convicts and twelve children. Also on board were a physician and his wife, emigrating to Australia. He was serving as ship's doctor. When the tide was at lowest ebb, rescue could have been easily accomplished, but Captain Hunter, the ship's master, refused help that was being urgently offered by French mariners on the beach, men who were experienced in shipwreck rescues. It appears that Captain Hunter was unwilling to give an order that would jeopardize his custody of the prisoners.

The ship wallowed helplessly on a sand bar throughout the stormy afternoon, within sight of the port of Boulogne, suffering a merciless pounding from the heavy waves of an incoming tide. At the crest of the tide she was still not free. Mr. Wilks, a British subject living in Boulogne, saw the ship not long after she ran aground, and learned that she was British. Like others on shore, he at first assumed that she would be freed by the flood of the tide, but when he saw that she was still in distress at six in the evening he wrote a hasty note to the British Consul in Boulogne, Mr. Hamilton, urging that he make arrangements to get aid to the vessel. The letter was delivered at about seven o'clock. The Consul took no action and did not make an appearance among those observing the struggling *Amphitrite* from shore until much later in the evening. Meanwhile, those aboard the ship knew they were in serious trouble, even if the authorities ashore who should have been most concerned did not. The crew of the *Amphitrite* put one longboat over the side. It would have, at the least, been capable of taking ashore the children and their convict mothers, and the wife of the ship's doctor. Apparently, she was the only woman on board who was not a convict. But the lady objected. She would not share her passage to safety with convicts. The ship's doctor, choosing to preserve his wife's dignity rather than her life, took it upon himself to order that no one be loaded into the boat. At ten o'clock that night the ship's hull gave way. All were engulfed by the sea. The physician and his imperious wife perished as did all of the female convicts, their children and all members of the crew except three. The captains of two small French boats, having put out into the dangerous seas of their own accord, were laying by the distressed *Amphitrite* when she broke up. They were able to fish from the stormy waters John Owen, Richard Rice and James Towsey, thus demonstrating that an organized rescue effort might have saved many more. These three crewmen survived to tell a board of inquiry about the unhappy events aboard the ship, which led to not even one of her lifeboats embarking. In the matter of there being no organized rescue effort, this same board of inquiry, in a remarkable exercise of rationalization, exonerated the dilatory British Consul at Boulogne of all blame.

According to an account of this sorrowful event in *The Times of London*, most of the prisoners aboard the *Amphitrite* were "Young girls, young women of small offenses, females who might have easily been reclaimed and led back to the paths of virtue." Sharing passage with them were twenty women from Scotland who were described as "hardened and most abandoned criminals."[11] In any event, the loss of the *Amphitrite* was a tragic loss to the colony in New South Wales, though hardly recognized there as cause for much bereavement.

Many of the early voyages to Australia were characterized by debauchery, drunkenness, rebellion and corruption. The marines who sailed out with the First Fleet were treated little better than the convicts. There appears to have been a deficiency of character and stability among convicts, marines, crew and commanders. Consider a listing by Jonathan King in his *The First Fleet, the Convict Voyage that Founded Australia*, of the "more interesting-frequently mentioned people" on board the *Alexander*, just one of the six convict transports:

Richard Asky, marine, court martialed for drinking at Tenerife, one of a gang of four who killed marine Tom Bullmore.

Surgeon in Chief John White, had an affair with convict Elizabeth Dudgeon.

Black John Caesar, convict rebel, bushranger, rapist and murderer.

William Dring, convict, looted wreck of *Sirius* spending a drunken night on board as she sank off Norfolk Island.

William Francis, convict, led an uprising on Norfolk Island.

James Freeman, convict, became public hangman rather than die when convicted of stealing flour.

Daniel Gordon, negro convict, flogged for stealing wine from contractor's agent Zachariah Clark of *Sirius*.

Lieutenant John Johnstone, marine, ordered severe punishments.

John Jones, caught sleeping with convicts.

Isaac Knight, marine sergeant, demoted for misbehavior in Cape Town.

William Long, First Mate, beaten up by convicts during uprising near Cape Town and fell from ship.

John Powers, convict, escaped briefly at Tenerife, led a rebellion below decks near Cape Town, committed more crimes in the colony before being hanged.

Lieutenant James Sharpe, marine, court martialed.

Lieutenant Shortland, Naval Agent for Transports, Commander of Division A of the fleet from Cape Town to Botany Bay and commander of commercial ships on return voyage, travelled on Supply before Cape Town.

George Thomas Shortland, Second mate, son of Lieutenant John

Shortland.

Duncan Sinclair, Master of *Alexander*, a weak and unpopular captain who lost control of his ship between Rio and Cape Town, and was superseded by the Agent, John Shortland.[12]

Ships of the First Fleet, under its commander and governor designate, Arthur Phillip, anchored in Botany Bay, but after a closer inspection of the shore, sailed up the coast in search of a deeper anchorage and more promising site for settlement. On January 20, 1788, the fleet put in at Sydney Cove, destined to become one of the greatest ports of the southern oceans. The anchorage was named Port Jackson, as was the colony established there.[†]

The good ship *Alexander's* passenger list, and other records, suggest that many of the convicts who disembarked from the First Fleet's ships at Port Jackson were perfidious fellows who had nurtured their criminality from an early age and offered little promise to be other than troublesome, if not dangerous, during efforts at settlement. But among them were inoffensive poor people whose crimes were motivated by need. Furthermore, within the convict group there must have been a hidden pool of decency and strength. To be sure, many of the convicts menaced and disrupted the good order of the settlement until they escaped, were hanged, or shackled and shipped off to Norfolk Island for good, but a greater number, to varying degrees, pitched in and did some part of this first task in the founding of the Commonwealth of Australia. What other conclusions are there to be reached when we consider the prodigious difficulties faced by First Fleet Commander and first governor of the colony, Arthur Phillip? Despite his best efforts, preparations for the voyage of the First Fleet had been appallingly inadequate. Most of the marine contingent that had accompanied the fleet refused to accept any responsibility for helping to maintain order after disembarkation. Instead, they set about exploiting their new circumstances as best they could. Some of them threw in with the worst of the convicts in bedeviling the settlement. And there were endless other difficulties. The woodlands, which needed to be cleared, were found to consist of trees that were almost impervious to the ax. Sources of fresh water from the interior were limited. The aborigines were resentful

---

[†] Botany Bay, five miles south of Sydney's harbor, became the reference commonly used in Britain for all convict settlements in New South Wales, even though no convict settlement was ever established there.

and could not be enticed. There was much illness, especially among the convicts. Crops failed; ships sent to Cape Town and to India for supplies were wrecked or lost at sea. Starvation threatened. When help finally arrived from England it came in the form of a shipload of sickly convicts, one of the unhappy remnants of the Second Fleet.[13] And yet, the colony survived. These facts tell us, first of all, that Arthur Phillip, who had been plucked from the obscurity of his modest Lyndhurst farm to undertake the task of commanding the First Fleet, was a remarkable man. Secondly, it is certain that he was accompanied by some redoubtable associates, that description of the cast of characters aboard the *Alexander* notwithstanding. But the most intriguing conclusion to be drawn is that among the convicts was much courage, strength and loyalty.

A few times in more recent decades, prison administrators have observed this phenomenon. Mutuality appears to be the key to its activation. It will occur sometimes when prisoners, asked for help by their keepers, perceive the reality of the need and show themselves capable of astonishing levels of responsibility and constructive achievement. This phenomenon has been observed at the sites of forest fires, threatening flood waters, prison uprisings and during the protracted development of innovative, politically vulnerable prison rehabilitation programs.[14]

Southeast Australia was sure to have been soon colonized in any event. But no less certainly, the first effort at Port Jackson in 1788 would have failed had it not been for the substantial help, indeed a certain measure of pioneer heroism, on the part of those wretched men and women who went out to Australia in chains.

When a semblance of organization was achieved at Port Jackson, the convicts were put to work in gangs on land-clearing projects, on roads, on the settlement's farms and on public buildings. Although convict voyages from England to the Port Jackson area continued until 1840, the numbers of convicts were diluted by the arrival of many free settlers who were given grants of land and other aids to homestead establishment. Some of the convicts were indentured to these free settlers. But then grants of land and assistance were also offered to convicts on completion of servitude. Many succeeded as homesteaders, establishing family dynasties and contributing to the healthy growth of Australian society.[15] Others, by no means equipped to undertake the wholesome rigors of pioneer farming, failed. Many of them, like James Vaux and Dickens' fictitious Magwitch, made their way back to England. Others were hired as prisoner gang guards, demonstrating a capacity for brutality learned at the other end of the lash, while still others became "bushrangers" or otherwise drifted into the wild labyrinth of southeastern Australia's flourishing criminal class.

In England the British government had an unassailable excuse for continued use of the hulks. They had become holding stations for convicted criminals awaiting transport to Australia. Until passage of legislation in 1855 authorizing penal servitude, offenders were not sentenced to terms of imprisonment, but many who went aboard the hulks with sentences to transportation never made the voyage. We can be sure that ordinance yard superintendents at Portsmouth and Woolwich maneuvered to delay transport of skilled workers among the convicts, for years if possible. Death from disease, debilitation and accident claimed thousands of hulk convicts who would otherwise have gone to Australia. The most fortunate of the convicts were spared the voyage by pardons.

The opening of Australia had allowed the resumption of convict transportation and thus, for some, a welcome alternative to long-term confinement on the hulks. Eventually, however, it was to have dismaying consequences for the more recalcitrant of the transportees. To be sure, harsh measures were taken against malefactors among the First Fleet convicts at Port Jackson, but during the time when there was only one colony, under the care and command of a man like Arthur Phillip, excessive punishments were not sanctioned. Sadism directed toward convicts, no matter what their offense, was not knowingly tolerated. With the spread of convict colonization, however, this kind of restraint was to evaporate. In England, voices of reform like those of Elizabeth Fry and James Neild, as well as the ardent influence of Wesleyan Christianity and the close proximity of liberals in Parliament like Samuel Romilly, had some mollifying effect on the misery suffered by prisoners in the hulks and gaols in the British Isles. Those humane influences seemed to wane, however, once the convict transports became lost from view over the horizon. Norfolk Island, a thousand miles from the east coast of Australia, was a place where some of the most egregious cruelties were perpetrated by such representatives of the Crown as John Giles Price and Lt. Col. James Morisset. Between the regimes of these two sadists, Captain Alexander Maconochie was to serve as commandant of the station. During his brief tenure, he introduced innovations in rehabilitation that were to be influential with penologists and reformers a century later. Although the beneficial effects of his efforts were undeniable, they were accompanied by more compassion than could be tolerated. Shortly after his departure in 1843, officially sanctioned brutality was resumed at Norfolk Island.[16]

In addition to the habitations of horror at Norfolk Island, Port Arthur and Moreton Bay, the colonial authorities who succeeded Arthur Phillip saw fit in 1824 to place at anchor in Sydney Harbor a decrepit, vermin-ridden old transport, the *Phoenix*, for use as a prison hulk. This hulk served as a holding station for the unfortunate wretches awaiting transport to the punishment settlements. Thus, a brutal microcosm of Britain's penal scheme was established at the other end of the world from the precincts of Elizabeth Fry and the other English reformers.[17]

After 1840 the transports did not disembark prisoners at Port Jackson or elsewhere in New South Wales. They were dispatched instead to Hobart in Van Diemen's Land, and Port Phillip Bay, where a nearby gold strike had caused the settlement of Melbourne to burgeon. Convict settlements were also established at Moreton Bay, eventually to become Brisbane, and Port Essington on the north coast. Throughout this period, contingents of recalcitrant prisoners were dropped off from time to time at Norfolk Island. Last to receive cargos of convicts from England were the settlements in Western Australia, where a desperate need for farm labor kept the doors open to convict importation in the Perth and Swan River areas until 1867.[18]

On May 24, 1857, the old teak-built merchantman, *Success*, dropped anchor off Williamstown in the Port of Melbourne. On board was a mixed company of convicts, ticket-of-leave men and free settlers. Rumors about a new gold find in the interior, north of Melbourne, resulted in the ship's soon being left in the harbor with hardly anyone on board to guard the shackled convicts. No cargo waited on the dock, nor would there have been a crew to manage passage to the next port. Meanwhile, due to the influx of gold seekers, many of them ex-convicts, crime in the vicinity of Melbourne had become rampant. On one day, the town's principal newspaper, the *Argus*, published twelve columns of notices of horse thefts. More serious crimes were everyday occurrences.[19] It was logical that the *Success* should become a convict hulk. With the ship's master and crew off in the bush looking for gold, authorities of the new state of Victoria had no problem reaching an accommodation with the owners.[†]

---

[†] A ship purporting to be the *Success*, fitted out as a floating museum, complete with wax dummies of suffering convicts, sailed to England and to the United States in 1912 and was on display at numerous ports. If authentic, she would have been more than 120 years old. The original *Success* was on display in the harbor at Hobart for several years after her deactivation as a prison hulk, but was not welcomed when she sailed to Sydney. She was scuttled at her moorings by irate citizens in March 1892. See Robert Hughes, *The Fatal Shore*, 600-601.

The Australian prison ship, *Success*

Unless they happened to have construction skills, prisoners who had made the voyage from England to the port of Melbourne aboard the *Success* were confined in makeshift on-shore lockups while elaborate refitting of the ship was done. Soon the sturdy old merchantman, which had been launched at Rangoon in 1790,[20] was converted into a far more formidable floating prison than any that had been seen at Woolwich or elsewhere in the waters of southern England. She was equipped with seventy-two cells fronted with iron grillwork. Most of the cells were seven by four feet. A few were seven by seven, purportedly for occupancy by honor prisoners, but since the prisoner capacity of the ship was established at 120, it is likely the larger cells were doubled more often than not.[21] Dark cells were installed and the ship was equipped with a sweat box, a Y post (for convenient laying on of the "cat") and the other accouterments of proper discipline. A more-than-adequate assortment of shackles, shot balls and chains were brought on board.[22] John Price, who had been one of the most brutal of Norfolk Island's governors, was induced to come out of retirement and take charge of Victoria's penal establishment.[23] Three other vessels had been acquired for use as prison hulks. The *Lysander* was the hulk on which women prisoners were held. The *Success* was the only Victoria hulk to be elaborately retrofitted.[24]

Twenty years before Victoria's hulk fleet was established in the port of Melbourne, legislation had been passed and regulations written in Great Britain that categorically forbade, in English prisons and convict hulks, cruelties of the sort that long continued to be commonplace in the Australian colonies. John Price had been allowed to retire honorably from his Norfolk Island post in 1850, even though the sadistic nature of his rule was well known. Indeed, it had been documented and called to the attention of colonial authorities by the Roman Catholic Bishop of Tasmania.[25]

Apparently, the authorities in Melbourne knew what they wanted. John Price did not disappoint them. For trivial offenses, prisoners on the *Success* were scourged, confined in airless, four-feet-high "black holes," and beaten indiscriminately by sadistic guards. The more tractable of the convicts lived in cramped, stifling quarters, and labored in quarries on shore without rest or refreshment, with eighteen-pound iron balls chained to their ankles. As reports of atrocities circulated in the community, the town's clergy and other responsible elements of the citizenry began to express their concern.[26] The *Melbourne Age* called for an inquiry into John Price's methods, but the *Argus* staunchly supported him. On a March morning in 1857, John Price made an inspection visit to the Williamstown quarry where gangs of convicts from the *Success* were at work. With his characteristic psychopathic arrogance, he strode in among a group of convicts who were accosting him with complaints and demands. They closed around him ominously. The guards who comprised his undermanned escort drew back. Using pickaxes, shovels and stones, the convicts struck him down. The assailants broke and ran, as did fifteen or twenty other prisoners who had been at work in the quarry but were in no way involved in the assault. As all were shackled, they were easily rounded up within a few hours. The records are not precise, but it appears that as many as twenty were hanged. John Price died on the day following the assault without regaining consciousness.[27]

Hulk convicts in England, under the successive administrations of Duncan Campbell, Aaron Graham, John Capper and, finally, Voules and Jebb, had suffered privation, suffering and sometimes, terror. But these agonies resulted from inattention, official myopia, incompetence, indeed from the irredeemable nature of the hulk system itself. They were not deliberately inflicted by those who administered the hulks. On the other hand, during his long years of service to the Crown in Australia, John Price, the son of a Cornish baronet, had committed, ordered or sanctioned many crimes against his fellow human beings that were more egregious than those for which most of the prisoners under his command had been convicted. He was one of the worst, but John Price's approach to managing prisoners was hardly unique among the men who were in charge of the Australian convict settlements during the transportation years.[28]

Rather than being a cause for increased ferocity in the treatment of the hulk convicts, the assassination of John Price precipitated a long-overdue inquiry. The result was that the hulk fleet in the port of Melbourne was officially deactivated before the end of 1857, the year in which it was established. It was necessary for a certain amount of shipboard confinement to be continued for a while, but without the degenerate influence of John Price.[29]


Just three months before the *Success* and her sister hulks in the port of Melbourne were deactivated — eleven years before the last shipment of convicts was disembarked in Western Australia — the *Defense* had burned in the Thames off Woolwich Warren and the last remnants of the English hulk establishment were shut down. The prison hulks of England and the convict settlements of Australia formed a parallelogram in the history of 18th and 19th century imprisonment, maintaining an integral, globe-spanning relationship for seventy years. In a sense, these two aspects of the British criminal justice system sprang from the same crisis, were argued for by the same advocates, and ridiculed by the same opponents. However ignoble the short-term intent, convict transportation to Australia played an important part in bringing about a glorious long-term result. Not so the hulks. Nothing gained there but shame, and yet, as we are to see, the "penitentiary house" alternative, argued for so ardently by progressive reformers and humanitarians, was to add its own chapter of shame to the history of imprisonment among English-speaking people, the legacy of which still lives.

# VII

## MR GRAHAM'S TRIBULATIONS

In 1802, Duncan Campbell finally decided to be unequivocal in advising the government that he no longer wanted responsibility for the convict hulks. His contract was not renewed. He died the following year,[1] an honored septuagenarian, who stood high among his peers in business, and among all the good folk of his community, but who seems to have insulated himself, throughout his long tenure, from the realities of the hulks. During his forty years as a convict transporter and hulk manager, he had made gestures in the cause of humanity from time to time, indeed, had spent a good deal of money in trying to reduce the misery of the wretched fellows committed to his care. What more could he have done? The attitude he displayed is one that has survived.

The Bunbury Committee, appointed and convened only two years after establishment of the hulks, had relied during the course of its inquiries, to no small extent, on John Howard's inspections. Legislation passed in 1778 authorized appointment of gaol inspectors, who would visit the places of confinement to which they were assigned no less often than once each quarter, where they were to "examine diligently" the state of these facilities.[2] But any reports of inspection of the hulks that may have been submitted by a government inspector during Duncan Campbell's tenure did not make their way into Parliamentary sessional papers and presumably did not capture the attention of anyone of influence in the government. With the departure of Duncan Campbell, appointment of an inspector who would, indeed, "examine diligently" the condition of the hulks and their operation, seemed the thing to do.

Aaron Graham had come to the attention of key members of Parliament because of his role as a young magistrate in the government's response to home port mutinies on board ships of the Royal Navy in 1797. He distinguished himself at the Nore, where the trouble first erupted. He was then dispatched to Spithead, where there had been a similar uprising. Graham was credited with having dealt with the mutineers in a firm but humane manner. There was no way whereby Richard Parker, the idealistic young midshipman who had been thrust into the leadership of the mutiny, could escape the gallows, but he did not die entirely in vain. Due in part to Aaron Graham's recommendations, inquiries were conducted by Parliament and the Admiralty into conditions that lay behind the mutiny. Some modest reforms followed.[3] Meanwhile, officials in the Home Office were impressed with Aaron Graham. He looked to them like just the man needed to serve as Inspector of the Hulks.

Graham was appointed on March 25, 1802.[4] It appears that he was either given, or took by his own initiative, more authority and responsibility than had been originally contemplated for him. After several years of calculated myopia on the part of the government toward the results of Campbell's mercenary administration of the hulks, it is probable that discomfort had developed. Division of responsibility among the Justices of Middlesex, the Court of King's Bench, Parliament and the Home Office, had made neglect inevitable, especially as this was a time of foreign wars and trying internal problems for His Majesty's government. Legislation passed before Duncan Campbell's departure effectively prevented the government from again contracting out management of the hulk establishment as a business enterprise.[5] Inspector Graham's willingness to remain in place and assume full command of the hulk establishment was undoubtedly welcomed, and it was pleasing to the authorities that he was asking for no change in title or increase in his salary of £350 annually. It was at this time that the Secretary of State for the Home Office became the senior official primarily responsible for the hulks. The Middlesex Justices gratefully relinquished their involvement, while the Justices of King's Bench continued a perfunctory sort of judicial oversight.

Graham managed the hulks for thirteen years. He took charge with considerable verve, but, as we shall see, his initial enthusiasm was seriously dampened, if not extinguished, by his discouraging encounters with the ponderous barriers to the reforms he clearly wanted to achieve. His experience was a classic example of the newly appointed, reform-minded administrator, defeated by entrenched forces of resistance within the system, a pattern that has become commonplace over subsequent decades.

At the time of Graham's appointment, the hulk establishment was somewhat smaller than it had been before, and would become again. It consisted of the *Retribution*, on the Thames at Woolwich, the *Captivity*, anchored on the Gosport side of Portsmouth Harbour, the *Laurel*, anchored off the Portsmouth docks, and the *Portland*, five miles distant in Langstone Harbour. Just as Graham was assuming command, the *Prudentia* was taken out of service at Woolwich, while a new acquisition for the hulk fleet, the *Zealand*, was stationed at Sheerness.

The *Captivity* and the *Laurel* had earlier been used for military prisoners.[6] Since they lay no great distance from each other in Portsmouth Harbour, they shared a hospital ship. Each of the other hulks had its own hospital ship.

By this time the hulk fleet consisted primarily of ships decommissioned by the Royal Navy, rather than retired merchantmen. The largest of them were the *Captivity*, which had carried 74 guns, the *Zealand* and the *Retribution* of similar size. Each of these hulks housed more than 450 convicts. The census of the *Retribution* reached 555 in 1809. The *Portland* and the *Laurel*, which were in the 50 gun class, housed fewer than 300 prisoners until the latter years of the Graham era.

Although Graham did not have to contend with an epidemic comparable to the gaol fever plague that assaulted the hulks during the first two years of their use, death from disease aboard the hulks (perhaps more frequently aboard the hospital ships) was commonplace. The *Retribution* was by all odds the unhealthiest of the hulks. From 1804 through 1811, 170 of her prisoners died (from all causes) as opposed to seventy of those assigned to the *Captivity*, a vessel of similar size.[7]

At the very beginning of his tenure Graham instituted significant reforms. The woefully inadequate food ration was increased. He was able to improve matters here without expense to the government by holding contractors who provided victuals and supplies to closer account, and by his more systematic approach to supervision of subordinates. Not long after his appointment in 1802, Graham issued detailed instructions to the overseers of the hulks that, when read today, reflect a remarkable grasp of sound fiscal and personnel management principles, and a surprisingly good understanding of inmate management problems. It appears that Graham learned some excellent lessons at the Nore and at Spithead as to the positive effects of honesty and humane treatment. He did not, alas, gain any miraculous insights as to how idealistic principles might be implemented with his staff of semi-literate guards and cynical, worn-out overseers, but his issuance of instructions to his captains, which provided something akin to a set of official regulations, was a much-needed measure.

The instructions required that either the overseer of each hulk, or his mate, be on board at all times. An occurrence book was to be kept, for recording incidents of significance, also for notation of the convicts sent ashore to work each day, the number and identity of those in the hospital, and other statistical information. Use of the hulk's boats for private purposes was prohibited, as was private utilization of inmate labor. The weekly menu was to be posted for perusal of the convicts, showing exact weight allowances of the items of food to be served. This practice had been urged by John Howard twenty-five years before Graham's appointment but never implemented. The instructions placed a great deal of emphasis on holding the supply contractors to account as to quantities and condition of victuals. There was specificity with respect to sick call and hospital admissions, religious services, duties of the chaplains, clothing issuance and sanitation. Hammocks were to be aired and lashed up each day, decks, above and below, washed down twice weekly, and no pigs or poultry were to be kept on board.[†] The instructions reflected much concern over matters of probity, prohibiting practices that had enabled employees of the hulk establishment to exploit their situation for personal gain. Graham's instructions also tell us that he was sensitive to fairness and objectivity in personnel management. Note Article 15 of the Instructions:

> You are to be careful that all the Officers and Guards punctually do their duty; and in event of any vacancy happening by death or otherwise, you are to direct the next officer in seniority to do the duty until I shall have had an opportunity of inquiring whether he is a proper person to fill it up. And as an encouragement to all on board, you are from time to time to send to me an impartial account of their behavior, so that I may be able on all occasions to approve of your choice of one from amongst themselves; and not be obliged to put a stranger over any of their heads. And it is to be understood by you, that in all cases where any person is appointed by me, that the moment he enters the Hulks, I have no longer any private knowledge of him; but if he neglects his duty, you are to treat him and report of him to me just as you would treat and report of any other person— In short, as you are answerable for the conduct of every one on board, you are to take care not to make any other distinction between them than such as shall be warranted by superior merit, which with me will ever be the strongest inducement to confirm your appointments.

---

[†] It is unlikely that an article of instructions regarding pigs and poultry would have been issued had there not been a practice of having farm animals aboard the hulks. Despite Inspector Graham's orders, there is evidence from at least one source that pigs were kept aboard the *Retribution* as late as 1809. See page 111 of James Vaux's *Memoirs* (London, W. Clowes, 1819.)

John Howard's recommendations with respect to lighter leg shackles had, at long last, been implemented, enabling Aaron Graham to replace the cumbersome, unsanitary sleeping platforms with hammocks. This was a beneficial change. The hammocks could be aired regularly and stowed topside during the day. But the use of hammocks also resulted in greater flexibility in the use of space below decks, making possible tremendous increases in the numbers of convicts housed on the hulks, with all of the added misery attendant to overcrowding, a classic example of the well-intentioned reform resulting in worsened conditions of confinement.

Another of Graham's improvements, while certainly worth trying, was a disappointment. By closing the main companionways and installing separate ladders to each of the decks on which hulk prisoners were housed, Graham hoped to give a measure of security to the less aggressive convicts. Before installing the ladders, there was no effective way to prevent the prisoners from having free range of all of the underdecks of the ship. From evening lock-down until dawn every prisoner had access to every other prisoner. Therefore, reasoned Graham and his colleagues, the practice of housing different categories of prisoners on separate decks was meaningless. The less-hardened men were subject to corruption. Old partners in crime could seek each other out for various evil purposes, and the weaker convicts had no protection against the predatory gangs that would rove throughout the hulks each night after lockdown.

Impelled by these considerations, Graham moved forward with his deck separation scheme soon after his appointment. The plan was first implemented at Portsmouth. The *Captivity* and the somewhat smaller *Portland* were fitted out with separate ladders to each deck. The companionways were closed. Similar modifications were then made on the *Laurel*, also at Portsmouth, and the *Zealand* at Sheerness. In February 1812, 218 prisoners were housed on the lower deck of the *Captivity*. Her next deck level was divided into three parts. One-hundred-eighty-seven prisoners were assigned to the main part, sixty-seven to a smaller area, and in the forward section of the deck, where the food was prepared, twenty-four more prisoners were housed. The *Laurel*, a smaller vessel, housed 150 on her lower deck while dividing the remaining 121 in separate areas of the two decks above. The records give us no figures for the *Portland* or *Zealand*, both of them three-deck vessels.

An effort to close the companionways and effect separation among convicts aboard the *Retribution* at Woolwich was a fiasco. It was reported to the Committee that "the convicts rose up in the night-time and tore down the work." The prisoner population aboard the *Retribution* consisted overwhelmingly of Londoners, offenders of the sort who would have developed all kinds of sophisticated illicit activities. The profitability of these activities depended on continued access to the whole of the below-decks areas of the hulk, hence the uprising and destruction of barriers between the decks. Having no officers in place to determine which of the prisoners were responsible, the hulk overseers apparently threw up their hands, perhaps after some measure of not overly provocative mass punishment. The entire sorry affair is reminiscent of the kind of incident that might happen in a present-day, overcrowded, understaffed, poorly managed American prison.

Aside from reducing the range of operations for the predators and shady entrepreneurs among the convicts, deck separation seems not to have been especially useful on those ships that did achieve it. The Select Committee commended Graham for his initiative, but was not very impressed with the results. If nothing else, Graham's deck separation effort demonstrated his recognition that unsupervised association of all prisoners below decks, whether predatory or weak, young or old, criminalistic or unsophisticated, was a serious problem. But he was not quite up to the task of developing an inmate classification system of the kind that so obviously should have accompanied the deck separation scheme. He continued to rely on separating the convicts on the basis of their length of sentence or remaining time to be served. Systematic information about convicts committed to the hulks was not provided. Therefore there could be no separation based on offense, prior criminal record or history of assaultiveness, and hence no reliable way to protect the weaker prisoners. At various times during the years that followed, attempts were made to categorize the convicts by having senior staff personnel make judgments on their behavior and attitude. This approach would have worked well on any hulk that happened to be blessed with a strong set of officers. Unfortunately, incompetence, roughness and unreliability were as often as not to be seen among line employees of the hulks throughout the eighty years of their use. The men who served as overseers of the hulks, surgeons and chaplains, may have done somewhat better, but, as we shall see, their efforts had limited usefulness.[8]

Graham's deck separation arrangements did not result in any alteration in the practice of locking down the convicts at night without supervision. Under these circumstances we can be sure that all the exploitative and predatory practices characteristic of all poorly supervised prisons continued to be commonplace after the evening lockdown. George Lee, who was confined aboard the *Portland* in Langstone Harbour in 1803, asserted that "The horrible crime of sodomy rages . . . shamefully throughout . . . ." He charged further that it was "in no way discountenanced by those in command." Jeremy Bentham became convinced by his sources of information that prisoners going on board the hulks at Woolwich were raped routinely, as something of an initiation ritual.[9] And yet throughout the history of the hulks there persisted a horrified reluctance to admit that weak and passive prisoners were ever raped by their fellows. The Select Committee on Penitentiary Houses dealt with the matter thusly in its 1812 report:

> Your Committee . . . have the satisfaction to observe, that with whatever misconduct (the prisoners) may be chargeable after they are locked down for the night, the Captains of the different Hulks all concur in disbelieving the existence among them of the more atrocious vice which rumor has sometimes imputed to them . . . . It is true that complaints of the prevalence of this vice, and of its having ceased to be held in detestation, have been sometimes communicated by letter, and otherwise, from prisoners to their friends when applying for assistance in obtaining their release, because they have found representations of this nature to be the most effectual means of exciting compassion, and stimulating their friends to exertions in their behalf; but whenever these complaints have lead to inquiry, the result has been a satisfactory disproof of the general charge, and in no one instance has any proof of individual guilt been established.

And thus the Committee's overly sanguine conclusion was based on their belief that the convicts themselves would prevent certain unspeakable outrages, not on any confidence in the efficaciousness of the deck separations.

Although the Committee chose to reject the thought of a significant incidence of homosexual assault, they could hardly put aside their concern about the general conduct of the hulk prisoners left unsupervised below decks so many hours each day. It must have been obvious that there was a great deal more to worry about than "prevalence among the convicts . . . of gambling, swearing and every kind of vicious conversation." The hulk overseers made it plain in testimony before the Committee that neither they nor any of their officers ever visited those parts of the ship in which the prisoners were confined ". . . except upon some extraordinary emergency." The belief was expressed that no guard nor officer ". . . could go down among the prisoners at night without risk of personal injury." All of the overseers claimed to have sources of information about prisoners' conduct below decks, but the information they had was of little use as the convicts who supplied it could not ". . . be brought forward to prove the facts (because of) the danger to which they would in that case be exposed of being ill-treated by their companions." On being asked whether convicts ever complained to him about mistreatment at the hands of others, the overseer of the *Captivity* stated that "it is a thing they do not dare to do in the *Captivity*, but in the *Laurel* (to which he had previously been assigned) they used to bring them up manfully." The overseer of the *Portland* did his best to persuade the Committee that mistreatment of convicts by other convicts aboard his ship was rare, then went on to outline what he was accustomed to doing when he observed "marks of violence."[10] It seems that his reaction was to cajole or badger information out of the hapless prisoner but to do nothing about the incidents reported. It is unlikely that victimized prisoners very often consented to name their tormentors. In any case, nowhere to be found in the lengthy report of the 1811-1812 inquiry is there mention of a prisoner being prosecuted, transferred or in any way disciplined for wrongful treatment of another prisoner. We do, however, have it on authority of another source that a prisoner was hanged at Maidstone for murder committed aboard the *Retribution* in 1809.[11]

The eighth article of Aaron Graham's General Instructions to his overseers required that all prisoners, except shoemakers and tailors employed on board the hulks, be sent to work ashore each day but Sundays. There seems to have been reasonably good compliance with this instruction at Woolwich during the first decade of the 19th century. There was plenty of work for the *Retribution's* prisoners at the Royal Arsenal and elsewhere on the Woolwich Warren. Work was also plentiful in the Portsmouth area. The labor of convicts from the *Portland* in Langstone Harbour, just east of Portsmouth, was greatly valued by British Army engineers then engaged in developing the arsenal at Cumberland Fort. Convicts on the *Captivity* and the *Laurel* moored in flourishing Portsmouth Harbour were in demand in the Portsmouth dockyard and across the harbor on the Gosport side as well. Aboard the *Zealand*, however, at anchor off Sheerness, there was much idleness. The *Zealand's* prisoner complement had increased to 500 by 1811. The dockyard at Sheerness was far less busy than those in the Portsmouth area or at Woolwich, and there were no major public works in progress elsewhere on the Medway. Available work ashore usually required fewer than half of the *Zealand's* prisoners. The overseer's practice was to call for volunteers each morning, 200 of whom he would send ashore for three or four hours of work. After the midday meal he would select 200 of those who had remained aboard during the morning for afternoon duty ashore.

At Sheerness and elsewhere, unskilled hulk prisoners were newly formed into work gangs each day. They bent their backs to the kinds of tasks done in the 20th century by forklifts, backhoes and bulldozers. The work was arduous except when nothing useful was at hand for the convict laborers to do, and they were allowed to dawdle away their time on make-work projects. Officials on the docks made good use of the few convicts who had skills in carpentry, metal-smithing and masonry.

As detailed and specific as they were, Aaron Graham's instructions did not address the lack of uniformity among the various stations where allowances and privileges were concerned. Authorities on the Woolwich Warren, at Cumberland Fort and on the docks at Sheerness and Portsmouth, chose to maintain independence in this regard. At Woolwich the value of the prisoners' daily allowances ranged from two-pence to four-pence-half-penny per day. At the Portsmouth dockyard, each man received allowances valued at two-pence and a farthing per day, with an additional two farthings worth in tobacco "for those who wanted it." The prisoners who worked at Gosport and Cumberland Fort received an allowance of biscuit, tobacco and beer in the value of a penny a day. The workers at Sheerness received nothing, probably because work was limited there, therefore not compulsory.

At Woolwich and Sheerness convicts were given, on release, a half guinea (ten-and-a-half shillings) and some clothing. At Portsmouth and Langstone Harbours the release gratuity was more generous, one pound, sixteen shillings, or about three times the amount given to releasees at Woolwich and Sheerness. Clothing was not officially a part of the release gratuity from the Portsmouth area hulks, but since the men were surely not released in convict outfits, it is likely that washed and mended clothing taken from new admissions were given to those who had nothing else suitable, a practice that continues today in American prisons.

Graham would have had no control over the allowances given to the convicts for their work at the dockyards on other on-shore work stations. He seems to have made no effort to arrange for uniformity in release gratuities.

In the course of fitting out for deck separation Graham had chapels built aboard the *Captivity*, the *Zealand* and, despite her small size, the *Portland*, contributing inevitably to the problem of overcrowding on those hulks. This fact was surely not lost on the long-suffering convicts. The *Laurel* was not given a chapel but arrangements were made for holding services on the spar deck, probably with the use of sail cloth canopies for protection against the frequent rains that fall on England's southern coast. It would have been reasonable to assign two chaplains to the Portsmouth area, where a thousand convicts were housed aboard three hulks, one of them a substantial distance from the other two. The *Retribution* at Woolwich and the *Zealand* at Sheerness, having prisoner populations half that number, were each given a chaplain. Neither of these men had to do the traveling between ships required of the Rev. Henry Donne of Portsmouth. Furthermore, the unfortunate Mr. Donne was required also to conduct services aboard the port commander's ship on Sundays and visit the sick aboard hospital ships in the Portsmouth and Langstone harbors. Mr. Donne testified before the Select Committee that he managed his extensive responsibilities by holding services for the prisoners of the *Laurel* and the *Portland* on alternate Sundays, with services read on the Sundays of his absence by an officer of the ship. He deserved better than to have been so thoroughly embarrassed before the Committee when the overseer of the *Portland* testified that the practice of having one of his officers "read the prayers" every other Sabbath day had been discontinued four years before.

Graham never did get his deck separation work done on the *Retribution*, nor was a chapel built for her. The likely scenario is that the carpenters and shipwrights arrived with tools and materials and well-wrought plans. They set to work constructing ladders to the separate decks, closing off the main companionway and framing out the chapel. But then they came to work one morning, a few days later, to find all they had done torn away by the convicts during the night. Whereupon, the workmen packed their tools and went home, leaving their bill with a thoroughly disgusted Inspector Graham, who seems to have made no effort to have them return.

In any event, the Rev. Mr. Samuel Watson, who had been given by his Bishop what may have been the most undesirable assignment in the Diocese of London, had no pulpit. Perhaps he had also been denied the gift of a strong and resonant speaking voice. He complained to the Committee that when he assembled the convicts on the spar deck for services most of them couldn't hear him. Among the disreputable company of London criminals aboard the *Retribution* it is unlikely there were many church goers. Those who did report topside on Sunday mornings would undoubtedly have been suspected of having other than religious motives.

Chaplain Watson complained to Aaron Graham with a verbosity that would have been irritating even during that era of florid expression. He mournfully reminded the Inspector of his prior assurances that a chapel would be provided for the *Retribution*. Graham's lack of sympathy with Chaplain Watson must have been influenced by his awareness of the far greater handicaps under which Chaplain Donne labored at Portsmouth without complaint, and by Chaplain Watson's insistence that he bore no responsibility for "personal communication" with the convicts, "except in cases of sickness." His attitude stood in vivid contrast to that of the Rev. Mr. Thomas Price, Chaplain of the *Zealand* at Sheerness. Chaplain Price would stay aboard his hulk for two weeks at a time, offering counsel to the convicts at every opportunity.[12] (This man's uncompromising effort to serve as an effective advocate for the boy convicts on the *Euryalus*, more than fifteen years after his service aboard the *Zealand*, is recounted in Chapter X.)

In 1811 and 1812, the House of Commons Select Committee on Penitentiary Houses conducted a long overdue review of the hulk establishment. Their report was hardly an unqualified endorsement of Graham's performance but, quite properly, criticism of him was restrained. Conditions aboard the hulks continued to be very bad, especially with respect to the lack of control over the behavior of the convicts toward one another. Members of the Committee were to express more concern about the corrupting effects of association between hardened criminals and less blameworthy offenders, than about predatory victimization of the weaker convicts. Indeed, as we have seen, there was a reluctance to accept that the latter was a problem. It would be fair to conclude, in any case, that while Graham's extraordinary efforts did not have altogether encouraging results, the horrors that persisted would have been worse had those efforts not been made.

It is unlikely that a more qualified or better motivated man than Aaron Graham could have been found for the task of attempting to elevate the hulk establishment to an efficient and humane level. He made a sincere and energetic effort over a period of years. A few improvements were made, but consider the observations of James Howard Vaux, bound for a second term of exile in Australia, who went aboard the *Retribution* at Woolwich in 1809. The reliability of Mr. Vaux's memoirs has been questioned, but for no better reason than that he was a convict. His account is consistent with facts known from other sources. Furthermore, it is significant that he saw so little need to complain about Newgate or the Australian prison colonies or other places of well-documented misery with which he was familiar, yet was constrained to write these vivid passages about his one year's experience aboard one of Aaron Graham's hulks:

I had now a new scene of misery to contemplate; and, of all the shocking scenes I had ever beheld, this was the most distressing. There were confined in this floating dungeon nearly six hundred men, most of them double-ironed; and the reader may conceive the terrible effects arising from the continual rattling of chains, the filth and vermin naturally produced by such a crowd of miserable inhabitants, the oaths and execrations constantly heard among them; and above all, from the shocking necessity of associating and communicating more or less with so depraved a set of beings. On arriving on board, we were all immediately stripped, and washed in large tubs of water, then, after putting on each a suit of coarse slop clothing, we were ironed, and sent below, our own clothes being taken from us, and detained till we could sell or otherwise dispose of them, as no person is exempted from the obligation to wear the ship-dress. On descending the hatch-way, no conception can be formed of the scene which presented itself. I shall not attempt to describe it; but nothing short of a descent to the infernal regions can be at all worthy of a comparison with it. I soon met with many of my old Botany Bay acquaintances, who were all eager to offer me their friendship and services, that is, with a view to rob me of what little I had; for in this place there is no other motive or subject for ingenuity. All former friendships or connections are dissolved, and a man here will rob his best benefactor, or even mess-mate, of an article worth one halfpenny. Every morning, at seven o'clock, all the convicts capable of work, or, in fact, all who are capable of getting into boats, are taken ashore to the Warren, in which the Royal Arsenal and other public buildings are situated, and are there employed at various kinds of labour, some of them very fatiguing; and while so employed, each gang of sixteen, or twenty men, watched and directed by a fellow called a guard. These guards are most commonly of the lowest class of human beings; wretches devoid of all feeling; ignorant in the extreme, brutal by nature, and rendered tyrannical and cruel by the consciousness of the power they possess. If I were to attempt a full description of the miseries endured in these ships, I could fill a volume; but I shall sum up all stating, that besides robbery from each other, which is as common as cursing and swearing I witnessed among the prisoners themselves, during the twelvemonth I remained with them, one deliberate murder . . . and one suicide; and that unnatural crimes are openly committed.[13]

The Select Committee was conscientious and thorough on the whole, during the course of its 1811-1812 inquiry. Committee members had observed that the hulk establishment continued to be something of a horror, despite several years of perhaps the best management effort likely to be available. Still, the Committee could not summon the resolve to recommend abandonment of the hulks, even though construction of the massive Millbank Prison was soon to begin, and the need for convict labor in the Australian settlements was approaching its height. The Committee covered its flanks by such unrealistic rationalizations as the conclusion reached on the matter of predatory homosexuality, and also by making a number of recommendations that, while constructive, were hardly calculated to put right much of what was wrong. The Committee's inaction with respect to the future of the hulks resulted in their expanded and continued use for another forty-five years. A more determined and convincing exposé of conditions on the hulks was eventually to occur, but before that time arrived, and before the British government finally faced up to the unalterable egregiousness of the hulk system, it was to suffer an unfortunate, three-decades-long experience with John Henry Capper, the man who was soon to take charge. And there was to be the embarrassment of Millbank Prison.

# VIII

## THE MILLBANK FIASCO

Aaron Graham's term of management ended in 1814. He had found his struggles with the problems of the hulks to be more daunting than those presented by the naval mutinies at Spithead and the Nore. The still-sorry condition of the hulk establishment at the time of his departure precluded his being given special honors. Although he had made a commendable effort, it is unlikely Graham even had much in the way of inner satisfaction over a job well done. His onerous tenure as manager of the hulk establishment may have had a part in breaking his health. He did not live long after leaving the job.[1]

Graham's successor was John H. Capper, a minor bureaucrat in the Home Office. His qualifications have been described as dubious, but they were certainly no more so than the qualifications of countless other individuals who hold, and have held, similarly responsible positions in the criminal justice field. He made a good beginning and introduced significant improvements but, as we are to see in later pages, thousands of prisoners on the hulks were to suffer fearfully before the thirty-two years of his unhappy regime came to an end.

Construction of the General Penitentiary at Millbank, Britain's first modern penitentiary, was begun during the last year of Aaron Graham's term as manager of the hulks. It was opened in 1816, culminating forty years of debate, agitation and procrastination. England's most eloquent and distinguished advocates of criminal justice reform, men like John Howard and Samuel Romilly, had for years urged construction of "penitentiary houses" in each major jurisdiction. Non-binding intent to build such facilities had, in fact, been expressed in the legislation that authorized use of the hulks as a "temporary expedient." The prototype, Millbank, a grotesque modification of an idea put forward by Jeremy Bentham, was badly planned and extravagantly built. The cost of its construction was enough to kill off any resolve in Parliament to staff it adequately. It proved rather quickly to be a colossal failure. Bentham would have been inclined to argue that its failure was the inevitable result of departures from the concepts he had proposed.

Jeremy Bentham is known primarily for his flawed, but surely prodigious writings on legal philosophy. He was also something of a self-styled Renaissance man, a visionary and an excellent amateur architect. In 1799 Parliament entered into a contract with him for conceptional development of a penitentiary to serve the London area. Bentham had acquired a tract of land on the Thames, anticipating such an opportunity. He must have been viewed by his peers as something of a crackpot, albeit a brilliant one.[†] In any case, there is no doubt about his understanding the importance of visual supervision in prison management. Borrowing an idea from his brother, an architect in the employ of the Czar of Russia, Bentham came forward with a plan that called for a gigantic, wheel-like *panopticon*, its housing areas observable from a central rotunda. This primary notion was accompanied by an array of other ideas, most of them ingenious but impractical. There were to be strategically placed mirrors to enhance observation of all the cells. The roof of the structure was to be of glass in order that the whole prison operation would be brightly illuminated (during the daylight hours at least.) Tubes were to be installed for spoken communication between the cells, the rotunda and the entrance sallyport. In addition to his architectural plans, Bentham's proposals included specific ideas on staffing, posting, feeding, and all other phases of prison management. His descriptions of these ideas were accompanied by lengthy treatises on philosophy and human behavior.

Bentham had been working on refinements of his panopticon idea for years and had become obsessed with them. He was not content to rely on the massive quantity of material he had set down on paper. Instead he harangued members of Parliament and officials of the Crown unmercifully. Much of the support he had gained deteriorated. The panopticon idea did not go forward. Bentham was devastated when Parliament broke off from an agreement made with him whereby he was to have supervised construction of the new prison and implementation of his ideas. He was

---

[†] To be found among Jeremy Bentham's writings is an essay entitled "Auto-Icons, or the Uses of the Dead," in which he suggests that dead bodies could be embalmed and preserved as statues. For example, the lane leading to a country gentleman's house might be adorned with the preserved and lacquered remains of his forebears, interspersed among the trees. See *Dictionary of National Biography*, (London: Oxford University Press), s.v. "Jeremy Bentham."

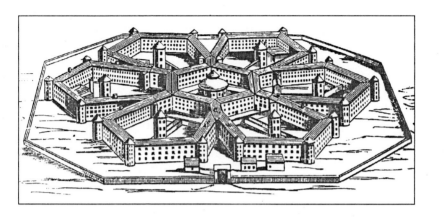

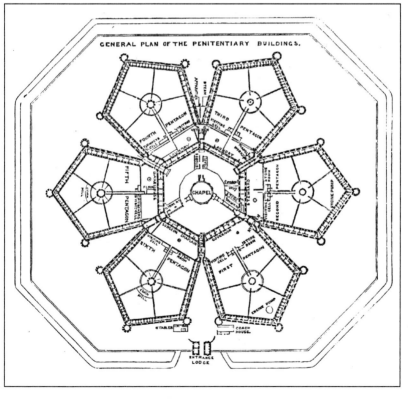

GENERAL PLAN OF THE PENITENTIARY BUILDINGS.

Millbank prison

convinced that George III disliked him and that the panopticon idea was laid aside because it was not given his Majesty's endorsement.[2] In point of fact, George III's interest in public affairs had long since declined to almost nothing.[3] It is more likely Bentham's aggressiveness and the bizarre character of some of his ideas had alienated Prime Minister William Pitt, Home Secretary Lord Dundas and others of influence who had been his initial supporters. In any event, the government took the building site off Bentham's hands and compensated him generously for his efforts. More conventional but exceedingly ill-devised plans were drawn up and England's first "penitentiary house" was built on a swampy tract on the banks of the Thames above Vauxhall (where the Tate Gallery presently stands). Construction began in 1812. There was partial occupancy in 1816. June 26 of that year is the date when the grand experiment was begun, but the structure was not finally completed until 1821. By that time massive disillusionment was already in evidence. The structure cost almost a half million pounds. It was among the largest and costliest public facilities ever built and, in that land of antiquity, was to stand less than a hundred years.

A near certainty is that Jeremy Bentham's panopticon idea would have failed, especially had it been faithfully executed under Bentham's direction. Yet it is doubtful that the results could have been as complete a fiasco as the General Penitentiary at Millbank was soon to become. According to Mayhew it was a "successful realization . . . of the ugly in architecture". A sprawling monstrosity, it rested ominously on the Thames side marshlands like a gigantic, squat, grey, six-pointed starfish. As a gesture to the panopticon idea, it was built around a central rotunda, a feature Bentham had devised as a means of supervising radiating galleries from a central station. But the Millbank design did not appropriate this advantage. A vaulted chapel was located in the rotunda, blocking all vision into the six massive, pentagonal structures that surrounded the center. Each of them contained a labyrinth of corridors, stairways and subterranean passages, giving access to a maze of cells and oddly placed workshops and storage chambers.[4] One old warder is reported to have used chalk to mark his way in order to avoid getting lost while on his rounds.[5]

During the 1960s, the concept of *unit management* came into vogue in American corrections. It is a concept based on recognition of how much more efficiently small institutions with small prisoner populations can be managed than large prisons. Unit management separates large prisons into smaller units for management purposes. The planners of Millbank did just about everything else wrong, but they were ahead of their time by a century and a half with respect to the concept of unit management. Mayhew described Millbank as a "collection of prisons." Pentagon Three was built specifically for women prisoners and used for women throughout the life of the penitentiary. The other five pentagons were used for separate classes of male prisoners.[6] Unit management is a useful concept. Its application at Millbank undoubtedly helped prevent a major disaster from becoming an unmitigated catastrophe.

A Committee of Management was appointed by the Home Office Secretary to run the new prison. George Holford, a Member of Parliament, and the Reverend J.J. Becker were to be the more influential members of the Committee. As we shall see, the ubiquitous interference of Mr. Holford was a heavy burden to be borne by John Shearman, the first Governor of Millbank, and several of his successors. Mr. Shearman's previous experience with the criminal justice system was a police court clerkship, but he was conscientious enough to inspect a few gaols in preparation for his new assignment. The Head Matron and a Master Manufacturer were other key officials.[7] Great interest and genuine hope were aroused by the opening of the new prison. The Grand Duke Nicholas of Russia was among the distinguished early visitors, as were the Bishop of London, the Bishop of Salisbury, dignitaries from Parliament and the Court system. In March of 1817 the Duchess of York paid a call. Her Royal Highness was allowed to observe women prisoners receiving religious instruction, was given a tour of the kitchen, the bakehouse, the washhouse and the laundry, "with the whole of which she was pleased to express her approbation."[8]

These visits occurred during the prison's honeymoon phase, a time when only a fraction of the 1,200 capacity had been reached. Within a year from the date of Millbank's opening, conditions had deteriorated. Thereafter, the prospect of a visit by a distinguished personage was inevitably anticipated with dread.

For more than forty years English reformers had been campaigning for a system of separate confinement. Millbank Penitentiary was the culmination of their hopes. It was viewed as the means whereby a new and more effective approach to working with lawbreakers in confinement could be demonstrated. Liberals and conservatives alike found hope in the prospect. Liberals, who were veteran critics of England's wretched punishment system, decried its inhumanity. They argued that the hulks as well as the Australian prison settlements were producing criminals by exposing youngsters and other first-time offenders to the pernicious influence of hardened criminals. Conservatives agreed with the latter complaint, but also blamed the system for its failure to inspire sufficient dread. Liberals and conservatives alike were persuaded that hard work needed to be a part of the new penitentiary approach. At Millbank elaborate arrangements were made for work in the cells and, with some misgivings, in the "associated work" areas as well. But, at the same time, the Committee of Management established principles that soon led to grave allegations of "tender-heartedness." Liberals were predominant on the Committee. Major Arthur Griffith made clear his view of the Committee of Management by describing Millbank as a "huge plaything; a toy for a parcel of philanthropic gentlemen, to keep them busy during their spare hours."[†]

And yet, however tender the hearts of the Committee members might have been, they failed to establish humane conditions of confinement at the new prison. Adequate funds for activation and operation were not forthcoming. The prison was to begin functioning with little better than a skeleton staff. Men recruited to become warders were of the lowest class. Moreover, they were underpaid and given no adequate training or supervision.[9] Consider instructions they were expected to follow:

"[The guard] shall enforce his orders with firmness but shall be expected to act with the utmost humanity towards all prisoners under his care. On the other hand, he shall not be familiar with any of the prisoners or converse with them unnecessarily, but shall treat them as persons under his authority and control and not as his companions or associates."[10]

The administrative staff of the penitentiary was thus faced with the task of finding people willing to work for wages not much above the poverty level and, at the same time, have a higher degree of skill and discernment than many university graduates would have possessed. Needless to say, it was necessary to recruit guards from among the same social classes that provided most of the prisoners. Undoubtedly, many of those employed were decent, well-meaning fellows, but inevitably, a significant number were brutal, or became brutal as result of their inability to handle the authority given them over their less-than-agreeable wards, a familiar story seen too often during succeeding decades. Medical care was inadequate; food was of poor quality; the housing areas, most especially the individual

---

[†] Major Griffith, an assistant governor of Millbank during the latter years, was an admirer of American penologist, Eland Lynds, perhaps without knowing that Lynds' name was to become synonymous in the United States with prison brutality. Griffith was, in any case, a hard-liner. While his vivid account of Millbank is a valuable source of facts, certain of his subjective observations are suspect.

cells, were improperly ventilated. We can be sure that deficient supervision and plant maintenance resulted in deterioration and filth throughout the vast reaches of the building.

The destructive effects of extended isolation of prisoners has long been recognized, even in the least progressive correctional settings, but in 1816 and for a good many years thereafter, there was a strong commitment to its efficacy. Penitential solitude was established as the key concept in Millbank's treatment program. There was ardent belief on the part of those who subscribed to the humanitarian point of view in criminal justice that separation of prisoners from each other would protect the weak from the predatory and prevent corruption of the young and unsophisticated. And there was conviction as well among Millbank's strongest supporters that Bible reading and religious instruction, accompanied by long hours of reflection in a solitary cell, would result in penitence. The penitentiary's *raison d'etre* was penitence.

In order to get work out of the prisoners and, at the same time, keep them in the solitude that was to produce a desirable measure of penitence, arrangements were made for work in individual cells. Cells were equipped with such additions as looms, sewing and cobbler benches, with some of the prisoners having to be content with the old standby, oakum picking.[†] Given Millbank's serious staff shortages, it is difficult to believe that the more realistic supporters of the experiment actually believed that even a fraction of the 1,200 prisoners Millbank was designed to hold could be given the necessary training and supervision to perform productive work as weavers, tailors, shoe makers or even oakum pickers. The advanced "classes" of prisoners were assigned to "associated work," with the shop supervisors having the grave responsibility of preventing all communication between their workers. When one considers Millbank's work program, a lamentable picture of futility is not hard to imagine. The Master Manufacturer was the second highest ranking staff member in Millbank's original table of organization. That personage was sacked early and often. Little wonder that there was continuous vacillation between solitary work, "associated work" and no work at all.

The attitude of redemptive Christianity that so strongly motivated the supporters of Millbank did not result in a compliant or appreciative prisoner

---

[†] Oakum was used for caulking ships and, at times, for stanching wounds during naval battles. Loose fibers of oakum were produced by the tedious process of untwisting and picking apart scraps of discarded nautical rope.

population. The convicts hated everything about the noble new experiment. The dreaded hulks were preferable, undoubtedly because there was never a successful effort on the part of the hulk operators to prevent association among the convicts. With all of the misery that characterized the hulks, there was camaraderie. Association among prisoners oftentimes resulted in the most vicious sorts of exploitation, but for most, association that brought dangers and sometimes terror and agony was preferable to long isolation from human contact.

During those periods of "associated work" at Millbank, conversation and all other efforts at communication between the prisoners were rigidly prohibited. To be sure, there was communication. A major design flaw had been failure to provide the individual cells with adequate ventilation. The solid outer doors had to be kept open much of the time, enabling the prisoners to shout back and forth to each other through their grill-work doors. Still, strictures on communications prevented the kind of camaraderie that would have made the long and dreary years behind Millbank's grey walls more bearable.

There were frequent riots and disturbances. During a riot that occurred early in 1818 the prison's governor was assaulted. Bow Street Runners had to be called in to restore order.[†] A later disturbance was especially embarrassing as it occurred in the chapel on a Sabbath morning when the Chancellor of the Exchequer was in attendance.[11]

In 1822, the year which marked full occupancy of Millbank, disruptions and disturbances among the prisoners had reached a point of near crisis. It was observed, moreover, that those prisoners who were compliant, were also depressed, listless and unproductive. Indeed no work was getting done. Illness was prevalent, as were real and feigned psychotic breakdowns. After reflecting on the discouraging situation, Dr. Copland Hutchinson, the Medical Superintendent, supported by Sir James McGrigor, Head of the Army Medical Board, arrived at a remarkable conclusion: *The prisoners at Millbank were eating too well.* He proposed a diet of thin gruel for breakfast, slightly more nutritious soup for the midday meal and thin soup for supper. Potatoes, which had been the saving grace of the diet, were no longer to be provided. It is astonishing that the Committee of Management, fifty years after Captain Cook had discovered the necessity of forcing rancid sauerkraut

---

† Henry Fielding, the novelist, was chief magistrate in Bow Street. In 1748 he organized the Bow Street Runners, who provided London with quasi-official police protection until establishment of the Metropolitan Police in 1829.

on the men who sailed his ships, approved Dr. Hutchinson's proposal. Needless to say, there was a serious outbreak of scurvy not long after the new diet was adopted.

It seems that Dr. Hutchinson was incapable of making a connection between his curious diet regimen and the outbreak of disease. Despite almost unmistakable symptoms of scurvy, he insisted that inadequate ventilation and the marshy location of the prison were the causes of the virulent illness. Medical consultants, obviously more competent than Dr. Hutchinson, were brought in by the Committee of Management (and eventually called to testify before the Select Committee). Recognizing scurvy immediately, they urged that oranges and other more nourishing food be added to the diet. The prisoners recovered from the symptoms of scurvy ". . . as by a charm," but within a short time disease struck again. The nature of the new malady that swept the prison was never determined with certainty by the medical consultants. Debilitating diarrhea was the most prevalent symptom. Evidence as to whether the disease was infectious was inconclusive. There was consensus among the medical experts that the prison was somehow contaminated and in need of "fumigation." Furthermore, the problem of poor ventilation in the housing areas of Millbank needed to be addressed, and measures were needed to overcome the effect of the prison's marshy, essentially unhealthy location. There was unequivocal agreement that, in its present condition, the prison was not fit for habitation.[12]

Plans to evacuate Millbank's prisoner population moved forward. Through the good offices of Home Secretary, Sir Robert Peel, the Navy Board made available at Woolwich the *Ethalion* for use as a prison hulk. Shortly thereafter the *Dromedary* was added. These two vessels took aboard a total of 467 male convicts. Two smaller vessels, *Narcissus* and the aptly named *Heroine* were prepared for reception of the women. Together, they were to house 167 women convicts. During the time required to make these hulks ready, a number of the women were moved to a public hospital in Regent's Park. On August 16, 1823, the first contingent of convicts, under heavy guard, was moved down to Woolwich by launch. This operation continued until the entire prisoner population at Millbank was removed, including the women who had enjoyed the brief interim at Regent's Park. About half of them were held briefly aboard the vessel *Desiree* before the *Heroine* was made ready. The Millbank women had been no less intractable than the men but, perhaps because they were stricken with illness even more gravely than the male convicts, their behavior became less troublesome. Indeed, whereas there was substantial improvement in the general health of the male convicts, once aboard the *Ethalion* and the *Dromedary*, the women on their two hulks were very slow to recover.

Throughout the several weeks of the evacuation process, disorder prevailed among the male convicts aboard the hulks and at the penitentiary. Griffith described Millbank during those days as a "bear garden."[13] Lockdown, a time-honored device for managing out-of-control prisoner populations, was undoubtedly used. To be sure, while locked in their cells at the penitentiary, the convicts' display of rebelliousness was limited to verbal abuse and refusal to work, but this was quite enough to have caused extreme grief. Being subjected to constant, colorful vilification was not pleasing to the staff. The Committee of Management, meanwhile, had to suffer the pain of recognizing no evidence of penitence or piety among the convicts. Behavior problems were to become more than just irksome after the convicts went aboard the *Ethalion* and *Dromedary*, neither of which had been modified sufficiently to afford strong control. Having to contend with fighting among the convicts, assaults on the officers and attempts to escape was the daily experience of staff aboard these vessels.

Millbank's hulk fleet at Woolwich remained under the control of the Committee of Management, which, remarkably enough, continued to have the confidence of the Home Secretary. The Governor of Millbank, Captain Benjamin Chapman, remained in residence at the penitentiary where he was to oversee remodeling and other efforts that were to be made there toward overcoming the unhealthy aspects of the location. The four hulks at Woolwich, provided by the Navy Board, remained under his nominal command, but for the purpose of actual supervision, the Committee of Management recruited Robert Kellock, who was then serving as first mate on one of John Capper's hulks at Sheerness. This unfortunate man had many years of experience with the hulk establishment. Without doubt he was a capable person, but there was remarkably little turnover among John Capper's hulk overseers. Denied command of a hulk of the regular hulk establishment, all at once Mr. Kellock found himself in command of the four Millbank hulks at Woolwich, crowded with prisoners who were either sick or in a state of near mutiny. The tone of his testimony before a House of Commons Select Committee suggests that he was a forthright man who was faced with an impossible task. Moreover, he had the misfortune to lose the services of the person who would have been his best lieutenant. Mr. Lodge, an exceptionally able Millbank employee, was drowned in an accident shortly after assignment as Master of the *Ethalion*. Testimony before the Select Committee indicates that Mr. Lodge was making good progress toward getting matters aboard the *Ethalion* under control. After his death, on November 5th, the semblance of order he had achieved disintegrated. At about this time, and none too soon, the House of Commons decided that the situation required attention. A Select Committee was appointed "to inquire into the State of The Penitentiary, Milbank."

Having been spared the benefit of Dr. Hutchinson's advice on nutrition, managers of the hulks on which the convicts were now confined fed them a more adequate diet. As the health of the convicts improved, words of self-congratulation were heard here and there and, for the first, last and only time in their long and baleful history, the English prison hulks were credited with contributing to the good health of their occupants. The conduct of the convicts did not improve, however, certainly not that of the males. During the spring of 1824, at a time when the Select Committee was taking testimony on the affair, convicts on the *Ethalion* and the *Dromedary* were on the verge of being out of control. The ravages of scurvy and diarrhea had imposed tractable behavior on many of Millbank's prisoners, but now that they were feeling better their keepers on the hulks no longer had that dubious advantage. With the exception of Robert Kellock, employees on the Millbank hulks had no experience in working with prisoners under the disadvantageous circumstance unique to hulk confinement. Furthermore, none of the Millbank hulks were fitted out with secure below-decks compartments as were those of John Capper's fleet.[†] Frustrations that had been, to some extent, pent up at Millbank, appear to have resulted in many months of near-riotous circumstances for the unfortunate masters of the *Ethalion* and the *Dromedary*. From knowledge of prisoner populations at all times and in all places, we can be sure that most of the convicts temporarily situated on the Millbank hulks would have preferred to settle down and nurture their hopes for improved circumstances. But a certain number of the convicts were so ruled by hopelessness and anger as to create ongoing chaos. They tore up the underdecks of the ships; they fought among themselves; they threatened and verbally abused the guards and masters, and fought like animals against efforts to restrain them. On one occasion, convicts on the *Ethalion* mounted an attack on turn-keys guarding the disciplinary cells, temporarily freeing

---

[†] The arrangements for separate group cells in the underdecks of the hulks are described in Chapter IX.

one of their companions. A state of disorder prevailed on the best of days aboard the "penitentiary ships," as these hulks came to be known. When vessels in the River Thames passed by, they were greeted by choruses of raucous catcalling and "hallooing."

In November 1823, at about the time of Mr. Lodge's death, three prisoners on the *Ethalion* executed a flawless escape plan. After gaining undetected access to a storeroom with an improvised key, one of them, a strong swimmer, stealthily exited through an unsecured port and let himself down into the water with a rope fashioned from spun yarn. He fetched a skiff that was tied to a nearby ship at anchor and towed it back to the hulk. His companions got aboard. They all floated silently away on a pre-dawn tide. One of the escapees was a boy of about thirteen. His family turned him in to the authorities and provided information that resulted in capture of the other two. But meanwhile, their success stimulated a frenzy of escape plotting and continued rebelliousness.[14]

Illness persisted among the women convicts. As late as March 1824, twenty of the one hundred and sixty-seven women confined aboard the *Narcissus* and *Heroine* were in a makeshift, shipboard infirmary. At about that time only thirty-nine out of four hundred and sixty-seven male prisoners were sick enough to be bedridden. The women prisoners deserved, and were accorded, far more sympathy than the men by the Committee of Inquiry. "The spirits of these wretched prisoners were said to be broken down;" the Committee was told. Matters were to improve for them as the government wisely decided to pardon most of the women rather than return them to Millbank. Some of the more deserving male convicts were also given "His Majesty's free pardon" while others, in large numbers, were transferred to the hulks of the regular fleet at Sheerness and Chatham and put on lists for transportation to New South Wales. Therefore, for their rebellious behavior, these prisoners were rewarded with what they had wanted in the first place. The women who were healthy enough were put to work making shirts. It is unlikely their production was significant, but the activity was helpful from the standpoint of morale and good order. No work or other constructive activity was provided for the male prisoners during their sojourn on the penitentiary ships. During lulls in the turmoil some of them would relieve their idleness by such projects as making playing cards from their prayer books. Their conduct continued to be "unruly to a degree, and in some instances to the extent of mutiny."

Whether predatory or engaged in through mutual consent, the practice of homosexuality among the convicts carried far greater risks than other kinds of misconduct, as the management of such behavior by way of kangaroo court proceedings had the blessing of the staff, and indeed was no cause of concern among the members of Parliament appointed to look into Millbank matters. Consider an excerpt from Captain Chapman's testimony before the House of Commons Committee of Inquiry:

> You mentioned that two or three instances had occurred on board the hulks, of crimes of a particular nature, did not the prisoners, speaking of them as a body, hold them in abomination? Completely so; and I am satisfied that if the perpetrators had not been confined, they would have been seriously injured by the other prisoners. Was there not an instance of a regular trial among themselves? Yes; they were assigned counsel or they defended themselves, and the judge regularly summed up the proceedings, and punishment was awarded. The punishment awarded was what the soldiers call cobbing? Yes, something of that sort.[†]

Late in the spring of 1824 a rumor spread that Parliament was on the verge of taking some action that would be to the advantage of the prisoners. Perhaps there were to be more pardons. There was a dramatic improvement in conduct, even though the expected help from Parliament did not materialize. Indeed, after reoccupation of the penitentiary, in the summer of 1824, Parliament repealed the bar to floggings, a response to the disorderliness that was resumed by prisoners returning to Millbank.

Substantial efforts were made during the time of its vacancy to improve ventilation and drainage at the prison. A healthier diet was provided and there was no reoccurrence of scurvy. Conditions just short of chaos continued, however. Governors resigned, or were dismissed and replaced, frequently. One of them, Mr. Nihil, was a deeply religious man who could not be dissuaded from his conviction that enforced piety would eventually have a redemptive effect on the prisoners. For a time he must have thought that his efforts were succeeding.[15] With respect to that period of Millbank's history, Mayhew observed that ". . . sanctified looks were . . . the order of the day, and the most desperate convicts in the prison found it advantageous to complete their criminal character by the addition of hypocrisy."[16] A governor of another sort was Mr. Groves, whose faith in the efficacy of brutality was similar in ardor to Mr. Nihil's faith in Christianity.

---

[†] "Cobbing" was a term used in the British Army in the 19th century for a severe beating on the buttocks, administered with a stick by one's fellow soldiers.

From 1816 to 1844, at which time the experiment in reformative incarceration at Millbank was abandoned, there was never a period that was not fraught with disorder and frustration. A contributing factor was the arrangement whereby the Committee of Management breathed constantly down the neck of every Governor that Millbank had during that period. Whether all of the Governors of Millbank were as incompetent as they seem now to have been is impossible for us to know, as they rarely made decisions without the risk of their being countermanded by "the Visitor," George Holford, Esq., Member of Parliament and major-domo on the Committee of Management. According to Griffith, spying on one another by the staff was encouraged by the Committee. As likely as not, prisoners would take complaints to "the Visitor" without first mentioning them to the staff, and officers were given orders by him and by other members of the Committee without consultation with the Governor.[17] The House of Commons Select Committee made a number of sensible recommendations, most of them aimed toward bettering conditions of confinement for the prisoners. These recommendations did not go far enough, however, and nothing was done to improve the unfortunate management organization. There was never to be observable progress toward the ideals first envisaged by those who had nurtured such high expectations for the concept of reformation through hard work and penitential solitude at the General Penitentiary at Millbank.

A decision was taken in 1844 to use Millbank as a utilitarian holding facility, a purpose for which it was only a little better suited than for a place of reformation. The name of the prison was changed from the General Penitentiary at Millbank to Millbank Prison, a rare official admission of failure.[18]

But it was not an admission that the concept of enforced penitential solitude was invalid. The failure of the Millbank experiment in that regard was attributed to the lack of adequate facilities for enforcement of total isolation.[19]

Construction of Pentonville, built between 1840 and 1844 on the north side of London, somewhat smaller in capacity than Millbank, required only £85,000, even though all of its individual cells were equipped with toilets and lavatories. These improvements, together with better ventilation in the cells, were seen as crucial factors for advocates of penitential solitude to at last demonstrate the efficacy of that concept. The model was to be set up with much greater care and specificity than had been used before. All of the inmates were selected from among young offenders, eighteen to thirty-five, who had been sentenced to transportation. The term at Pentonville was to be limited to eighteen months, no more, no less. Those who did well were to have ticket-of-leave status in Van Diemen's Land, and thus were to have opportunities akin to those of free settlers in the Australian colonies. Those whose adjustment at Pentonville was indifferent were to go to Australia with somewhat greater restrictions on their movements but would essentially be in ticket-of-leave status.[†] The Pentonville inmates who conducted themselves badly were to be assigned at the end of the eighteen months to one of the convict settlements in Van Diemen's land or on the Australian mainland. If the inmates knew anything about these establishments, the prospect should have motivated good behavior on the part of all but the most irrational. Unfortunately, individuals undergoing the stress of imprisonment cannot be counted on to act in the best interest of their future welfare. And, as it turned out, reducing alarming numbers of its inmates to a state of irrationality became an unintended specialty of the house.

Even an early epidemic of psychotic breakdown did not dampen the great confidence in the program planned for the new penitentiary. Pentonville was officially designated "the Model Prison." The Pentonville model prescribed a rigid regimen for its carefully selected convicts. As preparation for a new life in Australia, each young man selected for the program was to do a few hour's solitary work each day and spend the rest of his time in isolated silence, interrupted from time to time by an hour or two of sitting between the side screens of a chapel booth listening to sermons, prayers and scripture reading. During the brief exercise periods, and while marching through the corridors to chapel or for some other unavoidable purpose, the convicts wore masks in order that communication, even by facial expression, was prevented. The participants were expected to adhere to this regimen for eighteen months before sailing off to Australia.[20] Those who devised the Pentonville model inadvertently came up with an effective means of driving people crazy. For five years there was rigid adherence to the regimen.[21] Adequate means for enforcing compliance had been provided in the prison's construction. Consider Mayhew's description of the "refractory wards" at Pentonville. "

> Descending a small flight of stairs, we came to a narrow passage . . . here was a line of black doors . . . . These were the refractory cells.

---

[†] Sir Joshua Jebb was the principal planner of both the physical plant and rehabilitation regimen at Pentonville. See Chapter XIV.

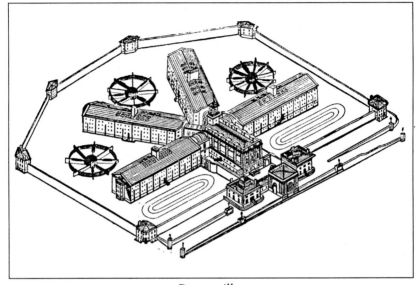

Pentonville

Chapel Services, Pentonville

The officer who accompanied us threw back one of the doors, which turned as heavily on its hinges, and gave forth the same hollow sound, as the massive door of an iron safe. The interior which it revealed was absolutely and literally 'pitch dark.' Not a thing was visible in the cell; and so utterly black did it look within, that we could not believe but that there was another door between us and the interior. The officer, however, introduced his lantern and then we could see the rays diverging . . . and streaking the darkness with a bright, luminous mist . . . . "Would you like to step inside," asked the warder, "and see how dark it is when the door is closed?"

We entered the terrible place with a shudder, for there is something intensely horrible in absolute darkness to all minds, confess it or not as they may; and as the warder shut the door upon us—and we felt the cell walls shake and moan again, like a tomb, as he did so—the utter darkness was, as Milton sublimely says—*visible*. The eyes not only saw, but felt the absolute negation of their sense in such a place. Let them strain their utmost, not one luminous chink or crack could the sight detect. Indeed, the very air seemed as impervious to vision as so much black marble, and the body seemed to be positively encompassed with the blackness, as if it were buried alive, deep down in the earth itself. Though we remained several minutes in the hope that we should shortly gain the use of our eyes, and begin to make out, in the thick dusk, bit after bit of the apartment, the darkness was at the end of the time quite as impenetrable as at first, so that the continual straining of the eyeballs, and taxing of the brains, in order to get them to do their wonted duty, soon produced a sense of mental fatigue, that we could readily understand would end in conjuring up all kinds of terrible apparitions to the mind.

The inordinate number of psychotic breakdowns at Pentonville did not result from commitments to the refractory cells so much as from the regular routine required of all prisoners. Dread of the "dark cells" was sufficient to ensure about ninety-seven percent compliance with the silent regimen. (Most of those in the three or four percent who were inclined to occupancy of the refractory cells were "boy convicts", some of them as young as twelve.)[22] But it was the silent regimen, designed as a preparation of prisoners for a new life in Australia, that produced an alarming rate of removals to Bedlam. Concern among Home Office officials responsible for Pentonville was sufficient to inspire some modification in the program, but not enough to greatly alleviate its egregious effect. Those who went to Bedlam were only the most pitifully reduced to insanity. Severe emotional damage was the likely effect on virtually all of the carefully selected young men who underwent the Pentonville regimen. The best of the Pentonville graduates who were placed on transports for the long voyage to Van Diemen's land were listless, vacuous fellows, poorly equipped to handle the demands that would be placed on them as ticket-of-leave men.[23] We have no data as to the numbers of them who ended their days at Port Arthur, Norfolk Island or one of the other convict stations that specialized in imparting despair and agony.[†]

The Millbank effort had been a failure, and now the notion of penitential solitude, implemented under the ideal circumstances provided by Surveyor-General of Prisons, Joshua Jebb at Pentonville, was having a clearly destructive effect on many of the young offenders it was designed to rehabilitate. Still, faith in the concept of penitential solitude was not seriously eroded. The notion continued to be a guiding principle throughout the period of transition from reliance on transportation and the hulks, to a policy of *penal servitude* in dry land English prisons, 1855 to 1867. Fortunately, there were some begrudging modifications. They were not as much due to humanitarian concerns as to belief that convict labor was too valuable a commodity to be sacrificed to a rehabilitative ideal. A sad irony is that the notion of separate confinement held promise for being a significant reform. Had it not been for the misguided conviction that deprivation of contact with other human beings would, in and of itself, be reformative, and had adequate prisoner classification practices been instituted, an untold measure of unproductive human misery could have been avoided. As to the more vexing question, more than a century has passed and we still do not know whether imprisonment and the reform of lawbreakers will ever become compatible.

Millbank prison, declared unsuitable for any reformative purpose in 1844, continued in use for a while, primarily as a holding depot for convicts bound for the Australian prison colonies, thereafter as a thoroughly inefficient facility for serving Britain's new policy of penal servitude. The prison was closed in 1892 and razed not long afterward. Consensus among members of Britain's criminal justice establishment is that Pentonville also

---

[†] Bethlehem Royal Hospital, founded in 1247, soon came to be called Bedlam more often than not. Thus we have the origin of *bedlam*, meaning uncontrolled uproar.

has long deserved to be honorably retired from service, but in 1993 it continues in use as a short-term prison. It has enlightened management and, by comparison with many metropolitan detention facilities in America, it is clean and orderly. Remarkably enough, the old prison serves its present function reasonably well. It also serves as a doleful memorial to good intentions gone tragically wrong.

# IX

## MR. CAPPER TAKES CHARGE

John H. Capper was appointed manager of the hulks on July 12, 1815.[1] Forty-one years of age, he appears to have been what present-day prison personnel would refer to as a central office functionary. During his long tenure as Superintendent he maintained a clerkship in the Criminal Department of the Home Office, a position he apparently had for some time before assuming responsibility for the hulk establishment.[2] The records indicate that he handled certain administrative duties related to management of the hulks, and therefore he is certain to have worked closely with Aaron Graham. Both Capper and Graham carried the title of Inspector during that time.[3] It is clear that John Capper was not altogether without qualifications for the job of Superintendent. Elevation of central office functionaries to high level management positions is hardly unheard of in the field of correctional administration. However qualified he may or may not have been, subsequent events suggest that Mr. Capper may have had the sponsorship of excessively loyal friends of high rank in the government, as he was allowed to become quite slovenly in performance of his duties, most particularly after his first eight years of service.

John Capper was the first *Superintendent* of the hulks. Aaron had managed the hulks as an *Inspector*. At the time of John Capper's appointment, the General Penitentiary at Millbank was under construction on the banks of the Thames, twelve miles upstream from Woolwich. Aside from the occasions when he would send prisoners to, or accept them from, Millbank, John Capper was to have no significant role in that prison's chaotic history. He is sure to have been well acquainted with the problems that besieged Millbank's Committee of Management from the beginning. None of his reports suggest opinions he undoubtedly had with respect to the troubled Millbank Penitentiary effort. Throughout his long career as a British prison official, John Capper doggedly avoided weighing in with opinions on matters that were remotely controversial. He was reasonably comfortable talking about construction costs, prisoner population trends and operational problems, but when it came to matters of philosophical principle, he was reluctant even to be on the safe side, preferring, it seems, to be on no side at all. His was not one of the multitude of voices that, during those times, expressed anguish over the harmful effects of "association" or glowing approbation for the notion of confinement in penitential solitude. When the 1823 scurvy outbreak inspired evacuation and en masse removal of Millbank's prisoner population to hulks at Woolwich, management of the vessels provided for them, the *Ethalion*, *Dromedary*, *Narcissus* and *Heroine*, was not entrusted to Mr. Capper. The "penitentiary ships," however, were anchored at Woolwich near, if not alongside, vessels of the regular hulk establishment. At the request of Millbank's Committee of Management, Capper directed preparation of the *Ethalion*, and perhaps the other vessels made available to the Committee by the Navy Board.[4] Thereafter he had no involvement in the Millbank evacuation. No references to the episode are to be found in the biannual reports submitted by Mr. Capper during 1823 and 1824.

The terms of John Capper's appointment were relatively generous. In addition to his salary of £400, he was given an annual compensation of £131 for maintenance of an office in his residence at Lambeth Terrace, a curious arrangement as Lambeth is no closer to Woolwich than was the location of the Home Office in Westminster. He was not deprived of his desk at the Home Office and, as time went by, he was to be at that location more often than at Woolwich or any of the other hulk stations. He had apparently gained considerable respect as an authority on imprisonment. His tenure coincided with an era of prison construction in England. The record suggests that he was dispatched from time to time to various proposed construction sites on missions for the Home Office. In 1835 a House of Lords Select Committee on Gaols and Houses of Correction called him as a witness in order to gain his views on a proposal to use Dartmoor Prison as a replacement for the Penitentiary at Millbank, and to question him on other matters. Dartmoor, built in 1806 on a desolate Devon moor to house prisoners of war, had lain empty for fifteen years. Mr. Capper informed the Committee about a "Survey and Estimate" that had been done, that £7,000 appropriated by Parliament for the purpose of looking into the Dartmoor question had not all been expended, and that Millbank's Committee of Management (unsurprisingly) did not support using Dartmoor to replace Millbank. He pointed out that a reactivated Dartmoor Prison had been considered for use as a "distinct Place of Punishment" rather than as a replacement for Millbank. Asked whether £100,000 would be sufficient to convert the old prison into a state of usefulness, his reply was that the project could be done for much less by using granite available on the 400-acre site, and taking the availability of prison labor into account. Capper responded to a number of other questions knowledgeably, exhibiting familiarity with costs, estimates, the status and condition of Dartmoor Prison and the organization of the Home Secretary's Criminal Branch. He skillfully avoided giving his views as to whether Millbank's function and mission should be moved to Dartmoor. The Committee asked for his views on other matters, including the advisability of setting up a "Sub-department" in the Home Office to handle all matters relating to prisons, the hulks and transportation to Australia. His responses reflect competence as well as a reluctance to press his views on the Committee.[5]

Earlier, the government had sent William Crawford, a prominent member of the London Prison Discipline Society, to the United States to study "Prison Discipline" and the concept of penitential solitude. As a result of the efforts of Dr. Benjamin Rush and his fellow Quakers in the Philadelphia Society for the Alleviation of the Miseries of Public Prisons, the concept had been implemented at the renowned Walnut Street Jail early in the century, and installed, presumably with refinements, at the Western Pennsylvania Prison in Pittsburgh in 1826. Crawford had liked much of what he saw (or was told) in Pennsylvania. He made a number of recommendations concerning the best approach to imprisonment and reformation in Great Britain. His views appear not to have been contrary to notions already well in place, especially with respect to the growing convictions about the efficacy of penitential solitude. The question arose in Parliament as to whether Dartmoor should be reactivated as a place where recommendations made in the William Crawford's report could be put into effect. The House of Lords Select Committee was appointed to examine this proposition. The Committee succeeded in gaining useful factual information from John Capper, but nothing more.[†]

It is clear, in any case, that John Capper was viewed as an expert in the field of imprisonment, though perhaps one who was more of an administrative specialist in the field than as one given to dealing with innovative concepts. There is little doubt that he spent much time during the latter years of his long tenure as Superintendent of the hulk establishment reposing at home in the interest of his frail health. But another

---

[†] Dartmoor Prison was eventually reopened, becoming in 1850 a principal facility for prisoners with lengthy sentences to "penal servitude."

reason for the well-documented neglect of his duties as Superintendent may have been his continuing to hold a Home Office clerkship. It appears he was frequently burdened with requests from Home Office officials to undertake tasks unrelated to his management of the hulks.

In 1823 John Capper obtained permission to employ as his clerk, his nephew, Robert Capper, a young London businessman. Consent for this appointment was as likely as not based on recognition within the Home Office of the multiple responsibilities John Capper was carrying. Nephew Robert was paid a salary of £270 a year. To begin with, he functioned as an executive assistant. In view of the nature of his background, we can hope that he also made an effort to learn something about the hulk establishment and about the British criminal justice system, for he was eventually to assume defacto management of the hulks.[6]

Aaron Graham, in his role as Inspector, had taken advantage of a vacuum and had assumed authority over the hulks in a manner that, while welcomed, had not been anticipated. On his own initiative he had drawn up detailed regulations and done his best to administer the hulk establishment accordingly. By contrast, Mr. Capper's duties were carefully circumscribed. He was not given responsibility for policy or for developing regulations. Instructions on hulk management were handed down in specific detail. And yet Capper may well have been the primary consultant to the Home Office in the development of policy. Indeed, given the nature of bureaucracy, it is as likely as not he wrote the instructions to himself. Whether Capper or some other Home Office functionary, the person who drafted the instructions had an easy job of it. He simply paraphrased a copy of the instructions Aaron Graham had issued to the masters of his hulks thirteen years before, in some instances using identical language.[7] That person may have, in fact, conferred with Graham, but this is doubtful. Graham's last report, submitted on November 18, 1814, has a look of finality about it.[8] In the appointment of John Capper, the Home Office was giving a job, previously held by Graham, a man of action, to more of a desk-bound sort, one accustomed to following the kind of guidance provided within the framework of bureaucracy. Graham had gained his reputation by way of his performance in an emergency, the Naval mutinies at Spithead and the Nore. Capper had gained his as a plodding, knowledgeable, competent bureaucrat. It is clear that the government had been sobered by the unhappy conclusions of the Select Committee in 1811 and 1812. Recognition seems to have dawned that the practice of confining offenders on the hulks was fraught with fundamental problems, that if their use was to be continued, there was a need for the establishment to be carefully monitored. It is reasonable that a man well known by senior officials in the Home Office, a person accustomed to following orders, should have been chosen to supervise the hulk establishment. It is an unhappy irony, however, that whatever resolve the Home Office may have had to provide the hulks with responsible oversight was to drain away, and to do so concurrently with a deterioration in the level of John Capper's effectiveness as Superintendent.

All too soon Capper was to demonstrate his remarkable gift in the art of obfuscation. As the years passed he was to rely on this gift more than any other in his management of the hulks, almost as if convinced that what Parliament, the Home Office and the British public believed to be true was of more importance than the truth itself. After his first several years as Superintendent, the distractions of other Home Office assignments, his ill health, and his misplaced confidence in Robert Capper, prevented his staying informed as to what was happening on the hulks. These circumstances may have helped him maintain an easy conscience. According to his always reassuring reports (and those written for him by his too-trusted nephew) the prisoners were consistently given "good and wholesome provisions", were generally healthy, were invariably treated "with great humanity" and in response, "conducted themselves in a manner that brought honor on their keeper(s.)" Furthermore, these reports were typically accompanied by five or six chaplains' reports, attesting to an amazing degree of contrition and piety among the convicts. Indeed it seems as though John Capper recruited chaplains on the basis of the hue of their rose-colored glasses. One would think that over the thirty-two years of Capper's reign there would have been, among the Church of England clergymen assigned to the hulks, more inclination to speak out truthfully about horrors they could hardly have failed to observe. The record provides us with no information as to how the hulks' chaplains were selected. An inevitable speculation is that the weakest men among the Anglican clergy were routinely assigned to hulks and prisons. One might further suspect that candid and critical observations were deliberately omitted from Mr. Capper's reports, but since chaplains' comments from all of the hulks were consistently included with the Superintendent's biannual reports, it appears that he simply was not significantly troubled with voices of protest from within the ranks on the subject of conditions of confinement. In the next chapter we will see the results of the protest that was rather inoffensively raised by Chaplain Price of the hulk *Euryalus*.

Especially toward the beginning of his term as Superintendent, Mr. Capper would have been exceedingly alert to the Home Secretary's wishes. (Henry Addington, the Viscount Sidmouth, was Home Secretary in 1815.) In his earliest reports, John Capper's inclination to tell his Lordship what his Lordship wanted to hear was more than a little noticeable, an inclination that eventually became his cardinal principle for managing the hulk establishment. It was a principle that served him well for many years. It was not so much a matter of Home Office officials' being deceived by the dubious representations that characterized Capper's reports as it was that they considered other matters of greater import. Taking John Capper's reports at face value was the least bothersome option for them. These were times marked by ominous social problems. There were food riots and other signs of serious unrest, and there was an increase in lawlessness throughout the country. The Luddite uprising in the northern counties sparked an uncharacteristically harsh reaction on the part of Home Secretary Lord Sidmouth. Until he left that office in 1821 he maintained a policy of unrelenting severity where matters of crime and rebelliousness were concerned. As long as John Capper was able to prevent his convicts from escaping in significant numbers and threatening the populace, what happened on the hulks was of small account to Sidmouth or to those who succeeded him in the Home Office. John Russell, who became Home Secretary in 1835, was a reform-minded man, but none of his efforts were to have a discernible effect on the hulks.[9] The Home Office took notice from time to time when Navy or Ordinance yard authorities complained about the fitness or availability of convict workers. This appears to have been the most significant, if not the only factor, which acted to the benefit of the hulk prisoners until near the end of the Capper era. After his promising beginning, John Capper's long reign was an era of neglect, nepotism, mismanagement and self-deception. The particulars are to be examined in later pages. But what of his efforts during the earlier years?

From the time the hulks were first pressed into service in 1776, convicts had been left to their own devices below decks after evening lockdown, with the unhappy consequences not hard to imagine. The deck separations effected by Aaron Graham had done little to improve conditions of confinement, or prevent what was deemed to be harmful association among them. Before Graham stepped aside as manager of the hulks, a Select Committee of Commons had asked the Commissioners of the Navy to develop plans for converting the hulks into more suitable prison ships. This work was done. Sketches for converting the underdecks of a 64-gun ship were submitted with the report submitted by Lord Bunbury's Select Committee on June 27, 1812. Having long used ships for detaining prisoners of war, the Navy had gained some experience with shipboard confinement. Given the brutal history of the British Navy's prisoner ships, one might wonder how valuable that experience was, if providing for more humane conditions of confinement was a sought-after goal. However that might have been, the Navy did a good job of developing a design for the hulks.

The first ship retrofitted was the 74-gun *Retribution*. It would have been necessary to up-size the design drawings, a task that was not difficult. Work on this project, done by the Navy at the Sheerness dock yard, was begun late in 1814, during the last weeks of Aaron Graham's tenure. It is unlikely that Inspector Graham, fast fading then, had anything to do with the project. The record does not tell us whether John Capper, from his desk in Whitehall, was involved. Quite probably he was. His appointment to the superintendency of the hulk establishment was to come a month or two after the remodeling of the *Retribution* was completed, and it would fall to him to oversee the task of remodeling the underdecks of other ships of the hulk fleet. The record indicates that he performed this job competently. His own work crews were to undertake the task of remodeling the smaller ships, while the Navy stood ready to do the work of converting any larger vessel that might be designated for complete retrofit. In either case, there would have been change orders, cost overruns and an array of other problems that would demand Superintendent Capper's attention.

The object in retrofitting the ships was to allow visual supervision of the prisoners during the evening and nighttime hours, an element of inmate management that had been entirely missing. Also to be accomplished was the separation of the prisoners into appropriate classes, thus creating a more meaningful prisoner classification system.

At the time John Capper became superintendent, the fleet consisted of hulks at Woolwich, Sheerness and Portsmouth. Among them were deactivated frigates as small as 50 guns, ships of the line as large as 74 guns, but not one vessel in the 64-gun class for which the Navy plan was specifically designed. It hardly mattered as the design drawings were easily adapted.

The design provided for housing prisoners on three decks. The lower deck (called the orlop in naval parlance) was to have eighteen secure bays, nine along each side of the ship, separated from a five-foot-wide central corridor by iron grillwork. The bays amidships were fifteen-by-eighteen

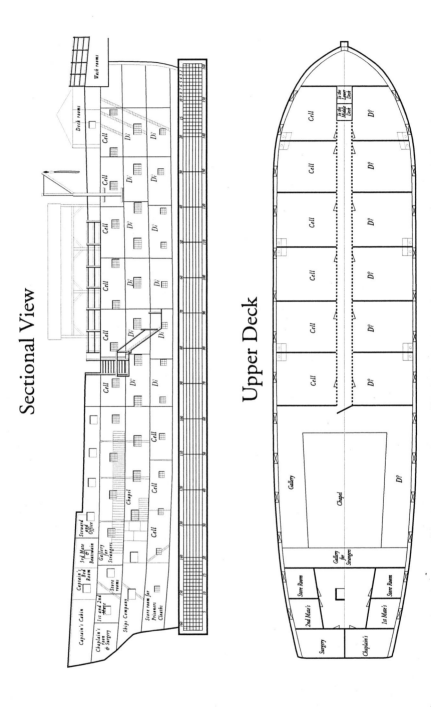

## Sectional View

## Upper Deck

Lower Deck

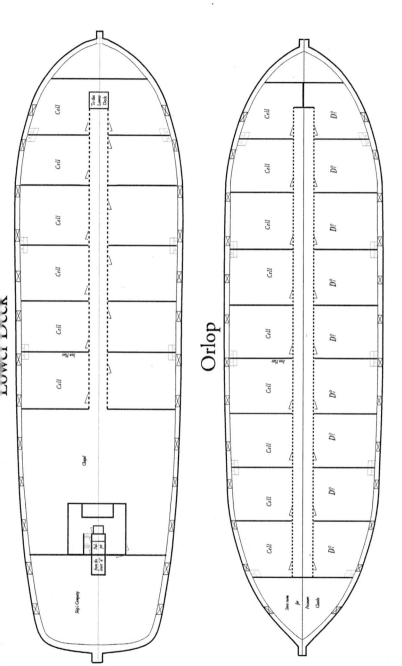

Orlop

Plans for remodeling naval vessels for service as prisoner hulks.

feet, slightly smaller toward the bow and stern. Ideally, even by early 19th century standards, no more than eight prisoners would have been assigned to each bay, but from the beginning, they were used for accommodating ten to twelve. The deck above the orlop, called the lower deck, was similarly arranged, except the ship's company's quarters and a large vaulted chapel occupied more than one third of that space, leaving room for twelve bays. The upper deck also had twelve bays, separated by a corridor. From the upper deck corridor the chapel gallery could be reached. Beyond it, in the stern of the ship, were storerooms, as well as quarters for chaplain, physician and two others. The captain's quarters were to be found at the stern of the spar deck. They included a bedchamber, a pantry and a commodious common room. Cabins for steward, boatswain and third mate were also in that area, as was the steward's office. A shed for hammocks to be stowed was amidships on the spar deck. Cook rooms and a wash house were situated in the forecastle.[10]

This arrangement is essentially what was done on the *Retribution*. The record is not clear as to whether the same plans were used for the *Leviathan*, which also underwent a major retrofit by the Navy. The problem of ventilation was not very well addressed by the Navy's design. In his October 1815 report to the Home Secretary, Mr. Capper made a clear point of having improved ventilation on the *Retribution* by replacing solid doors leading from lower-deck corridors to the chapel with iron grill doors, and by installing an iron grill door between the orlop corridor and steerage. One must wonder whether air flowing up from the bilge improved matters for prisoners confined in the orlop bays.

In any case, the plans described here for retrofitting the hulks represented dramatic improvements in their viability, especially those modifications that permitted visual supervision after evening lockdown. But whether the most critically needed improvements in conditions of confinement were to follow was another matter. The bays were to be woefully over-crowded and it is clear that convicts were still not adequately supervised. The midnight watch complement on the hulks would have been two officers, three at most. One of them may have been assigned to below-decks patrol but the emphasis would have been on surveillance of hatches and ports in order to make sure no one escaped during the night. Concern about the conduct of the prisoners would have been secondary. Furthermore, it is apparent from the record that the lowest sort of men were employed as warders. They were given no training and although, for the most part illiterate, they were expected to conform to detailed written instructions.

There was to be no consistent control of the behavior of hundreds of convicts huddled together at night in their dimly lit cells. For the weaker men confined in the underdecks of the hulks, the improvements meant that they now had to be concerned about being victimized by only eight or ten of their fellow convicts, rather than a hundred or more, as had been the case before. Furthermore, it was at least possible, if not probable, that an officer would appear in the corridor from time to time. Shortly, we will consider some of the prisoner classification efforts put forward during Capper's regime, aimed at improving conduct and reducing the corrupting effects of "association."

When Capper took up his duties as superintendent in the summer of 1815 he had a good deal more to be concerned about than the remodeling of the underdecks of the hulks. It seems, for example, that the captain of the *Retribution* had been caught, so to speak, with his hand in the till, and Mr. Capper was confronted with "Your Lordship's order for his dismissal." During his first year in office, Superintendent Capper completed an on-site inspection of the entire hulk fleet. It was not so large as it was to become later on. The *Justitia* lay at anchor off the Woolwich Warren, holding about 470 convicts. There were three hulks in the Portsmouth area, the *Captivity* in Portsmouth Harbour, the *Laurel* across the way at Gosport and the *Portland* at Langstone Harbour, located to the east of the Portsmouth peninsula. Together, these vessels held about 1,200. At Sheerness the newly remodeled *Retribution* accommodated about 450 convicts in separate bays, each holding eight to twelve. Thus the hulk establishment's prisoner count was then about 2,100.

In October 1815, John Capper recommended to the Home Office that alternative arrangements be made for convicts aboard the *Portland*. There was employment for only a third of them at Langstone Harbour. Moreover, the *Portland*, a venerable ship when placed in service as a hulk thirteen years before, was in poor condition and unfit for remodeling. Capper recommended that the Navy be asked to fit out a better ship and establish it at Sheerness. Navy officials there had advised him that four years' work would be available for 300 convicts at the Sheerness dockyard and that others would be employed by the Chief Engineer. This number of convict workers was needed at Sheerness in addition to those already employed from the *Retribution*. Capper was in good communication with the Navy during those days. He was invited to inspect the honored old warship, *Bellerophon*, then stationed on the River Medway. Liking what he saw, he described her to the Home Secretary as a 74-gun vessel ". . . of easy draft of water and lofty between decks."[11] Mr. Capper's recommendation was accepted. Responding to a petition from the Home Office, the Navy made the *Bellerophon* available. Her fitting out was completed in August 1816. Better ventilation was devised. Otherwise, her retrofit was identical to that of the *Retribution*. The cost to the government for retrofitting the *Bellerophon* was £1,200.[12] The government's cost for similarly fitting out the *Retribution* and the *Leviathan* does not appear in the records but if it was approximately the same, we must consider what the reaction must have been on the part of those in the government who had purse strings responsibility. Thirty-six thousand pounds had been spent on three old Navy ships in order that they might be used as prison hulks for a few years. The entire cost of the Pentonville Penitentiary completed in 1842, was £85,000. The *Bellerophon* was to remain in service for only nine years. As shall be seen in the next chapter, her role as a prison hulk was most significant during the last of those years. She disappears from the records in 1825. A fair assumption is that she went to the breaking yard.[†]

Retrofitting the *Retribution*, the *Bellerophon* and the *Leviathan* occurred when England's treasury had been drained by the long struggle against Napoleon's France, and trouble with her former colonies in North America. Furthermore, the exorbitant cost of constructing the General Penitentiary at Millbank was immediately in the offing. Unsurprisingly, the Home Office took another look at the manner in which the hulks were to be converted into more suitable accommodations for convicts. Capper proceeded with work on the *Captivity* and *Laurel* in the Portsmouth Harbour area, even before the extensive retrofitting of the newly acquired *Bellerophon* was completed at Sheerness. But those veteran hulks were to be given only seven compartments for separating prisoners.[13] The *Retribution, Bellerophon* and *Leviathan*, fitted out and placed in service at Portsmouth in 1818, may have been the last and only hulks to be retrofitted according to Navy plans; plans that provided for as many as forty separate compartments. Costs would have been an overwhelming consideration. The records do not provide us with cost figures for modifying the *Laurel* or *Captivity*, but

---

[†]  As a Royal Navy ship of the line, the *Bellerophon* fought bravely at Trafalgar. Only a year before she went into service as a prisoner hulk at Sheerness, Napoleon Bonaparte, after Waterloo, had surrendered to her commanding officer at Rochefort and had been conveyed to England. After about a week in port *Bellerophon* put to sea again where, off Berry Head, her renowned passenger was transferred to the *Northumberland* for the voyage to St. Helena. See pages 181-187 of *Waterloo: The Hundred Days* by David Chandler, Macmillan, New York, 1989.

the savings must have been significant. It is likely that surplus materials were obtained from the Navy or from dockyard managers, and some convict labor was used. In the absence of evidence to the contrary, John Capper should be credited with getting the work done on these two ships, and others that were to be fitted out less elaborately. The Navy was not significantly involved in work on the other hulks, most of them older and smaller.

While there was a major reduction in the number of compartments for separation on the *Laurel* and *Captivity*, arrangements were retained for supervising prisoners in their below-decks housing areas. This advantage, together with a crude means of prisoner classification put into effect by Capper, must have resulted in some improvement in the safety and welfare of prisoners. The days when eleven and twelve-year boys were locked down from sunset until dawn with adult offenders, some of them depraved and predatory, without the slightest effort at supervision, would not be seen again on the hulks. Something of an apogee in reform of the hulks had been achieved, although it was not sustained and hardly resulted in the hulks becoming commendable places of confinement.

The means of prisoner classification used by Capper were outlined for him in Home Office instructions. It was based on a "Character Book," an idea that began with John Howard about thirty years before. Every prisoner on the hulks was to be evaluated each quarter, thus:

Very Good ---------------- v.g.
Good --------------------- g.
Indifferent --------------- in.
Suspicious --------------- s.
Bad ---------------------- b.
Very Bad ----------------- v.b.

The instructions required that convicts were to be ". . . kept in separate divisions or compartments on board the respective ships . . . and upon no account . . . be allowed to mix with any other class than that to which they belong, after their coming on board from their daily labour."[14]

By January of 1819, convicts aboard the three hulks that had forty separate bays were being divided into twelve classes, rather than six.[15] It appears, therefore, that in addition to separating youthful prisoners from the adults, Capper set up separate classes for the youthful prisoners, prisoners who were eventually to have their own hulk. In separating the aggressive youngsters from the more passive ones, Capper was introducing an improvement many criminal justice jurisdictions had not come to until well past the middle of the 20th century, because of the mistaken notion that separation of juveniles from adults is somehow more important than separation of assaultive and predatory offenders, whatever their age, from those most likely to be victimized. Unfortunately, as we are to see in the next chapter, Mr. Capper's excellent advance in management of the boy convicts was soon abandoned, for reasons of expediency.

The efforts made toward improving prisoner classification and separation during the early years of John Capper's tenure are sure to have been effective in helping the well-disposed prisoners, whether adult or juvenile, serve their time in relative peace and safety. The hulk captains were inevitably to have trouble maintaining order in those areas of the ship where the "bads" and "very bads" were housed. On balance, however, the system provided significant advantages from the standpoint of prisoner management. No specifics were offered in the instructions as to how, or upon what basis, the "Character" designation for each prisoner was to be determined. They were, in fact, made at a deck muster on the first Sunday of each quarter with "Chaplain, officers and quarter masters" participating. A present-day correctional practitioner could hardly visualize a more fascinating scene than must have been presented by one of those giant, early-19th century shipboard classification committee meetings. In addition to the good that would have accrued from this classification system, crude though it was, there was this highly significant provision:

> By this mode of classing the convicts, they will be aware of the character given them by their officers, which it is hoped will be a stimulus to them so to behave themselves, as to lead to their removal into the highest class, from which class a selection is to be made every quarter in the most impartial manner, of one convict out of every hundred, who shall have served more than half the term of his sentence (calculating upon the whole number on board each ship) whom the overseer and Chaplain are to certify to you as the best behaved convicts, in order that you make further inquiries, previous to your reporting thereon to me, that I may be enabled to judge of the propriety of recommending them to His Majesty, as deserving of free pardons.

These instructions were issued in 1815. Before the end of that year the number of men considered for pardon each year as a routine aspect of the classification process was increased to two out of every hundred on board.[16] By no means were these the only pardons granted. After 1787 most of the prisoners who went aboard the hulks were ostensibly bound for New South Wales. Only a handful were discharged from the hulks each year except by pardon. But releases for all causes amounted to a substantial number. During the last three years of Aaron Graham's administration, more than 900 men were released by pardon from a prisoner population of about 2,000.[17] The proportion of pardons granted was to increase. About 500 pardons were granted during 1824 from a hulk population of about 3,000, as opposed to 1,885 prisoners transported to Australia.[18] Hence, convicts on the hulks that year would have had something better than one chance in four of escaping transportation and gaining release, depending on individual circumstances. Throughout the era of the hulks, the pressure of overcrowded places of confinement impelled the British government to maintain a liberal policy as to the granting of pardons. It was an eminently sensible policy. Most of the offenders committed to confinement or transportation during the era were not serious criminals and presented little or no threat to the public. Finding suitable candidates for pardon was not difficult. There are certain to have been unfair departures from merit in the award of pardons, but deserving individuals were released in large numbers—helping to keep the ongoing problem of prison overcrowding in Great Britain under some semblance of control. An additional benefit of profound significance was gained—alleviation of the abject despair that quite literally killed some convicts committed to the hulks during the early years. The more serious offenders, those with sentences to transportation of fourteen years or life, were not able to hold out much hope for pardon, but the prospect of a new life in Australia, though certain to be attended by suffering and sadness, was viewed with some sense of hope by thousands of wretched souls who experienced the misery of life aboard the hulks in English waters.

The evidence is that John Capper was a capable man. Had he exercised better judgment and given up superintendency of the hulks after six or eight years of service he would be viewed now as having left a respectable record. (Although, as we shall learn in the next chapter, he accomplished little toward alleviating the sad lot of the boy convicts in his custody during those early years.) Myopia and inattention on the part of Parliament and the Home Office and Parliament were no less to blame for the misery and neglect that characterized management of the hulks during all but the earliest years of Capper's long tenure.

Parliamentary inquiries into conditions aboard the hulks were conducted in 1828, 1831 and 1835. The earliest of them, conducted by a Committee on Criminal Commitments and Convictions, came closest to arriving at an accurate assessment, despite the dubious nature of its most prestigious witness, Samuel Hoare, Chairman of the Prison Discipline Society. Mr. Hoare had observed some idleness among convicts at work at the Portsmouth Harbour hulk station. His generalized conclusion was that the hulks encouraged indolence, and that the prisoners, as a consequence, were degraded. In Samuel Hoare's view, the degrading of prisoners was incompatible with rehabilitation. (He might have found more compelling examples of degradation had he visited a lower deck of the *Leviathan* after evening lockdown.) The Committee's conclusion from its admittedly superficial inquiry was that the hulk establishment was "very defective" and that it should not be continued without thorough examination by a special panel of inquiry. Three years passed before such a committee was empaneled. It was styled the Committee on Secondary Punishments. Any benefit, however, that might have been gained from the work of that committee was lost because of an isolated remark made by one of its witnesses, a youth of eighteen, identified in the record as "A.B." This lad had been pardoned after several years on the hulks. At first he had been assigned to the juvenile hulk, *Euryalus*, at Chatham, later moved to the *Retribution* at Sheerness. A.B. told the Committee of having worked, eaten and slept in irons, wearing the same issue of ragged "slops" for as long as eighteen months. He and his fellows on the *Retribution* were kept at dangerous tasks while on shore. Idleness was punished by double irons. Serious injuries on the job were commonplace. The convicts were frequently short rationed, and as often as not, the food was barely edible. A.B. did not complain of physical abuse, but having been confined for a time on the juvenile hulk, he was acquainted with "floggings on the breach" as part of the daily routine. When asked to compare his experiences on the two hulks, he did not hesitate to describe time spent below decks on the *Retribution* as "rather a jolly life." The irony of A.B.'s observation appears to have been entirely lost on the Committee. It conjured up images of the convicts dancing below decks, singing "flash songs," gambling and playing such games as "prick the garter." The "jolly life" comment appears to have reverberated throughout the halls of the British establishment, causing anguish to legions of righteous persons who then, as now, lived in fear that some poor wretch in confinement might somehow be allowed to experience a few moments of enjoyment. To be sure, the general outrage was not altogether unjustified. A.B. and others had given the Committee disquieting information about how trysts with female visitors had been allowed to happen on the quarter deck of the *Retribution*, and testified as to the prevalence of bribery.[19] These revelations resulted in the tightening up of operations at Sheerness, otherwise the Parliamentary inquiry of 1831 accomplished nothing of value.

The Lords' Select Committee, which conducted its hearing in 1835, heard testimony from one witness that must have raised mild concerns, at least, about the treatment of juvenile offenders confined on the hulks. Most of the testimony heard, however, concerned such matters as frequency of "Divine Services," and the annual salaries of various staff members. (Schoolmaster £60, assistant surgeon £70.) The Lords' Committee did not concern itself very much with conditions of confinement.[20] Ten years would pass before Captain William John Williams would be called on to conduct the kind of investigation that was needed.

The hulk *Discovery* resting on the bottom at low tide at the Deptford dock. Thirty years before becoming a prison hulk in 1824, *HMS Discovery* was Captain George Vancouver's ship during his voyages of exploration in the Pacific, most notably,

# X

## CHILDREN OF THE HULKS

In 1824 all of the adult prisoners on the *Bellerophon* were transferred to other hulks of the fleet, making that ship, which lay in the harbor at Sheerness, exclusively available for boy convicts. If John Capper's report of July 15, 1824, is accurate, none of the 350 boys who first went aboard was older than fourteen. It appears, in any case, that older juveniles were put aboard the *Bellerophon* within a few months. Periodic overcrowding was to be an inevitable disadvantage to there being a single ship for all of the boy convicts, as there was no option for population adjustments among hulks. A policy of regularly submitting for pardon a sufficient number of boys to keep the population down to a workable level might have turned that disadvantage into a benefit. The use of pardons was helpful to some extent, but at least one advocate for the boys, the Rev. Mr. Thomas Price, insisted that the government should have been less cautious in arranging pardons. Most of the young offenders on the hulks had been convicted of minor crimes and presented no significant threat to either person or property in the community. Mr. Price was the first to serve as chaplain on the *Euryalus*, the hulk to which the boys eventually were to be assigned. His view was that over-crowding and the resulting failure to maintain good classification practices defeated all hope of redemption for the boy criminals. As we are to see, he had additional complaints.

The *Bellerophon* was one of the ships remodeled by the Navy for use as a prison hulk. Since on-board workshops were not provided, it is clear that her being used exclusively for juveniles had not been anticipated. John Capper was under considerable pressure to effect a complete separation of the juvenile offenders from the adults. His designation of the *Bellerophon* as the juvenile hulk makes it clear that advocates for the boys had more than a little influence. Officials of the Navy, who had made the *Bellerophon* available and had remodeled her for the hulk establishment, could hardly have been pleased to learn that the convicts to be housed on her would be boys, who would not be available for work on the undermanned Sheerness dockyard projects. As we shall see, their complaints about this matter were addressed by John Capper at a later time.

The *Bellerophon* was equipped with forty separate housing bays in her underdecks, each of them suitable for eight or ten inmates. There were secure central corridors for patrol by the one guard assigned to below-decks duty during the night. All of the boys had work assignments on board, and thus it would have been necessary to appropriate some of the housing area for workshop space. Except for the lack of work space, the *Bellerophon*, as first modified, was suitable for the boy convicts (provided we accept the dubious premise that the confinement of several hundred undisciplined and deprived boys on an old ship at anchor, could ever be viewed as a suitable practice). In any case, Capper and his officers did not appropriate the advantages of the *Bellerophon*. The more aggressive boys could have been assigned to separate housing bays, and thus kept away from the youngsters most likely to be preyed upon during the night. But this approach to classification was not employed. Not wanting to put up with the frequent fighting that undoubtedly would have occurred had the stronger, more aggressive youngsters been housed together, the hulk officers chose instead to have the terrified smaller and weaker boys live in relatively quiet subjugation to their stronger bay mates.

In his first biannual report after the boys went aboard the *Bellerophon*, John Capper was pleased to inform the Home Secretary that they were "fully occupied with their respective trades . . ." and that "generally speaking," they were behaving well. A few weeks earlier, the Rev. E. Edwards, Chaplain aboard the *Bellerophon*, had reported to Mr. Capper that the boys were indeed working well at their trades, but complained about their "propensity to lying." It seemed to him that "scarce any confidence can be placed in anything they say." Apparently, this was the case, even though a hundred and forty-four of the boys would repeat the Church Catechism "from time to time" and "many verses of Holy Writ (had been) committed to memory." Chaplain Edwards lamented that among those who did not respond to religious instruction "many are very dull and others are reluctant."[1]

The boys were to have use of the *Bellerophon* for only about a year and a half. Toward the end of 1825 they were transferred to a new addition to the hulk fleet, the *Euryalus*, a smaller vessel that had been "specially fitted for them" and situated at Chatham, ten miles up the River Medway. "Specially fitted" undoubtedly meant workshop space was provided. And so the boys were moved from a recently retrofitted hulk that had once been a Royal Navy ship-of-the-line, to one that in its past incarnation had been a 34-gun frigate. Space had to be made for the workshops. It becomes clear, therefore, that the boys' hammocks were hung closer together from the low ceilings of the *Euryalus'* underdecks. Worse than the overcrowding was the loss of means to give adequate protection to the submissive boys. The *Euryalus* had undergone no retrofit. For the boy convicts, the worst days of Duncan Campbell's regime had returned. And yet it appears that by continuing to have a separate juvenile hulk, one that had been "specially fitted," John Capper avoided arousing concern among influential persons who might have been expected to have in mind the best interests of the boys. At the same time, he gained the approbation of Navy authorities by again assigning the *Bellerophon* to adult convicts who would be available for work on shore. At the expense of the boy convicts in his custody, John Capper achieved something of a *tour de force.*

During 1825 on the *Bellerophon*, the boys were reported to have produced "upwards of 6,000 pairs of shoes; 15,500 garments, and various articles of cooperage and bedding."[2] There is no record of their ever approaching this kind of production on the "specially fitted" *Euryalus*.

The Rev. Mr. E. Edwards, who served the boys as their Chaplain on the *Bellerophon*, had had no complaint about conditions of confinement on that hulk, preoccupied as he was with such matters as his young flock's lack of veracity. Chaplain Thomas Price, who was assigned to the *Euryalus* at Chatham at the time the boys were moved aboard her, was a different sort of man. A hold-over from the Aaron Graham era, Price had displayed an uncommon measure of dedication to his work as Chaplain aboard the *Zealand* eighteen years before being called on to serve the boy convicts on the *Euraylus*. Prisoners aboard the *Retribution* at Sheerness enjoyed the good fortune to have him for their Chaplain just before he was moved over to the *Euraylus*.[†]

Chaplain Edwards went to the *Retribution* in Thomas Price's place, but first took pains to advise him that he should expect no success in his work with the boy convicts. Chaplain Price was told that "such was the depravity of the Boys, that every attempt to moralize them would only terminate in

---

[†] Under Captain Henry Blackwood, senior officer of Lord Nelson's frigate squadron at Trafalgar, the *Euryalus* was the first to see the advance squadrons of the French and Spanish fleets come out of the harbor at Cadiz at dawn on October 20, 1805. Throughout the day she performed masterfully, stalking the enemy and keeping Nelson informed as to the movements of the enemy's ships. Her performance during the day of battle was no less commendable. See *Trafalgar: The Nelson Touch* by David Howarth, Atheneum, New York 1969, or any standard account of the Battle of Trafalgar.

disappointment." This prediction proved to be generally accurate, but Chaplain Price's view of the matter was that overcrowding, poor classification and an inappropriate approach to handling the boys were more responsible for their poor response than was their "depravity." In his first report he stated that the newly acquired ship, especially prepared for the boy convicts, was too small for the number of boys on board. Later he was to complain bitterly about Capper's decision to place the boys aboard a ship that did not have separated housing. Accustomed as he was to nothing more than pious, flowery optimism in his chaplains' reports, Mr. Capper could not have been pleased to have these observations. Very soon, however, he was to make a report that essentially confirmed Chaplain Price's views. On January 27, 1827, Capper reported to the Home Office that the boys on the *Euryalus* had "upon two or three occasions . . . committed outrages on the persons of some of the Officers." He added that the *Euryalus* was "too small to effect a proper classification, -- a measure which is absolutely requisite for keeping them in a proper state of discipline."[3]

Whatever progress may have been made in planning for adequate classification of the boy convicts was compromised when they were crowded onto the *Euryalus*. On January 1, 1827, Chaplain Price's report to John Capper consisted of one sentence: "I expressed myself so fully in my last Report, respecting the Juvenile Convicts on board the *Euryalus*, that I have nothing in addition to communicate for the past half-year, excepting that the facilities for their instruction and moralization have been still more impeded by the increased number of Prisoners." His next reports were a little longer but no less trenchant. On January 1, 1828, he wrote: "I feel I am under the necessity of further pressing upon your notice the subject of my last Report, in which I expressed it as my full conviction that no permanent reformation can be effected among the juvenile Prisoners . . . but by their being separated and classed according to age and character, and which will of necessity require that the decks of the ship be divided into suitable wards, and besides, that a more efficient system than the present be adopted, for the better ensuring the improvement of their morals,and furthering the objects the Government had in view in placing them there. The great importance of the subject will, I trust, be duly considered and meet the attention it claims." Six months later Chaplain Price wrote of improvements in the demeanor of the boys aboard the *Euryalus* resulting from some reduction of the population and from removal of certain of "the most turbulent and abandoned" of them, but he viewed the improvements of little consequence unless there was to be an adequate "plan of separation" on the ship. More significantly, he wrote of the need for the boy convicts to be "governed by persons competent to so highly important a charge;" leaving no doubt as to his view that those in charge of the *Euryalus* lacked that competence. By that time John Capper had had quite enough of Mr. Price. Two weeks later, in his report to the Home Office, he wrote: "I regret . . . to state, that the Chaplain has not given that attention to the Boys which I anticipated, on his being appointed to the *Euryalus*." On the first of January 1828, Chaplain Price pressed ahead, insisting in his report that the *Euryalus* be modified, as other ships had been, in order to provide for better classification and separation polices. He did not repeat criticisms of the overseer of the *Euryalus* in this report, but was obviously complaining about him through other channels. This was to be Chaplain Price's last report from the *Euryalus*.[4] He was replaced by a more compliant man, the Rev. H. J. Dawes. The courage Thomas Price persistently displayed in communicating with his Superintendent indicates he aggressively pursued his advocacy for the boys while on board the hulk. It can hardly be doubted that Chaplain Price's removal from the hulk *Euryalus* was a devastating loss to the boy convicts. This man may have been the strongest chaplain to be assigned to the English hulks during the first seventy years of their use.

No improvement in the behavior of the boys could be reported until the last of 1828, after a substantial number of the more recalcitrant boys had been shipped out to Australia. There had been an assumption that many of the most troublesome youngsters were too far along in their sentences to be sent out. Chaplain Dawes' opinion was that shipping out these troublemakers had a sobering effect on the boys who remained -- influencing better conduct on their part.[5] His view of this matter, expressed in his optimistic report of January 1829, indicates that a year's service had not enabled him to get to know the boys on the *Euryalus* very well. All other sources make it clear that most of the convicts on the hulks, whether young or old, were likely to pray ardently every night for the voyage to New South Wales.

In his report to the Home Office of 10 July 1828, Capper went out of his way to praise the overseer of the *Euryalus* and the newly appointed Chaplain Dawes, a transparent effort to further discredit the outspoken criticisms of the deposed Chaplain Price.[6] Unfortunately, we are not to know the specific points at issue between Chaplain Price and the overseer of the hulk to which they were assigned. One of them may have been the matter of corporal punishment. The boys were "caned with the birch" severely and often on the *Bellerophon* and during the first years of *Euryalus'* use as a hulk. Beyond that, as we shall see, the daily routine to which the boys were subjected would have been enough to assure serious management problems. In any case, the dispute between the overseer and Chaplain Price appears to have been an early example of the tension that has prevailed throughout succeeding decades between staff responsible for custody and discipline, and staff responsible for programs and services. That it was resolved in favor of custody and discipline is also consistent with the way such disputes have most often since been resolved in American and British prison settings.

The Rev. Mr. Dawes, the man with whom the intractable Mr. Price was replaced, was more in the mold of John Capper's other chaplains. No further candid reports were to be seen regarding conditions aboard the *Euryalus*. Indeed, except for Mr. Price's efforts, candor was almost entirely missing from the reports of Mr. Capper's chaplains. The chaplains were the only employees required to submit regular reports. Had they been encouraged to be forthright, the record of John Capper's thirty-year tenure as manager of the hulk establishment would have been less sketchy. But then, had the chaplains been allowed to make honest reports on a regular basis, it is unlikely Mr. Capper would have remained on the scene for quite so many years.

In his July 1831 report Chaplain Dawes observed that the boys had become noticeably less rebellious. He credited the improvement in their conduct to the "relaxation in the system of corporal punishment," which had been ordered by Mr. Capper some months earlier. Chaplain Dawes praised Mr. Capper for his wisdom in this matter, expressing the view that "these poor unfortunate youths are very far from being insensible to the influence of gentleness and kindness."[7] By this time the Rev. Mr. Dawes had been serving as chaplain on the *Euryalus* hulk for three years. He had made no complaint about the "system of corporal punishment" that had been relied on theretofore. Indeed, in earlier reports he had commented on the "excellent discipline observed on board the *Euryalus*, under the judicious direction of the Overseer."[8]

Children of seven and eight were frequently before the criminal courts of Great Britain during all of the hulk era. Minor thievery was most often the crime. First and second offenders, as often as not, were turned over to "friends" or family for punishment. Much delight was taken, for example, in beating up the child and locking him in a cellar without food or clothing for a day or two. Those who, with the court's blessings, administered such

Napoleon as a prisoner-of-war after his defeat at Waterloo, going aboard the *Bellerophon*

punishment, were as likely as not the same persons who taught the child to steal in the first place. Still, the child undergoing such mistreatment was spared a sentence to transportation. Sentences to transportation automatically resulted in commitment to the hulks. And if a child as old as ten or eleven went before a criminal court in Great Britain for a second or third time, charged with stealing something worth as much as a shilling, he could look forward to a sentence of transportation, and thus to some time in John Capper's custody. Few if any of the boys shipped out to Australia from the *Bellerophon* and the *Euryalus* were younger than fifteen. The younger boys had a reasonable hope for pardon. Otherwise, they could look forward to five years confinement on the hulk. Five *days* on the hulk *Euryalus* provided an experience one would not choose.

Wake-up call was at 5 a.m. A half hour was allowed for washing up, lowering and lashing up the hammocks and making ready for a hasty inspection. The boys were then marched to chapel where they took their seats in "profound Silence" while morning prayers were read by the schoolmaster. Breakfast was served in the wards at six o'clock. Each boy was required to "hold up his bread and give thanks." Clean-up time in the wards followed, with certain of the boys assigned to washing down other areas of the ship. At eight o'clock the boys settled down to work, most of them sewing together previously cut patterns of cloth, making crude jackets and pants for use of the prisoners on all the hulks. On the *Bellerophon*, during earlier years, the boy convicts are reported to have manufactured shoes and "various articles of cooperage and bedding." But these more difficult tasks were not continued after significant numbers of the older and more capable boys were shipped out to Australia. A system of supervision by the remaining older and stronger boys was, however, maintained. At nine o'clock each morning a ritual began where the "elder Boys" appeared before the overseer "accompanied by those of whom they complain." The unfortunate boys who were accused of various failings were thereupon punished either by deprivation of a meal, by being thrashed "moderately with the Cane," or by "solitary Confinement on Bread and Water, not exceeding Seven Days." We can be certain that such a system resulted in the weaker and less prestigious boys having to bear the brunt of most of the punishment meted out by officers aboard the *Euryalus*.

The boys fortunate enough to avoid involvement in the 9 a.m. tribunal, worked at their assigned tasks until the noon meal, served in quarters below decks. Modest portions of boiled beef were served three or four times each week. Burgoo or oatmeal gruel was standard fare. Breakfast was most usually a morsel of cheese and a chunk of brown bread, the quality of which varied greatly. The boys were given half an hour to eat the noon meal. Then they were "sent on Deck for Air and Exercise, but not permitted to make the least noise." This ritual was repeated after the end of the workday at five. Supper was at five thirty, followed by evening prayers and then lock-down for the night at eight.

According to Mr. Capper's reports, about a third of the boys were excused from work for three hours on weekday afternoons in order to have academic instruction. Chaplain Dawes conducted "Divine Services" for the boys on Sundays and Friday evenings. He visited the sick on board four times a week. A Church of England clergyman, Chaplain Dawes was assigned no duties in addition to his ministry to the convict boys on the hulk *Euryalus*. According to his own testimony he spent not more than two hours a day on board. His salary was £200 a year. The salary of the *Euryalus'* surgeon was £100; the schoolmaster was paid £60 a year, was given housing on board, but not food.

Mr. Capper and the hulk establishment had enjoyed a period of virtually no parliamentary scrutiny for several years when, in 1834, the House of Lords' Select Committee was appointed to observe the state of Great Britain's gaols, prisons and hulks. Mr. Dawes had been serving as chaplain to the *Euryalus* for eight years when he was asked during the House of Lords' inquiry his views as to the practice of confining the boys together in large groups as opposed to the use of smaller cells. His reply was, "I have had no experience enabling me to answer that question."[9]

During the *Euryalus* era, adult prisoners on the other hulks were occasionally "flogged on the breech with a cat [cat-o'-nine-tails]." Corporal punishment for the boys on the *Euryalus* was restricted to thrashing by cane. Aside from being spared punishment with the cat, the more effective device for inflicting pain, the record provides no information as to ways the boys may have been treated less harshly than the adult prisoners. The boy convicts were beaten far more often than the adults. (Grown-ups still tend to have few compunctions about beating children.) And, in some respects, the boys were subjected to a more agonizing routine than were the adult convicts. Most of the adults went ashore to work each day. For most of them the work was arduous. Their daily trips to shore were hardly pleasure excursions, but they did provide relief from the tedium and misery that characterized life aboard the hulks. The adult convicts were allowed to spend half of their shilling-per-week earnings for potatoes and extra bread. They had contact with free citizens, and engaged in various scams, which provided distraction, if not profit. The boy convicts never went ashore. They never had enough to eat; their cramped, squalid quarters below decks were miserable for all and offered no protection for the weaker boys. The work to which most of the boys were assigned was tedious and sedentary. By policy, they were denied outlet for the energy teen-age children require for good mental and physical health. The task of managing the *Euryalus* hulk was in some ways made easier by the pathetic physical and mental condition of the boys who went aboard. The physical development of many of them would have been retarded by malnutrition. Many of them are certain to have suffered from fetal alcohol syndrome or fetal alcohol effect. We can be sure that the officers on the *Euryalus* were not confronted with the problem of managing a physically vigorous or resourcefully rebellious group. Those in higher authority who from time to time looked into the situation with the boy convicts were beginning to develop misgivings, but so far as John Capper, Chaplain Dawes and the overseer of the *Euryalus* were concerned, the system worked. It worked because the boys were for the most part weak and passive. Policies were employed that bestowed generalized depression and despair, and stifled most of the energy and exuberance boys normally have. But the system did not work perfectly. Most of the reports submitted by Mr. Capper and his obsequious chaplain, Mr. Dawes, during the *Euryalus* era, speak of exceptions to the otherwise perfect behavior of the boys. Frequently, the boys were described as having been "refractory" or to have "committed outrages on the persons of the Officers." The system was never successful in crushing the spirit of all of the boys. Consider the beginning paragraphs of a letter written by Dawes to Capper, dated January 5, 1835, in which he confirms that there were indeed distressing exceptions to the piety and submissiveness of the boy convicts:

> In fulfilling my Duty of reporting to you on the Conduct of the unfortunate Youths imprisoned in the Euryalus, I am enabled to use the Language of general Commendation.
> It will not indeed be expected that in so large an Assemblage of Children, tutored in Crime as most of these unhappily have been, no Instances of Misconduct would occur; in truth, during the last Six Months numerous Offenses have been registered, but many of these were of a venial Description, though I am bound to add that

there have been some of an aggravated Character. If, however, a few such discouraging Cases are to be found, there are others which justify a sanguine Hope of permanent Amendment.[10]

The inquiry conducted in 1835 by the House of Lords Select Committee on Gaols and Prisons resulted in a substantial loss of faith in the program of reformation for juvenile offenders on board the hulk *Euryalus*. One of the witnesses interviewed by the Committee was Thomas Dexter, a Northhamptonshire shoemaker who, as a consequence of stealing a pair of shoes, spent time in Newgate and on the *Dolphin* hulk at Chatham. It appears that despite his criminal conviction he had been identified as a reliable person. He was questioned extensively about conditions in the gaols and aboard the hulks. During his confinement he had worked as a dockyard worker and shoemaker. Eventually, he was assigned as a nurse to the Chatham dockyard hospital that served the boys of the *Euryalus*. He was asked by the Duke of Richmond whether he thought the experience of being on the *Euryalus* hulk resulted in very many of the boys being reformed. His reply was: "I should most certainly say not; and frequently when I have seen it in a newspaper that a judge has sentenced a boy out of mercy . . . to the hulks, I have made the observation that was it a child of mine I would rather see him dead at my feet than see him sent to that place."[11]

It has been suggested that crew members in the British Navy, many of whom were as young as eleven, lived under worse conditions than those to which the prisoners on the hulks were subjected. It is true that seamen aboard the ships of the Royal Navy lived in constantly damp, cramped quarters, that their food was sometimes worse than that served aboard the hulks. It is true that British sailors of that era did not go ashore for months, sometimes years on end and were subject to more severe punishment than was meted out on the hulks. Furthermore, rather than having volunteered, many of His Majesty's sailors were victims of press gangs. But for them, especially after the mutinies at Spithead and the Nore, and the reforms inspired by Nelson, it was possible for a British sailor to retain some sense of purpose, pride and hope. Most of them did not have an easy, happy life to look forward to. But all of them could realistically dream of the day when they would return with honor to a familiar British shore. They had every right to idealize their prospects. Despair was the common condition for the boy convicts on the *Euryalus*. Their reputations were sullied for life. The best prospect most of them had was to survive the agony of the hulk long enough to qualify for a miserable five months' voyage to the other end of the world, where, in those alien surroundings, they would be set to work in chains or be given to the proprietor of a primitive, frontier farmstead for what amounted to a term of slavery.

Characteristically, John Capper took note of the new attitude in Parliament and the Home Secretary's office toward the *Euryalus* and quickly adopted that attitude as his own. In accordance with a House of Lords Committee recommendation, the policy pursued after 1835 was aimed toward reduction of the number of boys on the *Euryalus* and eventual deactivation of that hulk. Efforts to acquire a building site in the Chatham dockyard area for use as a facility for juveniles were never successful. But, at last, a clear understanding of the failure of policy toward juvenile offenders, as represented by efforts aboard the hulks, had penetrated the thinking of Home Office bureaucrats and key members of Parliament. Space at the Parkhurst prison was made available and in 1836 Dartmoor was also fitted out for the reception of prisoners. Priority was given for shipment of the older boys to Port Jackson and Van Diemen's Land. By July 1836 the number on board the *Euryalus* was down to 140.[12] Reducing the number further proved difficult, especially when impatient trial judges began sending children as young as nine to the hulks with sentences to transportation. In July of 1839 the number of boys on the *Euryalus* was up to 190, prompting John Capper to ask that a vessel be chartered for the transportation of the older boys to Australia.[13] His request was granted. Over the next three years six to eight hundred boys from the *Euryalus* made the long voyage to Port Jackson or Van Diemen's Land. About the same number of boys were transferred to Parkhurst Prison. Meanwhile, boys who previously would have been placed aboard the hulks with sentences to transportation, were being committed for terms of penal servitude at Parkhurst or Dartmoor. In the fall of 1843, Lord Nelson's proud courier, the *Euryalus*, went to the breaking yard, having given up the last of her boy convicts.[14]

# XI

## BERMUDA

Set in crystal waters, warmed by the sun, cooled by the gentle Gulf Stream breezes, adorned with sparkling beaches and lush vegetation, Bermuda is a shimmering paradise when experienced from the perspective of the privileged classes ashore, or the many thousands of tourists who have visited the colony during the 20th century. As we shall see, it proved to be something other than a paradise for the convicts on the Bermuda hulks.

In 1824 the Home Office acquired from the Royal Navy the deactivated frigate *Antelope*. After repairs and modifications, she was provisioned for a voyage and dispatched to the British colony at Bermuda with a cargo of 200 convicts. She was to become the first of a fleet of hulks to be stationed in Bermudian waters over a period of thirty-eight years, housing as many as 1,600 convicts in their steamy, vermin-infested underdecks. Bermuda was to continue as a hulk station five years beyond the time when fire aboard the *Defense* at Woolwich brought the hulk era to a close in England.

The *Antelope* dropped anchor at Ireland Island, which forms the upturned western toe of the Bermudian group. There was plenty of work there for the convicts — in the stone quarries and on the docks of the island's harbor. In 1826 the *Antelope* was joined in the waters of Bermuda by the *Dromedary*, one of the ships that had been provided by the Navy for the evacuation of Millbank Prison three years earlier. She arrived in the harbor at Ireland Island bearing a cargo of exceptionally sickly convicts. It soon became apparent that most of the wretched fellows were suffering from scurvy.

The unhappy results of the scourge could have been prevented had the ship been stocked with a few dozen barrels of turnips or pickled cabbage before setting sail from England. Here again we see the mystifying preference British prison authorities seemed to have, during the early years of the 19th century, for contending with outbreaks of scurvy among convicts after their occurrence, rather than taking simple preventive measures. The causes of scurvy had been known for almost fifty years. Immediately available products of Bermuda's vegetable farms enabled the hulk surgeons to bring the unnecessary scourge under control rather quickly.

Meanwhile, the *Antelope* was sailed up to St. George, where her relatively healthy contingent of 300 convicts was put to work at the dockyard and on other projects along the waterfront of the colony's principal town. Over the next five years the *Dromedary* was joined at Ireland Island by the hulks *Coromandel* and *Weymouth*. In 1835 the number of convicts on the four hulks in Bermuda was just over 1,100.[2] This number increased even though the *Weymouth* was deactivated in 1836 due to her decayed condition, and not replaced for several years. In 1853 there were 1,600 convicts on hulks in harbors situated at opposite ends of the Bermudian island group. The *Dromedary, Antelope* and *Coromandel*, still in service after more than twenty-five years, were joined by the *Medway* and the hospital ship *Tenedos*.[3]

All the unfortunate men confined aboard the Bermuda hulks were viewed as having been transported. They had no prospect for improvement in their circumstances as did the convicts on the hulks in English waters, most of whom were awaiting transport to Australia. The convicts transported to New South Wales or Van Diemen's Land had at least a remote chance of a favorable turn in their fortunes.

Many of the prisoners on the Bermuda hulks were serious criminals, considered to be too intractable even for the tender mercies of the Australian convict outposts. But others of them were Irish prisoners whose criminality was the inevitable result of poverty and despair. Captain Elliot, who served as governor of the Bermudian island group during 1848 and 1849, demonstrated atypical sensitivity to the unhappy circumstances of the convicts aboard the hulks. He was especially concerned about the Irish prisoners. In a dispatch to Home Secretary Earl Grey in June of 1848 he wrote:

I avail myself of this occasion to solicit the compassionate attention of Her Majesty's Government, so soon as any favorable conjuncture should present itself, to the case of the many . . . Irish prisoners recently arrived here. It will be remarked with anxiety, on examining the list of 704 prisoners, sent from Ireland, in the "Medway" and "Bangalore," that many of them were convicted of stealing food, and agrarian offenses; the first, no doubt, chiefly attributable·to the dreadful calamity which befell the poorer classes of people during the last two years, and the last in a high degree to the inflammatory practices of others, in the time of desperate need. Perhaps Her Majesty's Government may be pleased (taking all these circumstances into consideration, on the return of a state of comparative tranquillity in Ireland), to permit me to appoint a Commission in this colony, for selecting individuals from the Irish prisoners, whom it may be permissible to recommend for removal to Australia, on the ticket of leave or conditional pardon. These Prisoners are for the most part friendless men in humble stations of life, and your Lordship will feel that they are entitled to any extenuating considerations which I can advance in their behalf, whilst they are conducting themselves steadily and submissively at this depot.

Governor Elliot followed up on this eminently reasonable recommendation with a dispatch expressing especial concern about the large number of juvenile prisoners convicted in Irish courts and sent out on the *Medway* and *Bangalore*. He listed the names of sixty-eight Irish lads, many of them under sixteen, and one, a thirteen-year-old boy, who had been sentenced to fifteen years transportation for sheep stealing. Governor Elliot observed that "Poor and scanty food, and the hard things of their infancy, have for the most part left these lads with a lower stature and more childish appearance than their age would explain."[4]

The Home Office granted the Governor's request. A number of Irish prisoners were pardoned. They returned to their meager circumstances at home with grateful hearts.[†]

There was a striking difference between Governor Elliot's attitude and that of other men who governed Bermuda during the time of the hulks, even though all of them, during their terms in office, bore essential responsibility for management of the hulks in Bermuda. Governor Elliot visited the hulks and took actions aimed toward righting the wrongs he observed. Among these actions were instructions to the hulk overseers to arrange separation of the juvenile prisoners from the adults.

In response to orders from a relatively liberal Home Secretary, John Capper had separated juveniles from adult convicts in the English hulks

---

† In 1823 the Irish government established two hulks for reception of prisoners awaiting transportation; the *Surprize* at the Cove of Cork, the *Essex* at Kingstown. They were taken out of service in 1836 after an inspector pronounced them "most pernicious" and observed that "a worse form of prison could scarcely be devised." The British Home Office exercised no authority or control over the Irish Hulks, but it is likely that many of the Irish prisoners who were eventually sent to Bermuda — juveniles and adults alike — were first confined on the *Surprize* or the *Essex*. See R.B. McDowell, *The Irish Administration 1801-1914*, London: Routledge & Kegan Paul, Ltd., 1964 146-147.

in 1819. In 1824 he placed them on a separate vessel. Twenty-four years later, after Capper had left the scene, and the hulk establishment was in the hands of more competent management, Governor Elliot found it necessary to instruct the captains of the hulks to provide separate housing for a forlorn group of Irish youngsters and for the other juvenile prisoners in their custody. Theretofore, these children had been mixed indiscriminately with some of the most dangerous and venal adult criminals to come out of the trial courts of England during that era.

During the thirty-one years of his tenure, John Capper took no significant part in management of the hulks in Bermuda, even though Bermuda was a principal hulk station, ostensibly under his authority. His biannual reports to the Home Secretary included little more than the prisoner counts and other largely meaningless data about the Bermuda hulks. Two thousand miles of ocean separated Bermuda from Parliament, the Home Office and reform-minded persons likely to be in correspondence with the *Times of London*. For this reason disturbances, escapes and epidemics needed to be serious in nature to earn more than a perfunctory mention in Capper's reports, if indeed they were reported at all. To be sure, John Capper managed to get his kind of clergymen assigned to the Bermuda hulks. His chaplains' biannual reports were typically sycophantic. By contrast, as we shall see, the reports of J. M. Guilding, a chaplain assigned to the Bermuda hulks after Capper's departure, provide the most compelling information we have about the quality of life for prisoners aboard the Bermuda hulks.

Another source of information about the hulks in Bermuda comes from the *Jail Journal* of John Mitchel, the Irish firebrand patriot who in 1848 and 1849 served a portion of a fourteen-year sentence to transportation on the Bermuda hulks. He was removed from Bermuda and sent to the British convict establishment on the Cape of Good Hope when the authorities learned of a scheme cooked up by Irish partisans in New York to sail into Bermudian waters and liberate their hero. During most of his time of confinement in Bermuda, Mitchel was housed on the *Dromedary* in an Ireland Island anchorage known as the Camber. He was afforded all the amenities of a gentleman, despite his insistence that he hardly met the traditional British definition of that term. John Mitchel's *Jail Journal* contains scathing comment on the contrast between his treatment and that of his fellow convicts, many of whom were his compatriots. Most of his journal is devoted to musings about freedom, oppression, truth, courage, and the relative merits of life over death, but he has given us, as well, some enlightening descriptions of convict life in Bermuda:

> The 42nd Regiment of Highlanders is stationed here, and just before
> sunset, every evening, they muster on an esplanade right opposite to
> me, and march up to their barracks with bagpipes playing . . . . But
> upon the other side, upon the breakwater . . . is another muster, sad
> to see: many hundreds of poor convicts marched in gangs, some of
> them in chains, to their work, in the quarries, or the new government
> buildings. They walk, as I fancy, with a drooping gait and carriage.
> Their eyes, it is said, are greatly injured by the glare of the white
> rocks, and many of them grow "moon-blind," as they call it, so that
> they stumble over stones as they walk. There are always two or three
> of those belonging to this ship kept in irons for one fault or another,
> and the clank of chains is seldom out of my ears. Within the month,
> also, several of them have been savagely flogged: the other prisoners
> are all mustered to see this exhibition: and though I am never
> summoned to any muster, I can hear in my cabin every cut of the
> sounding lash, and the shrieks of the mangled wretches. I once asked
> the attendant who brings my meals what fault a man had committed
> who was flogged that morning. "For giving cheek, sir," answered the
> man: which means, using insolent language: but when I hear the
> officers or guards speaking to **them** (as when walking on deck I often
> do), it is always in an imperious, insolent tone and manner, even in
> giving the commonest order: which might well exasperate sometimes
> the tamest drudge. No wonder the poor fellows are sometimes
> provoked to "give cheek." Now, I am sentenced to the very same
> punishment with these convicts, yet here have I my cabin, my
> bookshelves, the attendance of a servant, wear my own clothes, go
> out and come in at my own times, am spoken to, not only without
> haughtiness, but with respect, and all because I am supposed to be
> (though I never said I was) a *gentleman*.[5]

Throughout the history of the hulks, being considered a "gentleman"
sometimes, but not always, resulted in better treatment. John Mitchel's
political constituency of perhaps a million Irishmen, situated on both sides
of the Atlantic, was the more likely reason for his singularly good treatment,
a fact that in no way invalidates his observations about conditions of life
for his fellow convicts.

An observer who represented a different point of view was Ferdinand

Whittingham. Captain Whittingham, a British Army officer, published an account of life in Bermuda based on observations made during an eighteen-month posting to the garrison in that colony.[6] He offered a view of the lives of convicts on the hulks that sharply contrasted with those given us by Mitchel and Chaplain Guilding. His contention was that the convicts had an easy life, indeed that they enjoyed more privileges and comforts than British soldiers or honest laborers back in England. Whittingham's account made no pretense of objectivity and appears not to have been based on much first-hand knowledge. His polemic is more persuasive as to the misery routinely experienced by British soldiers (though they paraded smartly) than indicative of the ease of the lives of hulk convicts in Bermuda. A draconian approach to dealing with civilian prisoners appears to have been the rule more than the exception among British military and naval officers posted to distant colonial stations during much of the 19th century. Consider the appalling practices of Major Joseph Foveaux on Norfolk Island and those of the more respected Charles O'Hara Booth, whose specialty was "breaking the spirit" of adolescent boys in mines of Port Arthur.[7] Perhaps a determination to make things harder on convicts than on soldiers, without wanting to improve the lot of soldiers (or sailors) contributed to the array of horrors documented at so many outposts of the British Empire during the reigns of Victoria and her two predecessors on the throne of Great Britain.

It appears that when any one of the succession of Home Secretaries who served the Crown from 1824 to 1862, would think about the Bermuda hulk station, he would think of it as a place to which troublesome convicts could be dispatched. There is no evidence that anyone in Whitehall ever had any interest in how the *Antelope*, the *Dromedary*, the *Coromandel*, or the *Medway* were being managed. The hulk overseers in Bermuda reported to the colonial governors. The record suggests that most of the governors were more inclined to Captain Whittingham's attitude toward the hulk prisoners than to the enlightened approach of Governor Elliot. In any event, we can be sure that all of the men who served in the post of Governor General of Bermuda during the hulk era were interested in having convict labor for the dockyards and for public projects. They would have insisted that the hulk captains do whatever necessary to prevent escapees from endangering the citizens and property of the colony. But, with few exceptions, they appear not to have been concerned about conditions of confinement aboard these disreputable old vessels, anchored along the edges of Bermuda's beautiful harbors.

Efforts of the colonial governors and the hulk overseers to protect the free citizens of Bermuda from escaped convicts were not always successful. Escape attempts were commonplace, even though successful attempts were exceedingly rare, if success is defined as unauthorized departure from the Bermuda Island group to freedom on some other shore. Such an accomplishment required that the escapee or escapees acquire a boat capable of remaining upright and afloat on the open ocean, and with a means of propulsion sufficient to negotiate the swirling surf and cross the coral reefs to the sea. This feat was accomplished a few times, only to place the would-be escapees in dismal circumstances more than three hundred miles from the nearest friendly landfall, the coast of North Carolina. Unless successful in a William Bligh style navigational achievement, the best hope escapees on the open ocean had was to be picked up by a foreign vessel whose crew and master were unfriendly toward British authority, and therefore willing to drop them off at some relatively hospitable foreign port. It was more usual for convicts who broke free of the island group to be apprehended by British patrol vessels and returned to the hulks for punishment. Sometimes the escapees would have had the bad fortune to avoid capture for a number of days, which meant that they were likely to have been parched by the sun, half crazy with thirst and not infrequently blinded by the glare of the sun.

The high probability of this being the fate of convicts who attempted escape, was viewed as one of Bermuda's principal advantages as a hulk station. A serious disadvantage, on the other hand, was that law-abiding citizenry of the islands were particularly vulnerable to outrages committed by escapees from the hulks. Escapes by the Bermuda hulk convicts were likely to pose more danger than escapes from the hulks in English ports. The majority of the prisoners on the hulks in England were men convicted of theft and other crimes against property, awaiting transport to Australia. A larger proportion of the prisoners sent to Bermuda, except those from Ireland, were violent criminals. Furthermore, a convict who succeeded in slipping away from his work crew on the docks of Woolwich or Chatham, for example, was most apt to make his way to London and do everything possible to melt into the teeming streets of the city that were so familiar to him. He would have friends who might help him (as well as presumed friends who might betray him). In any case, the practice of preying on innocent citizens would not often serve the interest of an escapee in England whose main desire was to avoid apprehension. Escapees from the hulks in Bermudian waters saw theft as the principal way whereby they could survive

The Bermuda hulk anchorages

and perhaps equip themselves for an attempt to quit the Islands. Theft by stealth was most often tried but theft by violence and threat of violence were resorted to all too often. Not many escapees entertained the notion of enjoying a life of freedom in Bermuda. No hulk convict could realistically hope to blend into the Island's small white population and avoid detection for very long, but there were those who tried to enjoy a semblance of freedom by living in forest or limestone cave, slipping out at night to forage for necessities and for liquor. Robberies were frequently perpetrated and, on more than one occasion, escaped convicts terrorized isolated house-holders into leaving food and provisions out at night for several days at a time before summoning enough courage to call on the Island's police authorities for help. Before his recapture, one convict escapee lived comfortably for six weeks in the basement of a grocery shop.[8]

When captured, escapees were subject to severe punishment. Mitchel recounts the fate of three convicts who escaped from the *Coromandel*, anchored off Ireland Island in 1848. They swam to shore, then made for the open ocean in a stolen skiff. When their boat became lodged on a sandbar they swam back to shore, stole some civilian clothing and managed to avoid recapture for two days. But recaptured they were, one of them dressed in the attire of a Bermudian lady. A portion of their penalty was to receive twenty lashes before the assembled company of the *Coromandel*, then to be rowed in turn to the *Medway* and the *Dromedary*, for an additional twenty lashes on each of those vessels; a modified version of the British Navy's by-then abandoned brutal practice of "flogging through the fleet"[9] (This event occurred two years after there had been a shocking exposure of excesses on the hulks at Woolwich, and dramatic reforms had been implemented, reforms that apparently did not apply beyond the shores of England.)[†]

During all of the years prison hulks were stationed in the waters of Bermuda, authorities there struggled with the problem of illicit contact between convicts who worked on shore and the free citizens of the Island. The contact took the form of trafficking in various kinds of contraband and, at times, assistance to convicts attempting escape. A few convicts were exceptionally skilled in carving and otherwise fashioning small objects of beauty that could be sold at good prices in Hamilton or St. George. Most of the them had no such skills. But among the convicts were ingenious fellows, capable of devising nefarious schemes from which unscrupulous

---

[†] See Chapter XIII

Bermudian dock workers could profit. The problem of illicit contact between convicts and disreputable free citizens was made worse by chronic understaffing of the hulks establishment, and the dubious quality of the men employed as warders and overseers.

Many of the men sent out to Bermuda from the criminal courts of England were tubercular or afflicted by other diseases. They were not often hardy countrymen, accustomed to good food and hard work in the sunny fields of Kent. Some of those who had come to Bermuda after confinement on the hulks stationed at English ports had developed some sinuous strength from exertions on the docks of Woolwich and Sheerness, but their general circumstances as hulk convicts were hardly conducive to the development of robust good health. Most of the English prisoners were Londoners, who had lived desperate, gin-sodden lives of survival in the slums of White Chapel or the Tower Hamlets. Almost none of them would have been in sound health.

Outbreaks of West Indian yellow fever swept the hulks from time to time. The worst of the epidemics occurred in 1853. It was believed to have arrived on a ship from Cuba, where the most severe onslaught of yellow fever in that islands' history was raging. The disease devastated Bermuda, claiming more than 650 victims. One hundred sixty of them were convicts on the hulks. The health of many others, civilians, soldiers and convicts, was broken by the disease. The suffering that was endured throughout the colony in 1853 had been standard fare for the convicts since the hulks first dropped anchor in Bermuda almost thirty years before. Four earlier epidemics of yellow fever had buffeted the hulks, adding to the chronic misery of consumption, scurvy and the innumerable afflictions that resulted inevitably from the wretched living conditions. At low tide the hulks would rest in the muddy sands along the edges of the harbor. Ventilation below decks was inadequate; sanitation was poor and adequacy of the food was inconsistent. Roaches and other vermin, liking the languorous climate, thrived in the underdecks of the Bermuda hulks, adding a dimension of misery that had not been experienced by men who had been confined on the hulks in England.10  The rats and roaches of England were smaller, less numerous and far less audacious.

Like the boys on the *Euryalus* at Chatham, juvenile convicts on the Bermuda hulks had work assignments on board. Most of the relatively healthy adults went ashore each weekday for five to six hours of labor in the quarries or on dockyard projects. We can be sure that certain of the work crews, not assigned to critical tasks, were allowed to loaf in the shade from time to time, and that their work was not always arduous. Others would have had the bad luck to fall under the supervision of hard taskmasters who took satisfaction in working their charges to the point of exhaustion. As observed by Mitchel, cases of ophthalmia struck from time to time, due to the convicts being given insufficient relief from the sun's glare on the sea and limestone cliffs.

Four years after the last use of convict hulks in English waters, the Bermuda hulks were still in service. In a report to the Directors of Convict Prisons in England, Chaplain Guilding had this to say:

Bermuda is the solitary exception under the British Crown where these dens of infamy and pollution are permitted to exist. Both on the score of civilization and humanity they have been everywhere else condemned . . . . If the hulks were so bad in principle that they have been totally abandoned in England, even with the careful supervision that the Home Government could bestow, what must they be in this distant colony, where abuses are more likely to grow up and far less likely to come to light? It is my painful conviction, after some years' experience of the matter, that the great majority of the prisoners confined in the hulks become incurably corrupted, and that they leave them, in most cases, more reckless and hardened in sin than they were upon reception . . . . Few are aware of the extent of suffering to which a prisoner is exposed on board the hulks, or of the horrible nature of the associations by which he is surrounded. There is no safety for life, no supervision over the bad, no protection to the good . . . . They are productive of sins of such foul impurity and unnatural crime that one even shudders to mention them . . . . A mob law, and tyranny of the strong over the weak, exists below, which makes the well-disposed live in constant misery and terror."[11]

The last of the Bermuda hulks was deactivated in 1862, two years after Chaplain Guilding's condemnation. Alas, he was incorrect in ascribing to Bermuda the dubious honor of having the last of the hulks. A hulk station, established at Gibraltar in 1842, was maintained after a fashion until 1875. Most of the prisoners sent to Gibraltar were housed in barracks ashore, where they were employed on public works. A hulk was continued in use as a hospital for the prisoners, however, until the very end.

# XII

## MR. DUNCOMBE ACCUSES

In 1847 John Capper had been manager of the hulk establishment for more than thirty years. Unquestionably there had been improvements since the days of Duncan Campbell. Conditions of confinement were, in fact, better than they had been under Aaron Graham's administration, even though Graham had been no less competent and far more energetic and conscientious than Capper. Most of the improvements under Capper flowed from the decision taken in 1817 to retrofit deactivated naval vessels with secure, separated housing below decks before placing them in service as prison hulks. Better classification and improved security for the prisoners was immediately achieved. And of greatest significance, separation made possible visual supervision of the prisoners in their housing areas.

Before this innovation there had been a period of more than forty years during which unseparated prisoners of all descriptions had been locked down for the night below decks without supervision. That infamous era had come to an end.[†] Thereafter, in the interest of their own safety and comfort, if for no other more admirable reasons, officers of the hulks took measures that were unavoidably beneficial to the prisoners. Sanitation below decks was improved, though never to a point that would approach acceptability by mid-20th century standards. In point of fact, revolutionary improvements were still needed. Most of the improvements that had been made, while significant, were modest and transitory. Neither the Select Committee nor the Home Office possessed sufficient resolve to put to an end permanently the dreadful conditions that continued to prevail on the hulks. There was a slovenliness of attitude — from the Home Secretary's office on down to the level of the mostly wretched fellows who had direct charge of the prisoners. After about five years in office, John Capper's efforts to effect improvements aboard the hulks began to slacken. It was

---

[†] An exception to the policy of providing the prisoners with separated housing below decks on the hulks, was John Capper's use of the *Euryalus* for confinement of juveniles from 1825 to 1843.

inevitable that conditions of confinement would deteriorate, and deteriorate they did.


During the latter weeks of 1846 a prisoner named William Mawman Brown, on board the *Warrior* hulk at Woolwich, initiated communication with Thomas Duncombe, Member of Parliament for Finsbury. He did so by writing detailed and graphic letters about conditions that prevailed on the hulks, then having a fellow prisoner give them to a certain Mr. Scott, a guard on the *Warrior*, for eventual delivery to the MP. It appears that Mr. Scott, in the interest of human decency, or perhaps for less commendable considerations, was willing to betray his trust as one of Mr. Capper's officers. We can be certain that there was a free flow of uncensored "kites" from the hulk convicts to friends, family, old partners in crime, and even public officials. It is doubtful that very many of the other letters were as detailed and compelling as those written by William Brown.[1]

Thomas Duncombe had been serving the borough of Finsbury in the House of Commons since 1834; he continued to do so until his death twenty-seven years later. From a moderately well-to-do Yorkshire family, Duncombe was elected as a Whig and threw in with the Radicals in Commons early in his parliamentary career. For many years he exercised his considerable talent in advocating for unpopular causes. Duncombe was well chosen as recipient of the information William Brown was proffering. The MP for Finsbury was not the kind of man who would ignore evidence of reprehensible neglect and mistreatment on board the hulks at Woolwich, for which the Tory government was responsible.[2] Duncombe did not take up the cause of prison reform on a permanent basis. He was something of a gadfly, without the morally compelling voice of a John Howard or a Samuel Romilly, and yet, where the hulks were concerned, he maintained interest just long enough to deserve credit for having contributed more to the eventual dismantling of the hulk fleet than any other member of Parliament.

As we shall see, the investigation that eventuated from Duncombe's reaction to William Brown's letters proved that most of the allegations they contained were exaggerated, if not entirely false. Mr. Bossey, the hulk surgeon who was the main target of the accusations and who was characterized by Brown as cruel and grossly negligent, was exonerated of the more egregious charges made against him. And yet, William Brown's letters were to have profound consequences. They set in motion events that brought an end to the English prison hulks, after one last dismal decade.

During the time he was engaged in sending his illicit communications to MP Duncombe, William Brown was serving as a nurse to the wretched prisoners aboard the *Warrior*.[3] This ponderous old vessel had been acquired by the hulk establishment in 1840. She had done her service with the Navy as a 74-gun Man-O-War. As a prison hulk, she was viewed as having a capacity for 600 convicts. In 1847 the *Warrior* was moored alongside the dockyard wharf at Woolwich. The other Woolwich hulks in service were the venerable *Justitia*, moored at the Royal Arsenal dock, the hospital ship *Unite*, anchored a hundred yards farther out from shore than was the *Justitia*, and the reception hulk *Wye*, anchored alongside the *Unite*. Early in the year, the much deteriorated *Wye* was taken out of service for repairs. She was replaced temporarily by a slightly more serviceable hulk, the *Morning Star*. The *Unite* was the designated hospital ship. The other hulks at Woolwich housed their share of sickly convicts, most of them ambulatory. A substantial complement of convict workers were employed on dockyard projects. There was chronic conflict between staff and convicts, arising from the complaints of the convicts who considered themselves too sick to work.

In addition to the Woolwich fleet, there were, in 1847, prison hulks stationed at the English ports of Gosport, Devonport, Deptford, Chatham and Portsmouth, as well as those in the waters of Bermuda and Gibraltar. But only the hulks at Woolwich ever came under effective scrutiny.

During those days substantial numbers of offenders were being sent by the criminal courts of Great Britain to the new dry land prisons to serve terms of *penal servitude*, an innovation in British criminal justice. The hulk stations at Gibraltar and Bermuda were still available, however, and many offenders, healthy enough to bear the long voyage, were cleared for transport to Van Diemen's Land and Moreton Bay, and were not required to bide their time on the hulks in English waters. These developments had altered the mission of the hulks in English waters. They had become the "invalid hulks," temporarily discontinuing service as holding stations for Australia-bound convicts. From 1843 until 1847, no convicts scheduled for transportation to Australia were sent to the English hulks.[4] The unhappy irony here is that, with few exceptions, the only prisoners housed on the notoriously unhealthy old hulks at Woolwich and Portsmouth during that period were prisoners not healthy enough to go elsewhere.

On January 28, 1847, Thomas Duncombe rose on the floor of the House of Commons and unburdened himself on the subject of the appalling conditions of confinement on board the hulks at Woolwich. William Brown had provided him with voluminous information, all of it compelling, some of it accurate. In order to support his call for a select committee inquiry, Mr. Duncombe first charged that the hulk Superintendent had made misstatements in the 1845 death statistics in an apparent effort to conceal the unhealthy state of the hulks. He charged further that an insufficiency of religious services were being provided for the convicts and that corporal punishment was being improperly and excessively used. The incensed MP then read into the record some of the woeful accounts of cruelty and neglect alleged by his informant.

First there was George Monk, "a lunatic," hospitalized on the *Warrior* with a broken leg. According to MP Duncombe's information, this man had recently been "allowed to lie in bed in his own water and filth until such time as a large piece fell out, putrid with his urine, from the bottom of his back bone." He had been handcuffed to his bed much of the time. Due to his mental status, he was eventually moved to the insane asylum at Bethlehem.

Next came the unhappy story of "An old man of the name of Peter Bailey." It appears that this pitiful fellow, lying on his bunk in a state of severe infirmity, talked to the surgeon, Peter Bossey, about his "life of the most simple nature," and his dread of death away from his home. He asked that he might be visited by a clergyman of the Wesleyan Methodist faith, seemingly in hope that through some near-miraculous act of kindness he would be able to go home. According to Duncombe's informant, Mr. Bossey had laughed at the old man and said to him, "It is of no use your imagining that you will ever go home, for home you will never see; you will die on that bed you are lying on . . ." Allegedly, the surgeon added further words of scorn. Before dying a few days later Mr. Bailey said to the informant, "He has broke my heart."

MP Duncombe next told his colleagues about William Theobald, an epileptic and a man who suffered from a "great weakness of body." Observing him in the course of a protracted seizure one day, the surgeon, Mr. Bossey, announced that he intended to cure him of his epilepsy. He proceeded to pour cold water over his head, a procedure that had no effect. The next day Mr. Bossey informed Mr. Theobald that, should he have another fit, he could expect to be "well flogged." The prisoner died shortly thereafter. Apparently, the informant did not tell MP Duncombe whether Mr. Bossey had carried out his threat to have the man flogged.

And then there was the case of James Brandish, described by the informant as "a maniac." He was admitted on board the *Warrior* "while in a fit, roaring out lustily." On seeing him in this condition, Mr. Bossey laughed at him and then told him that such behavior would not do. Later, on the occasion of a similar fit, Mr. Bossey said to him, "It's all gammon, Mr. Brandish. I will have you well flogged if you don't alter your course." The informant had told of this man's having been handcuffed to his bed in his own filth much of the time, causing him to suffer the same dreadful experience as that of Mr. Monk, in having a piece of urine soaked, mortified flesh fall out of his back. He was frequently threatened with floggings by Mr. Bossey before he died — all of this according to MP Duncombe's informant, Mr. Brown.

In his letters Mr. Brown told the MP of three other cases, one of them particularly horrifying. William Cooper came to the hulks with a grossly enlarged liver. Mr. Bossey chose to treat the condition by punching and squeezing the protrusion, explaining to his apprentices that in this way he intended to break loose the collected fluid that was the cause of the enlargement. The prisoner, who had been ambulatory on admission, died a few days later as a result of Mr. Bossey's radical treatment.

Henry Heighton, a consumptive prisoner, was accused of malingering by Mr. Bossey, and ordered out of his bunk and back to work. He died a few hours later, declaring to his companions moments before death that he was "a murdered man."

The last such tale of horror that had been related to MP Duncombe by his informant concerned the melancholy events just before and immediately following the demise of Henry Driver. This man had been sent down to the hulks from Millbank because of his infirmities. He too was declared to be a "schemer" by Mr. Bossey and put to work. He died four days later. According to the informant, Mr. Brown, "This unhappy wretch had no sooner departed this life than the body, still warm, was carried over to the dead-house, and the knife [put to] work, operating and dissecting. Entrails taken from the body were thrown into the river, where dozens had gone before. When the dissection was over the vacuum was filled up with flannel, then sewn up for the jury to sit on." (One is inclined to visualize a number of somber gentlemen sitting together on the flannel-stuffed corpse of a dead convict.)

In addition to accounts of the alleged mistreatment of these unfortunates,

Thomas Duncombe, Member of Parliament

MP Duncombe passed along to his colleagues in Commons certain other grisly allegations concerning the handling of corpses. The chaplain, it was said, seldom, if ever, visited the dying. Convict nurses, on the other hand, watched them "with the eyes of a hawk." When judgment was made by a nurse that some poor wretch had drawn his last breath, the body would be hauled out of its bunk and laid on the deck, so that the bedding could be ransacked for money and other valuables. Then, with still no pronouncement of death by a physician, the body would be conveyed to the death-house for dissection, a place where buckets containing various body parts were apt to be found here and there about the floor, and the remains of deceased convicts were otherwise subjected to appalling casualness. Among the convicts on the hulks at Woolwich there was a conviction that when a man's illness became life threatening, little or nothing was done to save him, because of a wish on the part of the medical officers in charge to have a good supply of cadavers for the schools of anatomy.

From the information provided him by his informant, MP Duncombe was convinced that the coroner's inquests that were conducted into deaths among the hulk convicts were little more than gestures toward the requirements of the law. Furthermore, he pointed out that the hulks' medical officers had obviously been repeatedly in violation of the Anatomy Act, which prohibits dissection of a corpse until forty hours after death.[5]

Before making his speech on the floor of Commons, Thomas Duncombe had communicated to the Home Secretary, George Grey, something of his concern about conditions aboard the hulks, but without divulging very much of the shocking information that he was to reveal in his speech before the House. He had asked the Home Secretary to take the lead in requesting a select committee on the part of the Crown. This the Hon. Baronet declined to do. Apparently, he had offered instead to have a departmental commission look into the situation. Duncombe was dissatisfied with this approach. Much to the chagrin of the Home Secretary, he laid out his accusations in a speech on the floor of the House of Commons and thus before the British public.[6]

A motion made by him before the House of Commons, which would have required appointment of a select committee, failed on a vote of 44 to 121.[7] But there had been a public debate. Despite having prevailed on the vote in Commons, the Home Secretary had little choice other than to pursue the matter. He did so by having an associate write a letter to John Capper on January 29, 1847, the day after the debate in Commons, calling his attention to an article that appeared in the *Times* that day, exhaustively detailing Thomas Duncombe's disturbing allegations. Capper was instructed to report on "any of the matters which fall within your own knowledge, or upon which you can furnish information or explanation." The letter indicated the probability of a "special inquiry" but made it clear that, in any case, the Superintendent's comments on the allegations were required.[8]

During these events Superintendent John Capper, then past seventy and in poor health, was confined to his bed in Lambeth Terrace. Nevertheless, a comprehensive response, bearing his signature, was on the Home Secretary's desk within eleven days, making this declaration: "To all these charges I beg leave to give a most positive and distinct contradiction . . . . The prisoners are not hid from public view, as in a gaol, but work daily and openly in the presence of hundreds of individuals . . . who must of necessity be perfectly aware of any acts of cruelty toward them . . . . The visitors, also, on board the hulks are numerous, and they have invariably expressed themselves in terms of approbation at the cleanliness and order apparent to every one." The report then provided a reasonably credible explanation of what had appeared to MP Duncombe to be misstatements in the 1845 death statistics, and used the logs to discredit charges of an inadequate offering of religious services. The least persuasive aspect of the report was its effort to justify the degree to which corporal punishment was being used. It appears that officers on the hulks had been condoned in unlimited use of "a birch on the breech," thus circumventing regulations then in place that severely restricted floggings as a means of discipline. The report invoked Mr. Capper's concern about the problems being encountered in properly overseeing the convicts on the hulks with a substantially reduced complement of officers. It appears that staff cuts had been made by attrition, as even then there had been some fairly serious discussion about the breakup of the hulk fleet. And then the Capper report proceeded, on a case-by-case basis, to dispute each of the allegations of mistreatment of sick convicts that were detailed in the *Times*. An attached report prepared by the surgeon, Mr. Bossey, provided most of the details.

Yes, it had been necessary to cuff the hands of the "lunatic," George Monk, to the sides of his bed, but only to prevent him from injuring his broken leg, a condition he suffered before being admitted on board. The charge of his having lain in his own filth for days on end was denied, but it was true that he suffered from severe bed sores.

The charge that Mr. Bossey had been heartless in his treatment of the terminally ill Peter Bailey was denied. Mr. Bossey had thought it the course of kindness and honesty to disabuse the pitiful old convict of any hope that he might be released to die among his friends at home. And rather than laughing at the old man and scoffing at his request to be visited by a Wesleyan Methodist clergyman, Mr. Bossey, himself a Methodist, had arranged two such visits. The Capper report was appended with copies of letters from the clergyman, confirming this assertion and praising the surgeon for his kindness and concern about the spiritual welfare of the dying convict.

With respect to the treatment of William Theobald, the report asserted that pouring cold water on the head of a person experiencing an epileptic seizure was an accepted practice. The charge that Mr. Bossey threatened to have the man "well flogged" was denied.

Also denied were the allegations of cruelty and incompetence in the treatment of the "maniac," James Brandish, who had indeed been admitted into the hospital "while roaring out lustily," or that there had been anything inappropriate about the treatment of William Cooper's enlarged liver, or Henry Heighton's consumption, or the unspecified illness from which the "malinger," Henry Driver, had died. The report characterized the "threats of flogging, repeated more than once in this case [as] a mere fabrication."

Mr. Capper's report was less convincing in its defense against the charges of misconduct in the handling of the remains of deceased convicts, even though a letter from Her Majesty's coroner for the County of Kent was offered, putting forward the view that Mr. Bossey and the other authorities had not been in violation of the Anatomy Act, and that otherwise he had no complaints about Mr. Bossey's performance in disposing of the dead.[9]

The report submitted by John Capper was comprehensive and, on balance, convincing. In point of fact, it had not been prepared by the Superintendent, but by his nephew and assistant, Robert Capper. For all intents and purposes, Robert was by then managing the hulk establishment without much help or interference from his ailing uncle.[10]

The request for the report, sent to John Capper from the Home Office on 29 January 1847, had stated that "Sir George Grey will probably think it necessary to institute a special inquiry." Undoubtedly the Cappers hoped that by submission of such an exhaustive and persuasive report in response to the allegations, the Home Secretary would be reassured and would allow the matter to rest or, at most, to order a departmental inquiry that would prove to be as perfunctory as such inquiries had been during past years.

The Home Secretary's decision in this matter might have gone either way. We are not to know what factors influenced him to order the inquiry. It is unlikely that the English prison hulks would have continued in use indefinitely, even if Sir George had accepted the Capper report at face value. Had he taken that decision, however, it is unlikely that we would have come fully to know the extent of the misery and mismanagement that so pervaded the hulk establishment during the thirty two years of the Capper regime. There was to be no parliamentary select committee inquiry. That question had been settled by a vote in Commons immediately in the wake of MP Duncombe's allegations. Instead, the Home Secretary dispatched the following letter to one of his prison inspectors, Captain William John Williams:

Whitehall, 6 March, 1847
Sir:
Statements have been recently made respecting the treatment of the Convicts in the Hulks at Woolwich, which require investigation. I thought it right in the first instance to refer those statements to the Superintendent of Convicts, and to call for a Report from him upon the several allegations which they contained. I, at the same time, intimated to him, that I should probably feel it my duty to institute a special inquiry after I should have received his Report.

In pursuance of this intention, I request that you will undertake the duty of making close and thorough investigation into the general treatment and condition of the Convicts in these Hulks, especially with reference to the statements in question; a copy of which, and of Mr. Capper's Report upon them, I enclose for your information.

You will conduct the inquiry in the manner which appears to you best calculated to elicit the fullest information on the several matters to which it relates. All the officers connected with the Convict Hulk Establishment will be directed to attend your summons, and to facilitate your inquiry; and you will have access to any documents, the inspection of which may be required.

You will obtain such evidence from persons unconnected with the Establishment as you think necessary, and as you may have it in your power to procure.

It is my wish that Mr. Duncombe, who is in possession of

information on this subject, should have the opportunity of attending the investigation, and that every due facility should be afforded him of suggesting topics of inquiry, and of putting questions to witnesses.

You will report to me the results of your inquiry, with your opinion upon the matters referred to you, and with any observations or suggestions with respect to future conduct of the Establishment.

I am, Sir,
Your most obedient humble servant,
G. Grey[11]

The Home Secretary demonstrated political skill of a high order by bringing the Government's severest critic into the center of the process. It was a deft stroke. Of more significance, it appears that Sir George had decided he could no longer ignore the intimations he had undoubtedly been hearing, long before MP Duncombe's broadside, and had developed genuine concern about conditions aboard the convict hulks. Having warded off the prospect of a parliamentary select committee inquiry, he decided to give some teeth and meaning to a departmental investigation. It is unlikely that the selection of Captain Williams was a casual choice. Select committee inquiries and the inquiries of the Crown's prison inspectors had in the past been useful in encouraging better performance on the part of the hulk managers and in preventing a downward spiral in conditions of confinement for the convicts, but none of the past inquiries had penetrated to the core of the problem. All of them had been, to some extent, victimized by obfuscation on the part of the hulk managers. The difference this time was the ability and determination of the man whom the Home Secretary, Sir George Grey, called on to conduct the investigation.

# XIII

## CAPTAIN WILLIAMS INQUIRES DILIGENTLY

In March 1802, when Aaron Graham was asked to examine the hulk establishment, he was not a member of the British government's cadre of prison inspectors. However, on his assignment to the task he was given the title *Inspector of Prisons*. He held no other title during the twelve disheartening years he served as manager of the hulks. From the time of Graham's departure in 1814 until the appearance of William John Williams thirty-three years later, none of the innumerable Inspectors of Prisons who were assigned to routine inquiries into conditions aboard the hulks during John Capper's long tenure ever made any impact. In 1847, John Perry, an Inspector of Prisons, was to give evidence of his own incompetence when he testified that he had visited the hulks at Woolwich eight or ten times during the three years previous to Captain William's inquiry, without seeing "any want of cleanliness" or other significant failings on the part of the hulk managers.[1]

It seems likely that the Home Secretary, Sir George Grey, knew William John Williams was something more than just another member of the government's cadre of prison inspectors.

Captain Williams began taking evidence aboard the *Justitia* on the twelfth of March, 1847, seven days after the date of the Home Secretary's letter instructing him to initiate the inquiry. With little respite, the inquiry continued aboard the *Justitia* through April 1. After a well-deserved long weekend, Williams moved the inquiry to the *Warrior* hulk where he and Thomas Duncombe resumed examination of witnesses, doing so for four days before returning to the *Justitia*. Seven more days of evidence were taken before the inquiry was adjourned, *sine die*, on April 23, 1847. Ninety-eight witnesses were questioned, sixty-four of them convicts. The others were employees of the hulk establishment at Woolwich or persons who had some connection with the hulks. Robert Capper was questioned first and perhaps most exhaustively. He was recalled four times. Peter Bossey, surgeon and principal medical officer for the hulks at Woolwich, was called to the stand ten times. (Incidentally, Bossey's name is incorrectly spelled *Bossy* throughout the records of the inquiry.) Other witnesses, including chief accuser, William Mawman Brown, were recalled several times.[2] From the thoroughness of the report submitted by Captain Williams to Sir George Grey on May 28, 1847, it is clear that on the days between March 12 and April 23, not devoted to taking formal evidence, Williams was inspecting the vessels and probing every aspect of John and Robert Capper's administration.

Pomp and prestige were to have no part in these proceedings. It is probable that the shipboard hearings were conducted in the quarters of the overseers. These quarters on both vessels were reasonably commodious. As there was no need to accommodate lawyers, jurors or spectators, the use of a large chamber was not required. Member of Parliament Thomas Duncombe was a vigorous participant during most of the inquiry, sharing the questioning with Captain Williams.

In addition to the infirmities that kept him at home in bed, Superintendent John Capper undoubtedly suffered from considerable anxiety during these days. He would have been told by his nephew during the early stages of the inquiry that this Williams fellow was acting as though he intended to get to the bottom of things — especially discomforting as it isn't likely either of the Cappers knew what the bottom of things might hold. And there was to be the vociferous presence of Thomas Duncombe at the hearings. The Superintendent's reputation as a responsible public servant, which despite all he had managed to maintain for more than thirty years, was in jeopardy. In any case, because of his illness and infirmity, he was not called and took no part in the inquiry.

In his report on the inquiry, Captain Williams pointed out that much of the testimony was "prolix, desultory, and contradictory," the result, in his view, of its not having been taken under oath. Some of the witnesses were over-eager to testify, and inclined to embellish. Others, especially those who wanted to put the administration of the hulks in a more favorable light, were exceedingly reluctant, with the sought-after facts having to be dragged out of them.[3] Consider this exchange between MP Duncombe and Robert Capper during one of the younger Capper's several appearances in the witness chair:

Duncombe:   Did you not [fire] Captain Hatton on that day?
Capper:        Certainly not.
Duncombe:   You did not mention it to him?
Capper:        He knew it before I came down.

Duncombe: From whom?
Capper: By a letter from the Superintendent.
Duncombe: From you?
Capper: I am not the Superintendent.
Duncombe: Do you mean that John Henry Capper wrote that letter?
Capper: He signed it?
Duncombe: Who wrote it?
Capper: I wrote it.[4]

Over the course of many days and several return appearances by Robert Capper, Captain Williams elicited from him a substantial body of information of the sort that was hardly in accord with the notion that the prison hulks at Woolwich were being administered competently. It was learned that Robert, the son of John Capper's brother, was appointed Clerk to the Superintendent of the prison hulk establishment by Sir Robert Peel in 1823. His being permitted to have his nephew as Clerk, an important junior executive position in the hulk establishment, is consistent with evidence which indicates that John Capper was highly regarded in the Home Office during those early days of his tenure. Despite growing misgivings about the hulk establishment, John Capper continued to enjoy a substantial residue of respect up until the time of Captain Williams' inquiry. Nephew Robert's appointment had come twenty-four years before, toward the end of the time during which his uncle had functioned effectively as manager of the hulks.

John had demonstrated a considerable measure of competence during those first five or six years in giving general oversight to the program of remodeling the underdecks of the prison hulks, working closely and energetically with the Navy. Moreover, throughout the years of his administration, John Capper was viewed as one of the government's more knowledgeable experts on dry land imprisonment. He appears not to have especially relished this role, but neither, apparently, did he object to having assignments that clearly interfered with his duties as Superintendent of the hulks.[5] Robert Capper, undoubtedly an intelligent and energetic man, arrived on the scene at a time when his Uncle John felt a need to relax and turn over some of his more stressful duties as manager of the hulks to a younger, hardier man. At this point John Capper would have been wise to give up his superintendency of the hulks, and perhaps continue with his clerkship in the Home Office. His choosing instead to hang on as Superintendent, while allowing his unqualified young kinsman to act as his surrogate for most of the following twenty-five years, was a tragic mistake.

Captain Williams was to expose several embarrassing facts about John Capper's conduct as Superintendent, and about the unseemly circumstances of Robert's role as *de facto* acting Superintendent. Williams' report describes an appalling range of other deficiencies in the administration of the hulk establishment at Woolwich.

But first, Captain Williams addressed the specific allegations that had been made by Thomas Duncombe on the floor of Commons and then had been reported in distressing detail by the *Times of London*. Duncombe's colleagues in the House of Commons would have been most specifically interested in what the inquiry gleaned with respect to these horrifying allegations. Each of the allegations was investigated with excruciating thoroughness. Captain Williams confirmed the contentions in John Capper's report with respect to the "lunatic," George Monk. The evidence revealed that restraints on this man were necessary to prevent his further injuring a broken leg. Furthermore, he accepted as substantially accurate, although "somewhat exaggerated," testimony of a convict nurse indicating reasonable efforts to keep the poor man's bed cleaned up. Captain Williams was critical of Peter Bossey's long delay in having Monk transferred to Bethlehem.

Information passed along to MP Duncombe alleged that the dying pleas of the pitiful old convict, Peter Bailey, had been ridiculed by his attending physician, Peter Bossey — that Mr. Bossey had laughed at the man's death bed request to be visited by a Wesleyan Methodist clergyman. Again, the denial in John's Capper's report proved valid. Mr. Bossey, himself a Wesleyan Methodist, prevailed upon his own pastor to visit Peter Bailey, not once, but twice.

The accusation concerning the epileptic convict, William Theobald, was that Mr. Bossey had poured cold water on his head and threatened to have him "well flogged" for feigning seizures. Evidence taken by Captain Williams established that the cold water routine was standard practice for attempting to break a seizure, and the allegation that the surgeon threatened to have the man flogged was "unsupported, and appears under the circumstances, improbable."

Information provided to MP Duncombe about the "maniac," James Brandish, was that Mr. Bossey had laughed at his peculiar antics, squeezed his jaws in an attempt to prove that he was feigning his inability to open his jaws, and threatened to have him too, "well flogged," furthermore, that Brandish had been forced to lie in his own filth with hands shackled to the sides of the bed, causing him to lose hunks of mortified flesh from his back, as in the case of George Monk. Captain Williams made an especially careful investigation of this matter. The reported events had occurred two years before, and Brandish was long since dead. The testimony established, to Captain Williams' and MP Duncombe's satisfaction, that Mr. Bossey's treatment of this convict had been responsible. There was no doubt the man was neglected and ill-treated, but it was Mr. Bossey who took vigorous action in an effort to put things right.

William Mawman Brown had made accusations of cruelty and neglect in each of these cases, as well as in the cases of William Cooper, Henry Heighton and Henry Driver. In each instance Captain Williams established that Brown's allegations were for the most part incorrect. In the course of investigating these matters, however, Captain Williams gleaned evidence of pervasive mismanagement in the hulk establishment at Woolwich. Before the inquiry ended, this evidence was to become overwhelming. Furthermore, a number of embarrassing misstatements of fact in John Capper's report (written by Robert) were to be revealed by the evidence. One example — William Mawman Brown had alleged that a "lunatic" by the name of Timothy Hetherington had been repeatedly flogged on board the *Justitia*. In their report, the Cappers had claimed that their officers and medical staff had no knowledge of the man's record of insanity. Williams documented the falsity of that claim, but was unable to place specific culpability, probably because the events in question had occurred more than three years before. Certain other charges of "improper punishment" mentioned by MP Duncombe in his speech on the floor of Commons were not proved but, as we shall see, the inquiry was eventually to raise serious questions about John and Robert Capper's slovenly policies in the administration of corporal punishment.

With the influential Thomas Duncombe at his side, Captain Williams had systematically examined and resolved the MP's well-publicized charges against the Government's administration of the hulk establishment at Woolwich, finding most of them without substance. But in the course of making that determination, he gave the MP cause to consider himself vindicated. A plethora of shocking facts were established. MP Duncombe had apparently not even suspected the worst of them. He had made his case, rather stridently, on the basis of invalid allegations. Nonetheless, he appears to have been satisfied with the measure of embarrassment the Government had to endure. He was able to claim that his report on the floor of Commons, alleging intolerable conditions in the hulks at Woolwich, had been proven correct, though perhaps erroneous as to some of the specifics.

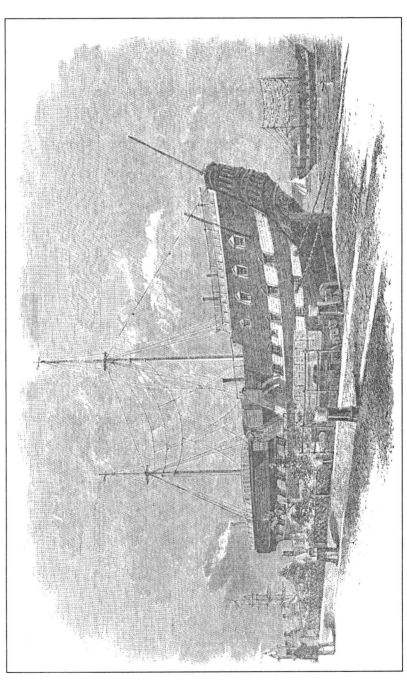

The *Warrior*, Woolwich 1850

Having made the original charges and participated in the inquiry, Thomas Duncombe undoubtedly gained prestige among influential anti-government liberals in Great Britain, including those in the prison reform movement. But there is no record of his having ever again shown significant interest in prison reform. For that matter, his biographer makes no mention of the key role played by Thomas Slingsby Duncombe in the 1847 inquiry, which exposed the essential futility of the hulks and precipitated the beginning of the end.[6]

Neither Duncombe or Williams considered William Mawman Brown discredited by the largely empty results of the investigation into his proffered information. The evidence given during the inquiry by Robert Capper, by Brown himself, and by others, indicated that he had passed the information along to MP Duncombe in good faith, but was clearly at fault in giving too much credence to tales told him by other convicts. Brown was an American who had been convicted of forgery. He was an intelligent man who had established a good reputation with most of the employees of the hulk fleet at Woolwich. On one occasion he had intervened to save an officer from an assault. For the most part he had worked as a clerk, having been given far more responsibility than Captain Williams thought appropriate. Brown developed his disapproval of the chief medical officer, Peter Bossey, after going to work aboard the *Warrior* as a nurse. He had observed Bossey's insensitivities on a number of occasions and soon formed the opinion that Mr. Blythe, the other medical officer, was by far the better and more caring physician. He intensely disliked Mr. Bossey and was inclined to believe the worst of what he was told about him by other convicts. He also carried a bad opinion of Robert Capper, having had a rather ludicrous encounter with him over a matter of illegal pockets in his (Brown's) trousers. During the inquiry Captain Williams questioned Brown extensively on matters that could be corroborated. Despite his obvious bias he proved to be a useful witness.[7]

At the time he gave his evidence before the panel of inquiry, Robert Capper had been on the job quite long enough to have become an expert on imprisonment in his own right. But his testimony reveals that he did not become a bona fide expert, except to the extent of learning what he needed to know in order to help his uncle maintain a canopy of pretense over the misery and decay that characterized the whole of the hulk establishment. Over the years, and especially during the weeks he was given to prepare for the inquiry, he absorbed an impressive amount of information about the hulks at Woolwich, but it appears to have been organized in his mind around the need to fend off criticism, rather than the need to make improvements.

Robert testified before the panel of inquiry that his salary was £270 per annum, only £20 more than his beginning salary.[†] About ten years before the inquiry, he had gone into the grocery business with his brother in London, a half day's journey from Woolwich, but not so far from the Home Office in Whitehall where the Superintendent spent most of his working hours. Robert explained to Captain Williams that his pay as clerk to the Superintendent was insufficient for his needs. He conceded that he spent enough time in his grocery business in the Strand to be considered a part-time employee of the hulk establishment, furthermore that most of the work he did as Clerk was performed at a desk in the Home Office, not at Woolwich.8 An annual salary of £270 would have been considered more than adequate for the kinds of duties Robert mentioned as within his realm of responsibility. Williams and Duncombe are sure to have been exasperated on learning that he was collecting these wages while giving something less than full time to the job.

The Transportation Act, 5 Geo.IV.,cap. 84, included provision for appointment of "one fit and able person to be assistant or deputy to [the Superintendent of Convicts in the Hulks] at one or more of the [hulk stations] and to be constantly resident at or near the place or places to which he shall be appointed."9 The residence requirement of the law may explain why Robert Capper never sought to be named Deputy Superintendent, and why John Capper, so far as we know, never put his nephew's name forward for the appointment. It is clear that Robert was quite unwilling to move to Woolwich from his comfortable house at 87 York Road in Lambeth, or for that matter, to fully commit himself to his responsibilities as *de facto* deputy to the Superintendent.

Robert Capper's appointment as clerk was requested by John Capper at a time when he would have done well to have asked that a qualified deputy be appointed and established in residence at Woolwich. Asking instead for permission to hire nephew Robert was a mistake that had appalling consequences for more than two decades. But John Capper thought he was doing the right thing because of two considerations that were of crucial importance to him; he knew that his nephew, Robert, was an exceptionally

---

[†] In his report to the Home Secretary, William John Williams gave Robert Capper's annual salary as £257. Robert testified that he was paid £270. In any case, it is clear that he was paid not less than £250 nor more than £270 per annum during his twenty-four years of employment as clerk to Superintendent of the Hulks.

capable young man, and he knew that Robert could be counted on for an absolute, filial loyalty.

Even if Robert had been willing to move to Woolwich, he did not have qualifications, at the time he was first employed, of the sort that would have enabled John Capper to reasonably request his appointment to the post of Deputy Superintendent. Concern about nepotism appears not to have been a factor. At no time during the course of the inquiry did Captain Williams or Thomas Duncombe question the propriety of Robert Capper's employment of his nephew as Clerk.

Facts not disputed are that in 1823 Robert Capper was appointed by the then-Home Secretary to the post of Clerk to the Superintendent of Convicts in the Hulks, the appointment having been requested by the Superintendent, Robert Capper's uncle. Secondly, that in addition to his duties as Clerk, Robert was given responsibilities and authority that would normally be in the province of a Deputy Superintendent.

Consider the following testimony of Robert Capper before the panel of inquiry:

Williams: What are your duties?

Capper: Keeping the correspondence and accounts, and attending to all matters that are required to assist the Superintendent in execution of his duties.

Williams: The Superintendent is unable to attend from ill health, is he not?

Capper: Entirely so, and he desired me to express his regret that it is quite out of his power to leave his house.

Williams: Is it a fact, that he has been for some time incapacitated from attending to his duties through ill health?

Capper: For a few months past.

Williams: Have you done his duties?

Capper: I have done more in consequence of my relationship to him, than I should have done for any other Superintendent.[10]

Robert took pains at every opportunity during his many hours of testimony to depreciate the importance of his role as Clerk to the Superintendent. He admitted to the panel of inquiry, however, that for several years he had been in the habit of signing the Superintendent's name to official documents, and that his rendering of his uncle's signature "was recognized as of equal weight in giving directions." Moreover, there was no escaping the fact that if anyone was in charge of the hulk establishment at the time of the inquiry, it was Robert Capper, and that he had been in full charge since June 1846, at which time John Capper had taken to his bed in Lambeth Terrace.

Although John Capper did not appear before the panel of inquiry, certain facts were established that must have been embarrassing to his colleagues in the Home Office as well as to him. In addition to an annual salary of £400, the Home Secretary had been paying John an additional £131 annually for maintaining an office at his residence. He had not, in fact, had an office at his house for a number of years, but there had been no discontinuation of the extra compensation. In giving evidence before the panel of inquiry Robert Capper had tried to put the best face on this situation by pointing out that samples of non-perishable foodstuffs and other stores were delivered to the Superintendent's residence from time to time for his perusal; moreover, that certain records were stored there. Captain Williams was not impressed. He deemed the arrangement to be a major irregularity, and noted that it had not been sanctioned by proper authority. It appears that Captain William's remarkable dedication did not, however, result in his asking outright why officials in charge of financial accounts in the Home Office had failed to notice that, while showing up for work in Whitehall every day, John Capper was continuing to draw an annual income that was increased to the handsome amount of £531 by the no-longer justified office rent increment.

Captain Williams took a dim view of John Capper's having had a desk built by a convict on the *Warrior* and delivered to his office in Whitehall. It is difficult to tell from William's report whether his main concern was about the propriety of the convict carpenter's building a desk for the Superintendent, or the lack of security for the convicts who delivered it. There were four or five of them, all dressed in "liberty clothes" who, with two officers, went along on the ship's boat to Westminster Bridge. One of the officers remained with the boat while the other accompanied the convicts as they conveyed the desk to the Home Office on their shoulders. There was no attempt at escape and there is no indication that John Capper ever took possession of the desk as his private property. In the light of so many truly reprehensible matters that were exposed by his inquiry, it is surprising that Captain Williams would have raised questions about this benign affair. It is typical of the kind of peccadillo that occurs every day in American penal settings.

Of more significance, Captain Williams concluded that "the visitorial duties of the Superintendent [had] been most imperfectly performed." Due to his illness, John Capper had made no visits since June of 1846. Before that time he had been accustomed to making visits to the hulks at Woolwich on occasional Sundays, "his absence from the Home Office being more convenient on that day, and the convicts being also disengaged from labour." Records of these visits were not regularly kept, and they appear to have been casually conducted, frequently without a muster of the convicts on deck.

Consider testimony given by Robert Capper before the panel of inquiry on the matter of visitation:

Williams: When you have visited the hulks, has it been for the purpose of inspecting?

Capper: Yes; seeing that things were going on properly.

Williams: The Superintendent has certain periodical visits to perform, has he not?

Capper: Yes.

Williams: Have you performed them for him?

Capper: When he has been unable to come, I have occasionally come down in his stead.

Williams: During the last two years, how many times have you been down instead of the Superintendent?

Capper: I cannot speak exactly from memory, probably five or six times during the two years.[11]

The Transportation Act, 5 Geo. IV., cap. 84, contained a provision requiring that the Superintendent "personally visit and inspect (the prison hulks in English waters) four times in every year, or oftener if occasion shall require, and [that he] distinctly examine into the state of such places of confinement, the behavior and conduct of the respective assistants or deputies, overseers, officers and guards, the treatment and condition of the prisoners."

For more than two years John Capper had not been actively involved in managing the hulk establishment, and it appears that for much longer than two years he had failed to meet the requirement of the law concerning quarterly inspections of the hulks. At the time of John William's inquiry, the hulk establishment in England consisted of the *Warrior*, the *Justitia* and the auxiliary vessels at Woolwich, the *York* at Gosport and the *Stirling Castle* at Portsmouth. In addition, John Capper was ostensibly in charge of the four hulks then stationed in Bermuda and the *Owen Glendower* at

Gibraltar.[12] A characteristic lack of concern was displayed by Thomas Duncombe, by the Home Secretary, by other members of the government and, for that matter, by Captain Williams, about the convicts unfortunate enough to be confined in Her Majesty's prison hulks beyond the shores of England. The attention now was on Woolwich. The Superintendent would not have been expected to make inspections of the overseas hulks, and the panel of inquiry had not been authorized to look into the matter of the hulks at Portsmouth and Gosport. To have expanded the inquiry to those ports would have imposed logistical difficulties. There was quite enough to be found out about conditions aboard the hulks at Woolwich.

Early during the course of Robert Capper's testimony the panel of inquiry turned its attention to the matter of corporal punishment:

Williams:   In cases of corporal punishment, who awards that?
Capper:     Corporal punishment by the "cat" is always approved by the Superintendent.
Williams:   But with regard to corporal punishment of any sort?
Capper:     The Overseer [the hulk commander].
Williams:   He hears the case and awards the punishment?
Capper:     Yes.
Williams:   Is that under the 15th section of the 5 Geo. IV., chap. 84?
Capper:     Yes.
Williams:   You were about to make some distinction as to corporal punishment?
Capper:     Corporal punishment with the "cat" is never inflicted without the approbation of the Superintendent.

After some testimony about the "punishment book," Captain Williams attempted to learn something of how the Superintendent determined whether punishment with the "cat" was justified:

Williams:   You cannot speak, I suppose, as to the ordinary mode of adjudicating these punishments?
Capper:     Not being present, I cannot speak of my own knowledge.
Williams:   You do not know whether the prisoners are called before the Superintendent, and evidence heard?
Capper:     I cannot say, never having been present.
Williams:   I am to understand that it is only in cases where the

corporal punishment is inflicted by the "cat," that it is referred to the Superintendent?

Capper: Yes, always so.

Williams: When the entry is "18 stripes with the rod," it has not been referred:

Capper: No, it is considered a minor punishment.

After a time, MP Duncombe, less patient than Captain Williams, took up the questioning:

Duncombe: I see the regulation here is an order issued by Lord Normanby: "If any convict at labour, or otherwise, should misbehave himself, the officers and guards appointed over him are not to beat him, but in ordinary cases, to use mild and persuasive means to induce him to alter his conduct; and if this should fail, the Overseer is to punish him on board the ship, according to the nature of his crime, either by reducing his daily allowance of provisions for a time not exceeding seven days, or by confining him in a dark cell with no other provisions than bread and water, for a time not exceeding seven days, or by moderate whipping; but in no case is such a whipping to take place upon adult prisoners until you [the Superintendent] are made acquainted with the nature of the offence for which the punishment is proposed to be inflicted, and your approval thereof is obtained." Do you mean to say, when prisoners suffer corporal punishment with the birch that this regulation is not acted up to?

Capper: Never, and never was; it never was intended to apply to it.

Duncombe: How do you mean? Moderate whipping means with a birch, does it not?

Capper: I cannot say what it means.

Duncombe: How should you read it? Do not you read these regulations as intending that any corporal punishment should be submitted to the approval of the Superintendent before inflicted?

Capper: It has always been read as applicable to inflictions by the cat on the back.

| Duncombe: | I know that such has been the practice, but is not that practice illegal? |
| Capper: | I cannot say that it is. |

At this point Captain Williams resumed the quesitoning.

| Williams: | All you can say is, that that rule has been interpreted that in cases where the corporal punishment has been inflicted with the birch rod, it has not required the approval of the Superintendent, but when inflicted with the cat, on the back, then it requires the sanction of the Superintendent? |
| Capper: | Yes, invariably. |
| Williams: | Whether legal or not, you do not give an opinion? |
| Capper: | No. |

This exchange occurred early during Robert Capper's appearance before the panel of inquiry. It established in the minds of Williams and Duncombe an understanding of Robert Capper's position. He was to be questioned more exhaustively than any other witness, and it was clear that, out of loyalty to his uncle, he was determined to concede nothing, even in the face of the obvious.

The evidence taken by Captain Williams, nonetheless, exposed serious excesses in the punishment of convicts. Throughout most of John Capper's long tenure as Superintendent, no limits were placed on the severity of beatings except when the "cat" was used. Robert Capper testified that his uncle had put a stop to excessive beatings with the birch rod two years before commencement of the inquiry. When asked about a recent instance in which a prisoner had been given eighty lashes with the birch, Robert replied simply that the incident should be considered "a solitary case." By such responses Robert continued, throughout the course of the inquiry, to dig a somewhat deeper grave for his career as a prison official. In addition to frequent punishments by use of a birch rod, whippings with the dreaded "cat" were administered from time to time on orders from the hulk overseers. Prior approval of the Superintendent was not sought, but the Superintendent was given a routine notification by letter after such punishments had been inflicted. Robert Capper was thus not in a position to say that his uncle had no knowledge of these clear contraventions of the regulations.[13]

Written in a manner intended to reduce the use of corporal punishment, the regulations permitted confinement of prisoners in a dark cell, on bread and water, for as long as seven days.[14] The hulk overseers did not hesitate to employ this means of disciplining prisoners, and even the most conscientious reformers in England seemed not to understand the agony and psychological damage that can result from such punishment. The principal hulk surgeon, Peter Bossey, was willing on more than one occasion to improve on that punishment, in the interest of what he considered to be the appropriate means of managing an insane prisoner. In his report to the Home Secretary, Captain Williams wrote:

> Upon my first visit to the hospital ship (the Unite), I found a violent lunatic, George Wilson, confined in what is not inaptly termed the cage. This cage, situated at the head of the ship, in the lower deck, is of irregular shape, having a frontage of about 14 feet by 3 1/2 feet, and scarcely of sufficient height to admit of a man to stand upright. The front is secured by open iron bars, and being elevated about 18 inches above the floor, the inmate is exposed to the full view of the patients. This place has been ordinarily resorted to for unmanageable insane prisoners, and also on some occasions for prisoners under punishment, as in the case of James Venn, who was kept in it for two months.

Surgeon Bossey's attitude toward mentally ill prisoners was puzzling to Captain Williams and would be puzzling to present-day prison administrators. A characteristic practice for decades has been for the prison administrator to do everything possible to rid himself of unstable, troublesome prisoners, by packing them off to the appropriate facility for mentally ill offenders. Conflict between mental health facility professionals and prison staff over this issue is an on-going, unvarying phenomenon. A very different situation pertained at the Woolwich hulk station. Rather than sending disturbed and irrational convicts to the insane asylum at Bethlehem on the strength of early symptoms, Peter Bossey would, for months, even years, keep convicts on board the hulks who were described as "maniacs" and "lunatics." He would do so even when cruel and extreme measures were required to control them. James Venn was the unfortunate (and undoubtedly troublesome) man who, in addition to having been confined to the cage for two months without exercise, had recently been given eighty lashes with a birch rod, the incident that Robert Capper had characterized "a solitary case."

Consider the following exchange between Captain Williams and Peter Bossey:

Williams:   What is the object of retaining lunatic prisoners in the hulks?

Bossey:    The removal of a lunatic, in my opinion, depends much upon the degree of intelligence and tractability that he exhibits; there are many cases of unsound mind in Union houses and other establishments who are not placed in the public county asylums as insane persons, and yet they are known to be persons of weak intellect, but generally quiet and manageable. I have considered such persons as invalid patients, in consequence of their weak mind; but persons who are under delusions and unmanageable, or dangerous, I have found it my duty to remove. I certainly cannot consider it my duty to incarcerate in a lunatic asylum an individual who is, more or less, in that condition.

In his report to the Home Secretary, Captain Williams responded to Peter Bossey's convoluted view of this matter with a statement of pristine clarity: "I decidedly dissent from Mr. Bossy's opinion . . . . I consider that a convict of unsound mind, as soon as his unsoundness of mind is ascertained to the satisfaction of the medical officer, to be no longer a fit or proper inmate of a penal establishment."[15]

Captain Williams found other causes for concern about Bossey's performance. Williams' observed that "a very large proportion of the convicts were affected with spongy gums and other symptoms of scurvy." He lamented the absence of vegetables in the diet. Bossey testified that he had long considered inclusion of potatoes in the diet as important. When asked why he did not press this point on the Superintendent, his characteristically lame reply was "the subject of the dietary was hardly within my peculiar province." Captain Williams did not hesitate to make recommendations that the chief medical officer should have insisted upon long before. He recommended the addition of three-quarter pounds of potatoes to each man's daily rations, six ounces of cooked pork in place of the poor-quality cheese that was customarily served, and substitution of cocoa for gruel once a day. The latter recommendation would not have made the diet healthier, but would have contributed greatly to morale. These recommendations add to the evidence that Williams was an astute prison man. He understood the importance of nourishing and reasonably enjoyable food in the successful management of a penal establishment. He understood this principle even better than had such estimable fellows as John Howard and Aaron Graham.

It seems that sanitation was another matter that Peter Bossey did not consider to be within his "peculiar province." Captain Williams found the hospital ship, *Unite*, to be filthy from stem to stern and that the convicts who were her patients were "begrimed with dirt" and "infested with vermin." He found similar conditions on the *Justitia*. For more than twenty years the *Justitia* had been under the command of William Hatton. Although Hatton had been "superannuated" shortly before the inquiry began, he was called as a witness. He demonstrated skill in dodging much richly deserved blame for a number of dubious practices, but he could not escape having allowed his ship and the convicts aboard her to become filthy beyond reason over the two decades of his command. Moreover it was established that he had more than once bullied Mr. Bossey into approving the birch caning of mentally disturbed convicts. On a number of occasions he had had prisoners scourged with the "cat" without approval. He assured the panel of inquiry that he always sent word to Mr. Capper of his intent to punish with the "cat," and that he would assume approval if he heard nothing in return. No records were produced, however, to support his testimony.

Having been "superannuated" rather than fired for cause, as he should have been, William Hatton was able to slink off somewhere and live on his pension in reasonable comfort. Robert Capper had been wise to get rid of this wretched officer before the inquiry began, but his having been tolerated in such a responsible position for more than twenty years added more weight to the burden of culpability the Cappers were accumulating on their shoulders.

Henry Masterman, overseer on the *Warrior*, was a different kind of man. He had had the appointment as overseer only since January 1847, but had served as acting officer in command of the *Warrior* for fourteen years (at a substantially lower salary than the salary of his unworthy colleague on the *Justitia*). His ship was much cleaner than the *Justitia* and his approach to working with the convicts far more reasonable than that of Hatton. To be sure, his management performance fell short of being exemplary, clearly reflecting the Superintendent's lack of guidance. Mr. Masterman felt the heat of Captain Williams' disapproval for having destroyed a letter written by a prisoner that was meant eventually for the attention of MP Duncombe. He was convincing, however, in contending he did not know the identity of the intended recipient, and the letter contained flagrantly false information. In any case, no information was developed during the inquiry that sullied Masterman's reputation as one of the hulk establishment's more responsible employees.

In addition to problems exposed with respect to medical care, policy toward mentally disturbed prisoners, disciplinary practices, food, sanitation and, most importantly, management oversight, Captain Williams identified deficiencies in a whole range of other areas. He did not like the irreverent treatment of deceased prisoners or the fact that they were buried in unconsecrated ground. The lack of attention by clergy to dying prisoners was distressing to him. He was obviously a devout man, dissatisfied with the lack of attention to the spiritual needs of the prisoners. If Captain Williams took time to read the pious pronouncements submitted to the Superintendent by the hulk chaplains so faithfully every six months during the Capper era, he was obviously unimpressed.

No formal set of recommendations was submitted to the Home Secretary with Captain Williams' report. He chose instead to make his suggestions and recommendations, perhaps twenty-five to thirty of them, in the context of his narrative. Captain Williams did not recommend that the hulk establishment be abandoned.16 Perhaps he believed that, with proper management, the system could be retrieved. In any case, one must conclude that in addition to his uncompromising determination to get at the truth, he possessed an inclination to charity that caused him to stop short of where he might have gone in his condemnation of the Capper administration. Williams was clearly not a bureaucratic fussbudget, obsessed with rules and regulations. A chapter-and-verse recounting of the ways in which the Cappers, their chaplains, medical officers and hulk overseers were in specific violation of the rules and regulations issued by the Home Secretary in 1839, with the culpable individuals identified by name, would have made his report even more devastating than it was.† Such an approach is likely to have occasioned more severe sanctions against the Cappers and their minions. Perhaps Captain Williams was more of a gentlemen than he should have been (in the contemporary American sense of that word). However that might have been, Williams performed an incalculably valuable service to British society. The daunting array of flaws and failings he exposed settled the issue. Use of the hulks for confinement of prisoners could not much longer be defended — could not much longer be tolerated.

---

† See Appendix B.

# XIV

## THE END OF A VOYAGE TO NOWHERE

During the mid-19th century, criminal justice policy and practice in England underwent a revolutionary change. Reliance on transportation as the primary means of dealing with convicted offenders was in its final decline. Having served for decades as baleful adjuncts to the practice of transportation, the hulks too were doomed. Resistance to the notion of a system of "convict prisons" on English soil was stubborn, but destined to be overcome.

There was no more influential agent of the new direction than Sir Joshua Jebb. A career army officer, detached from military service early in his career, Jebb eventually became Great Britain's preeminent authority on imprisonment. He was knighted in 1860 in recognition of his contributions to civil justice in England. Jebb was not inclined to invoke humanitarian principles in his advocacy of improvements in the manner of confining criminals. He was more concerned about efficiency. His conviction was that efficiency, discipline, proper design of facilities, and the right way of doing things, would result in better conditions of confinement. Needless to say, the hulks were anathema to him.

Jebb had earned his commission through studies at the Royal Military Academy in Woolwich. The record does not suggest that he developed special interest in the prison hulks during his days as a cadet, but unlike most people in England, he was aware of their existence. As a strong-minded young man, he is certain to have formed opinions about the shackled convicts he would have seen shuffling around the grounds of the Royal Arsenal, and the dilapidated old vessels to which they returned each night.

Jebb served creditably as an engineering officer in Canada and the West Indies, demonstrating on those assignments, and during later postings at Chatham and Birmingham, an impressive ability to learn technical skills. He became a competent surveyor, an explosives specialist and an expert in defense construction design. More likely than not, he had some responsibility for military prisoners during his years of regular army service, but we cannot be sure just how he became interested in civil imprisonment. The relatively humane attitudes he eventually embraced were hardly typical for a career army officer. He came to his views on imprisonment from a different perspective, but they were views that coincided with those of prominent reformers of the time, men like Samuel Hoare, Thomas Buxton and, most particularly, William Crawford.

Crawford was the most respected member of the group that comprised the London Prison Discipline Society. He was secretary to the Society and, for a number of years, edited its voluminous annual reports. He came to be knowledgeable about imprisonment in England and was in the forefront of those who advocated the separation of offenders in confinement. In 1837 the Home Office sent Crawford to America to observe the operation of the Pennsylvania system of prison discipline, viewed in England as having applied the concept of penitential solitude most successfully. Unfortunately, his visit to Pennsylvania came before there was much inclination on the part of American penologists to look at the results of their methods objectively. During the course of his observations Crawford depended on what he was told and what he was shown. His preconceived convictions were confirmed. When he returned to England he submitted a highly praised report that convinced virtually every remaining unpersuaded person of influence in the British government that the correct approach to imprisonment depended on silence and separation. The concept of penitential solitude already had wide adherence. The failure of Millbank was attributed to causes that in no way discredited the concept in the eyes of its advocates. Crawford and Jebb, who were in the leadership of that group, became close associates.

In order to have available a competent advisor on prison design and construction, the Home Office arranged with the Army for the services of Lt. Col. Jebb. He was given the title, Surveyor-General of Prisons. Crawford and Jebb were the principal figures in the design, construction, and eventually the administration, of Pentonville, "the Model Prison." Jebb took the conceptional sketches Crawford and his fellow reformers had been working with over a period of years, drew up detailed plans and supervised construction of the prison from first turn of the spade to completion. Still under the influence of Crawford's adamant insistence on silence and separation, Jebb devised the ingenious, but tragically flawed phase system that was installed at Pentonville. The regimen began with a long, emotionally damaging period of total isolation. Most of the young offenders who survived this phase of the system were reduced to a state of profound listlessness, which looked sufficiently like *penitence* to be pleasing to the men in charge at Pentonville. These apparent good results were undoubtedly reported with great satisfaction to the Surveyor-General. From the beginning, Crawford's views on the efficacy of separate confinement had made good sense to Joshua Jebb. It was a concept that continued to be ardently supported by some of the most thoughtful and compassionate men in England.

Jebb was a tough soldier. He was also a devout and honest man who sincerely wanted to implement the most effective approach to reformation. He appears not to have been especially perceptive, however, where human psychology was concerned. As a planner, he was least competent in the development of motivational schemes. Clearly, he did not have creative instincts like those possessed by Sir Walter Crofton, who was engaged during this same era in developing the "Irish System" of penal reform. Still, Her Majesty's government was well served by Joshua Jebb's energy and by his formidable range of skills. He was not without imagination and certainly did not lack practical judgement. He was convinced that a period of silent isolation was important, but that it should be followed by "associated" labor at the prison or on public works.[†] He had a healthy determination to emancipate his country from its dependence on prisoner transportation and to shut down the hulks. The extensive prison construction program undertaken in England under Jebb's leadership during the mid-19th century was driven by these convictions.[1]

*Justitia*, unofficial flagship of the English hulk fleet, had bad luck with her last two captains. William Hatton had served as her overseer for twenty-four years before being discreetly "superannuated" by the Cappers just before William John Williams began his devastating inquiry into the hulks at Woolwich. Under Hatton's command, the *Justitia* had deteriorated into a condition of filth and disorder. The convicts confined in her underdecks, "begrimed with dirt" and "infested with vermin," frequently fell victim to Captain Hatton's penchant for administering severe punishment, including unauthorized and illegal scourgings with the "cat." The main consequence he suffered for his two decades of cruelty and mismanagement was that he

---

[†] The young offenders who survived eighteen months of isolation at Pentonville emotionally intact, and with some remaining physical strength, could look forward to the voyage to Van Diemen's Land where they would be in ticket-of-leave status.

had to begin living on his pension sooner than planned. In December 1846, William Hatton was replaced by Richard Loader. Having had long experience in lesser posts with the hulk establishment, Loader was viewed as a reliable man. In view of all that had been revealed during the course of William John Williams' inquiry, there was good reason to hope for improvements on the neglected old *Justitia*. But alas, it appears that Captain Loader's previous assignments had not included responsibility for handling money. Now he was entrusted with some of the cash appropriated for administration of the *Justitia*. In May 1848, just a year and a half after assuming his new post, Richard Loader absconded with just over £855 in public money. After a few months, not liking the life of a pecunious fugitive, he gave himself up. For his crime, he was sentenced to seven years transportation.[2]

As we shall see, Captain Loader's betrayal of his trust was but one of a whole array of vicissitudes with which the new management of the hulk establishment had to contend.

The impact of William John Williams' Report of Inquiry was substantial, but without substantial injury to the more culpable parties. John Capper was allowed to resign "in consequence of age and declining health" with a pension of £240 a year. Robert Capper was asked to step down from his post as clerk to the Superintendent. Astonishingly enough, he was given an annual pension of £130.[3] Such unjustified generosity gives rise to speculation as to the quality of the high-placed patronage the Capper family continued to enjoy, even after exposure of the debacle John and Robert had created in their management of the hulk establishment. Also pensioned off was the chief medical officer for the hulks at Woolwich, Peter Bossey. He had never fully discontinued his medical practice in the town during his service with the hulk establishment and undoubtedly retired to comfortable circumstances. It is hard to imagine his experiencing nostalgic wistfulness over the loss of his hulk prisoner patient load, and it appears that the inquiry's findings as to his less-than-distinguished service to the Crown during those twenty-two years, were not publicized widely enough to cause him undue embarrassment.[4] Appointed to replace Peter Bossey as chief medical officer at Woolwich, was a surgeon of the Royal Navy. The new man was assigned to full-time duty with the hulk establishment.[5] William John Williams had been sharply critical of Bossey's being allowed to serve as chief medical officer to the hulks at Woolwich while maintaining a private practice.

John Capper's replacement was Herbert P. Voules, another of the government's prison inspectors. It is not unlikely that William John Williams was offered the job. More than anyone else he knew what a hopeless slough the hulk establishment might prove to be for a new Superintendent, sufficient reason for his turning down the offer, if indeed such an offer was made.

Having had no effective leadership for twenty-five years, the hulk establishment had become a self-sustaining web of accommodation among the groups of individuals that comprised it. The overseers were firmly established, as were their ranking lieutenants. Long tenure was more the rule than the exception. The overseers had been virtually unsupervised during most of the Capper era. Tensions arose from time to time between overseers and medical officers. The medical officers were the only officials on the scene with any authority to interfere with the manner in which an overseer might choose to manage the convicts on his hulk. But it behooved all to resolve conflicts without disturbing the balance. The convict subculture was an important element of the accommodation. Free laborers who supervised the on-shore convict work parties were integral to the subculture, as were the common guards on the hulks. Severe punishment of malefactors among the prisoners was commonplace, but the record suggests that those subjected to punishment were almost invariably guilty of insubordination, threatening or assaulting officers, or other offenses that might jeopardize the accommodation. The birch rod seems to have been most often employed against prisoners who were rebellious, disorderly, out of control and, all too often, emotionally disturbed. Rarely to be seen was punishment of prisoners because of depredations against other prisoners, or because of involvement in nefarious schemes that victimized other prisoners. We can be certain that such nefarious schemes abounded. For twenty-five years the accommodation was maintained; the organism that was the hulk establishment lived and breathed, with the weak, the sick and the powerless elements of the convict population paying the whole price. Thus it can be said that circumstances of England's mid-19th century prison hulks bore striking similarities to those that characterized American penitentiaries a hundred years later.

In the wake of William John William's unsettling revelations, the Home Office took action that interfered with the accommodation. The unfortunate Herbert Voules was selected to serve as point man. The result was an era of disorder that had not been seen on the hulks for decades. Many old hulk hands were "superannuated" or fired. The new officers employed were given to understand that the regulations were to be followed.

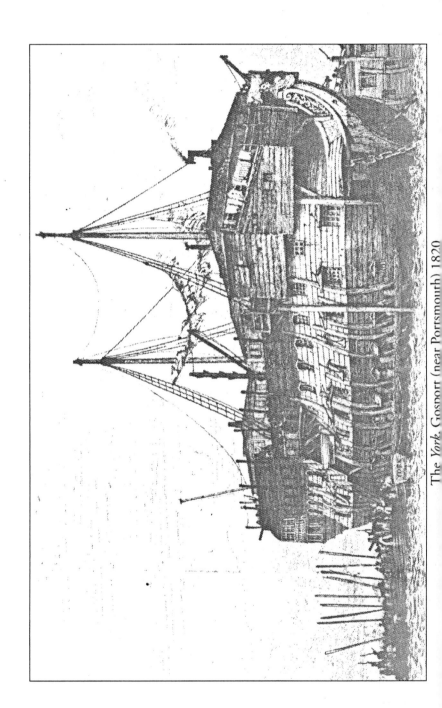

The *York*, Gosport (near Portsmouth) 1820

And many new officers were hired, as the practice of relying on free laborers for supervision of convict workers onshore was discontinued. This change interfered with trafficking in contraband and other patterns of connivance between the convicts and their accomplices. And then Mr. Voules decided to discontinue giving convict workers their earnings on a regular basis, but rather to hold on to money owed the prisoners until discharge or embarkation to the colonies. His reasoning was that substantial improvements in the diet (those recommended by William John Williams) removed any need for convicts to purchase extra bread or vegetables.6

These and other changes initiated by Herbert Voules were commendable, but the immediate and ongoing results were discontent and unrest that at times broke out into open rebellion. Maintenance of control in a penal facility is achieved by close allegiance to the necessary policies and practices. Reestablishment of control after it has been lost, and after subcultural patterns are developed, becomes a profoundly more complex and difficult task.

Serious trouble first broke out, not at Woolwich, but on the *York*, anchored at Gosport, southwest of Portsmouth Harbour. According to Voules, "eight or ten thoroughly bad men obtained complete influence over the rest of the prisoners." They established a "system of terrorism," which undermined discipline on the ship, and caused many prisoners who had been "well-conducted" previously to join in a general spirit of insubordination and rebelliousness. Apparently, prisoners were refusing to go to work and were threatening the officers. Control of the *York* was about to be lost. On December 9, 1848, fifty-three of the more vociferous troublemakers were moved to Millbank, an action that may have prevented a murderous outbreak of open rebellion. Voules complained about the government's having failed to regularly transport troublesome prisoners to Australia. The policy of giving priority to the most hardened offenders had, for a time, been abandoned. Also discontinued was the practice of allowing well-behaved prisoners to work out half their terms of transportation at English hulk stations, then recommending them for "free pardons." Instead, healthy prisoners who stayed out of serious trouble were sent out to Australia with tickets-of-leave after serving periods of time specifically set by the Managers.7 Two "scales" were established, one of them applicable to prisoners who conducted themselves just passably, the other for those whose conduct was judged to be "exemplary." For prisoners with sentences of seven years, the least severe of the transportation terms, Scale No. 1, required service of three years in England, first in

separate confinement, then in work status at a hulk station. The most
severe term, a life sentence to transportation, meant eleven-and-a-half years
in England before embarkation to the colonies in ticket-of-leave status.[†]

Taking into account good-time award practices that have prevailed
throughout succeeding decades, we can be sure that virtually all reasonably
cooperative prisoners were marked down as "exemplary," and therefore
eligible for Scale No. 2, which significantly reduced the time they had to
serve on the hulks before embarkation in ticket-of-leave status:

Scale No. 2.

Minimum period of penal discipline applicable to prisoners whose
conduct is exemplary:

7 years—a period not less than 2 years.
10 years—a period not less than 3 years.
15 years—a period not less than 4 1/2 years.
20 years—a period not less than 6 years.
Life—a period not less than 7 1/2 years.

A *Notice to Prisoners Under Sentence of Transportation* issued by the
Managers in 1850 described the two scales, and outlined (none too clearly)
a number of other ways whereby remission could be earned.

By the late 1840s, a ticket-of-leave man in Australia had good prospects,
better than those that would have been available to him in England. Some
would have accepted any opportunity to get off the hulks, but only the
more adventurous and dissatisfied would have wanted to go to an unknown
future on the other side of the world, leaving their families behind. The
government addressed this concern, but only for those who had financial
resources. The wives of prisoners who qualified, and children older than
fourteen, were given passage to Australia for seven pounds, ten shillings;
younger children for about half that.[8] The cost for a family of four would
have been more than £20, an amount on which that same family could
subsist in England for three or four months. Many was the ticket-of-leave
man who left his family behind, hoping to scrimp together enough of his
earning in Australia to someday bring his loved ones out. More often than
not, it was a forlorn hope.

Needless to say, the reforms of Joshua Jebb and his fellow Managers

---

[†] A life sentence to transportation was considered expired after twenty-four years.

were attended by much sadness and anger. The new policy in administering terms of transportation was viewed as calamitous by hundreds of hulk prisoners who had counted on being granted pardon after serving half their terms in England. In view of this policy, and the many unsettling corrective actions in inmate management that were taken after the Williams exposé, there is little wonder the hulks were visited by so much discontent and disorder.

The hulk prisoners least reluctant to go to Australia were the more criminalistic fellows, visualizing better opportunities there than what they were experiencing on the hulks, and not understanding that they might be better prospects for Norfolk Island than for finding gold or establishing sheep stations. As we shall see, some in this category were designated for Norfolk Island before embarking. The well-behaved prisoners, men most likely to contribute to the orderly development of the colonies, prayed earnestly for free pardon in England.

There had been frequent shifts in the government's policy on choosing offenders for transportation to Australia. It took a while before the idea of establishing criteria and sticking to them took hold.

In the spirit of sweeping out the old in favor of the new, Herbert P. Voules was given the title, Manager of the Convict Hulk Establishment. John Capper's official title had been Superintendent of the Several Ships and Vessels for the Confinement of Offenders under Sentence of Transportation. He and others would modify that title from time to time, to fit the circumstances.9 Mr. Voules held his title only one year. Ostensibly, he was in sole command during 1848. But then, for the year 1849, the report to the Home Secretary on the hulk establishment was submitted jointly by J. Jebb, D. O'Brien and Herbert P. Voules, reflecting the establishment of a directorate. During the following year Voules disappeared from the scene, as did O'Brien. The term *Manager* was pluralized, then discarded with the establishment of an agency of government known as the Directors of Convict Prisons. After 1849 the overseers of the hulks took their orders from the Directors rather than from a manager or superintendent of the hulk establishment. In practical terms, the man in charge was the redoubtable Joshua Jebb. He was named Chairman of the directorate, and effectively was in charge of imprisonment in England. He remained in charge long after the last of the prison hulks in English waters was abandoned.10

From the beginning of his involvement, Jebb made clear his belief that the hulks did not provide a viable means of confining prisoners, that their use should be viewed as a holding operation, and should not be tolerated much longer. Herbert Voules did not call for abandonment of the hulks in his first and only annual report, but he enhanced Jebb's position by illuminating problems for which there were no solutions.

Voules was on the scene long enough to vividly experience some of the trouble that resulted from stirring the pot. It was not a change in inmate management policy, however, that caused the most serious early crisis of the new regime. During the fall of 1848 cholera struck the *Justitia* and the hospital hulk, *Unite*. In contrast to the way in which Peter Bossey is likely to have managed matters, the new medical officer, Dr. Dabbs, slept on board the *Unite* and spent all of his time attending sick prisoners on both stricken ships until the visitation of the disease had run its course. It is a tribute to his management of the outbreak that not one case of cholera appeared on board the *Warrior*, which was moored just upstream from the cholera-ridden *Justitia* and *Unite*. Moreover, the outbreak did not result in a high incidence of mortality.

Indeed, the most prominent casualty of the visitation of cholera was the hulk *Justitia* herself. For several years this most venerable member of the hulk fleet had been anchored close to a swampy stretch of shoreline at the lower end of the Woolwich Arsenal. She had settled into the mud and apparently was not floating free even at the flood of the tide. The *Unite* was anchored close by. "Noxious vapour arising from the marshes" was wrongly blamed for the cholera outbreak and thus a decision was made to move both hulks to a healthier place. The *Unite* was successfully towed upstream for a way, but the *Justitia* refused to be drawn up out of her marshy abode. After the worst of the cholera outbreak was over, prisoners aboard the *Justitia* were moved upstream to two deactivated navy ships at the Woolwich dockyard. An inspection of the *Justitia* proved there had been far more neglect of her upkeep than Captain Williams had observed in his inquiry. She was judged to be unfit for reoccupation by convicts or for any other purpose. Thus ended the long and pernicious career of the *Justitia* as a prison hulk.[11]

The loss of the *Justitia* would hardly have been lamented had an adequate replacement been at hand. Instead, a thirty-year regression occurred when the Home Office decided to arrange with the Navy for indefinite use of the *Hebe* and a deactivated frigate, the *Wye*. Half of *Justitia's* 400 prisoners were already on board the *Hebe*. The other half, those on the *Sulphur*, were moved over to the *Wye*. The new acquisitions were smaller ships and neither had divided underdecks. Therefore, the prisoners aboard them were once again subject to the appalling conditions that had characterized the hulks during the days of Duncan Campbell. Indeed, so far as physical discomfort was concerned, conditions were worse. The underdecks of the "temporary hulks" were only five feet, six inches, and five feet, eight inches in height. Many of the prisoners were unable to stand or walk upright. Whether tall or stunted, all of the prisoners confined in the cramped underdecks of these ships suffered from a lack of adequate ventilation.

There was one mitigation, undoubtedly flowing from the philosophy of Joshua Jebb. After the directorate assumed responsibility for the hulks in 1849, in place of Herbert Voules' sole command, one warder was assigned to night patrol on each deck of the *Hebe* and the *Wye*. During the early years, when all of the hulks lacked below-decks separation and the convicts were left to their own devices throughout the night, officers were not foolhardy enough to venture below. They were not required to do so. Jebb insisted on recruiting better-qualified people, saw to it that they were trained more adequately and had higher expectations of them. He was not entirely successful in upgrading the quality of employees on the hulks, but the fact that there was a sufficient number of men capable of serving in the underdecks of the *Hebe* and the *Wye* during the night is a credit to his effort. Jebb called these men *warders*, not guards. (His hulks were commanded by *governors*, not overseers.) By following William John Williams' recommendation that the prisoners' hammocks be hung lower to the decks, some improvement in visual supervision was gained on all of the hulks. Gaslight, another of Captain Williams' recommendations, was installed on the *Warrior*, but apparently not on the *Hebe* or the *Wye*.

In reporting on the year 1849, the Directors were honest enough to concede that "unsurmountable difficulties" continued to exist in using the "temporary hulks."[12] Even among the most enlightened of prison authorities, willingness to abide deplorable conditions (pending hoped-for improvements) is still often to be seen, after more than a hundred years. In 1849 the hulk managers recognized that conditions in the underdecks of the *Hebe* and *Wye* were indeed deplorable, but then the *Defense* was being fitted out at Portsmouth. She would soon be sailed round to the Thames and, perhaps within three or four months, be available at Woolwich for accommodation of the 400 prisoners then confined in the cramped and fetid underdecks of the "temporary hulks." The arrival of the *Defense* hulk at Woolwich in 1850 alleviated the worst of conditions there. In the view of Joshua Jebb and his fellow Directors, that newly retrofitted vessel also served to strengthen their argument for construction of on-shore prisons, and for shutting down the hulks. Their contention was that: "The hulks have not even the advantage of economy." The cost of retrofitting the *Defense* had been almost nine thousand pounds sterling. The Directors' report for the year 1848 called attention to this fact as well as to the ongoing cost of maintaining a hulk, substantially greater than the cost of maintaining on-shore facilities, taking into account the number of prisoners that could be accommodated in a hulk, as opposed to a prison on shore.

Jebb liked the idea of an on-shore prison at or near the site of each hulk station. A point he attempted to make with the Home Secretary was that a single prison, requiring only one governor and one deputy governor, but confining twice as many prisoners as could be handled on the largest of the hulks, would result in savings of £700 per annum in salaries alone at each station.13 Meanwhile, the *Warrior* hulk at Woolwich was on her last legs.14 More likely than not Jebb was unaware of the extent of her deterioration, or he would have emphatically brought the matter to the Home Secretary's attention. *Warrior* housed 400 prisoners. If she was to be replaced, another major outlay would be required. Jebb recognized that arguments based on economy were more likely to be effective than those that invoked the miserable conditions under which the convicts were confined. In any event, because prison bed space on shore was coming on line more slowly than Jebb had anticipated, the *Warrior* was kept in service long after her condition warranted her being mercifully towed away to the breaking yard.

There is no record of the Home Secretary's defending the viability of the hulks, but there were influential members of Parliament who clung to the belief that if convicted criminals could no longer be promptly transported to the colonies, they should at least be kept on board ships. More than a few prestigious figures in the government found abhorrent the notion of further sullying the shores of England with expensive buildings for the purpose of housing criminals. But Joshua Jebb had set a course from which he was not to be deterred.

For a number of years before Jebb and his fellow Directors of the Convict Prisons took over, the most troublesome prisoners at Millbank and Pentonville were routinely transferred to the hulks. The Directors found it unreasonable that the hulks should be required to deal with "the refuse of all the convicts confined in the Government prisons," in addition to large contingents of "invalids," men judged to be too sick or frail for transportation to Australia. (All too often, "invalids" were among the most unruly of the prisoners.) In 1849 a reversal in policy was adopted. Prisoners at the on-shore prisons were required to demonstrate good behavior in separate confinement during a period of probation before being sent to the hulks. For many prisoners, relief from isolation, and the opportunity for assignment to public works on shore, would have made the hulks preferable to separate confinement at Millbank or Pentonville, despite the hulks' well deserved reputation for misery. The prisoners who conducted themselves well and worked hard on their work assignments for the required period of time were listed for transport to Australia in ticket-of-leave status. Those who gave trouble were returned to solitary confinement on shore. Misconduct thereafter was likely to result in the unenviable fate of a voyage to Norfolk Island — below decks and in chains.

By the end of 1849 conditions of confinement aboard the hulks had improved. While hardly transforming them into pleasant places of abode, reforms resulting from William John William's exposé, and the efforts of Joshua Jebb, had ameliorated the horror that had characterized the hulks, in varying degrees, for seventy-five years. At the same time, changes in policy that had accompanied the reforms continued to stimulate bad conduct. Herbert Voules, during his one-year regime, then Joshua Jebb and the other Managers, may have had to contend with more tumult among the prisoners than the Cappers experienced during the whole of their long reign. (There is some uncertainty about this question because, where troubles with the convicts were concerned, John Capper was not inclined to candor in his bi-annual reports.) In any case, it is clear that in trying to put the house in order, Voules, Jebb and the Directors paid the price for the laissez-faire laxness that characterized the thirty-year period during which the Cappers were in charge.

In pursuit of their new policy, the Directors sent seventy-one troublesome prisoners to lockdown status at Pentonville during 1849. In December of that year sixty men, identified as having been "ringleaders in violent and mutinous conduct," were loaded aboard the *Eliza* for the long and woeful voyage to Norfolk Island. In talking to the prisoners left behind, Jebb's warders and governors are not likely to have spared the disagreeable details as to what could be looked forward to at that prison colony. In their report to the Home Secretary covering events of 1849, the Directors were able to say that these actions had had "a very salutary effect;" adding, however, that "with the very imperfect means of supervision and control which the Hulks afford, we must expect irregularities amongst the prisoners." This proved to be an apt observation.[15]

Beginning in 1848, reports to the Home Secretary on the hulk establishment were filed annually, rather than on an biannual basis, as had been the practice during the thirty years of John Capper's reign. His reports were typically characterized more by obfuscation than hard information. They consisted of the Superintendent's memorandum, some statistical returns, and reports from each and every one of the obsequious fellows who served as chaplains on the hulks during Capper's time. Capper's overseers had not been required to file written reports. (It is interesting to contemplate what Captain Hatton of the *Justitia* would have had to say for himself.)

Although reports were required less frequently, the format was significantly improved. In addition to the report of the Directors, reports were included from the governors, medical officers and chaplains. Useful information and valuable insights were thus gained. In January 1850, F.T. LeTouzel, who served as Governor of the soon-to-be-deactivated *Wye* and *Hebe* hulks at Woolwich, observed that: "The conduct of the convicts has been far from satisfactory in many cases, but some excuse may be offered for them from the nature of their place of confinement. [Consider] the consequent temptation to crime and opportunities to avoid detection, from being congregated in a flush-deck five feet six inches high, in numbers varying from 100 to 190." Henry Masterman was governor of the *Warrior*, whose underdecks, unlike the temporary hulks, had been modified into bays, each housing eight to ten prisoners. He did not consider this arrangement to offer adequate protection. "In my opinion," he observed, ". . . it would be more advisable that they should only associate while at labour, and be kept separate at night; this would greatly improve the discipline, removing the well-disposed from the contamination of those who are lost to all sense of their position and future prospects." Chaplains' reports submitted after 1848 were of a refreshingly different character than those submitted twice yearly for the three previous decades. Chaplain Hanna, who served the *Hebe* and the *Wye*, made a strong case for adding books to the prisoners' library that were not "exclusively religious." The Rev. George William Livesay, chaplain to the *Briton* and *Sterling Castle* in Portsmouth Harbour, made clear his conviction that "it is hopeless to expect a hulk to become a school of moral reformation." Chaplain Martin reported having had visits by convicts in his cabin on the *York* at Gosport 354 times during 1849, and to have made more than 700 pastoral calls to convicts on the "invalid hulk," *Defense*, before she was taken round to Woolwich. His modest claim was that he "always endeavored to impress on them some useful truth. . . ."[16]

Alas, improvements in the character and dedication of personnel of the hulks, made by Voules, Jebb and their associates, were not sufficient to forestall continued unrest and rebelliousness. Jebb and his Managers had mixed success in recruiting warders. Some of them were reliable; others were prone to indolence and tippling gin while on watch. On one occasion at Woolwich a disturbance was precipitated by a fight between two officers. (The prisoners' role was mainly limited to lustily cheering on the combatants.) A number of escapes from the hulks occurred, a matter sure to have been especially disturbing to the Home Office. Firings and hirings, in quest of stable personnel, became a frustrating preoccupation with Jebb's administration. Chaplain Martin's commendable efforts notwithstanding, the *York* at Gosport was the scene of some of the most serious trouble. The second officer was assaulted and seriously injured by a prisoner during an affray that broke out on that hulk not long after Herbert Voules was given command of the hulk establishment in 1847. A new Governor was placed in charge of the *York*, but trouble continued. In June 1848 an officer was murdered on the docks by a hulk prisoner. Captain I. S. Whitty was dispatched to Gosport by the Home Office.[†] It was on his urging that the transfer of fifty-three troublesome prisoners was made. In order to separate the ringleaders, transfers to Bermuda and Gibraltar were also made. There were dismissals of certain of the less competent officers. The result of these actions was a period of relative tranquillity at Gosport, lasting about a year.[17] The *York* was sailed across to Portsmouth in time to be at hand when trouble aboard the *Sterling Castle* erupted in 1850. According to the *Times of London*, the uprising among prisoners of the *Sterling Castle* was "put to an end on Monday evening by the superintendent of the ship seizing up and flogging several of the ringleaders. . . ." But then the "emeute" on board the *Sterling Castle* "was followed by one on board the *York* . . . when the convicts refused to go to work, and commenced with the legs of their stools to batter the bulkheads and to use all sorts of abusive language to their keepers." The uprising was brought under control after two of the ringleaders were dragged out from their quarters and flogged. One of them was reported to have asked for a glass of water after two dozen lashes, then to have told the warder with the cat to have another go at it. Another dozen lashes were sufficient to convince him to use his good offices among

---

[†] Captain Whitty, one of Joshua Jebb's more trusted associates, was later to serve as Governor of Portland Prison and as a Director of Convict Prisons.

the convicts, as the authorities strove to restore order.[18] And so it appears that, while Jebb and his Directors were laying stress on the importance of abiding by the regulations, officers aboard the hulks during this time of tumultuous enlightenment were not hesitant to ignore the regulations when they saw fit to do so.

In 1855 Jebb's public works prison at Portsmouth was completed. All of the *York's* prisoners were moved to the new facility. A few sick men were held on the hospital hulk, *Briton*, for a time, and the *Sterling Castle* was kept in service with a reduced prisoner count for another year. But the troubles that had plagued the Gosport and Portsmouth hulk stations for eight years finally came to an end. Work crews from Portsmouth Prison, all consisting of former hulk convicts, were set to work breaking up the *York*, a task they undertook with zest.[19]

Perhaps because Woolwich was in closer proximity to the imposing eye and hand of Joshua Jebb, most of the troubles at that hulk station were of a minor nature by comparison with those at Gosport and Portsmouth. For several reasons Jebb and his Directors had delayed deactivating the *Warrior*, even though that hulk was literally having to be patched together with tar and canvass to prevent her falling apart.[20] In addition to complete retrofitting for convict use when first acquired from the Navy in 1840, she had been equipped during Voules's administration with gaslight. More important than anything else, she accommodated 400 prisoners. No suitable prison site had been found at Woolwich, but construction of a new prison was soon to begin at nearby Chatham. A mutiny broke out on board the *Warrior* a few days before Christmas 1851. Prisoners took control of the underdecks of the hulk and were not dislodged until a contingent of Royal Marines were called to the scene. Thirty-eight of the insurgent prisoners were identified as having provoked the uprising. Heavily ironed, eighteen of them were put aboard the hospital ship. The remaining twenty were conveyed in police vans to Millbank. The *Times* observed that "The military displayed great forbearance under the most provocative circumstances, as the whole of the convicts were armed in some shape or other, and it was only the sight of the bayonets and the caps on the nipples of the percussion locks half-cocked which checked their movements, and ultimately restored some degree of order." Earlier in its account, the *Times* had given emphasis to its description of the "provocative circumstances" by reporting some of the rebellious convicts, "who had got hold of pipes and tobacco, commenced smoking." [21]

A period of relative calm prevailed for several years after the 1851

Christmas mutiny, but Jebb wanted no complacency to creep into the thinking of Home Office officials where the hulks were concerned. In his report for the year 1853 he wrote: "Each succeeding year's experience of the hulks, as places of confinement for convicts . . . only serves to strengthen the conviction as to their unfitness for carrying out these [reformative] objectives. Whatever may be done to enforce discipline outwardly and to promote good order and regularity by fear of punishment and hopes of reward, there is an undercurrent of depravity beyond the reach of human power to control . . . ."[22]

By 1855 most of the diehard resistance to shutting down the hulks had been overcome. Jebb had his on-shore prisons. Portland had a capacity of 1,500. Portsmouth Prison and a poorly designed facility thrown up at Chatham, each housed more than a thousand. New prison construction at Dartmoor provided room for 500 "invalids." Parkhurst had capacity for 550 juveniles. Together, Pentonville and Millbank housed about 1,600 prisoners. To augment available prison capacity in England, the Home Office rented cell space from the local gaols at Wakefield and Leicester.[23] A new convict prison was soon to be under construction at Woking. Joshua Jebb's controversial ticket-of-leave and *Release on Order of License* programs were established. As early as 1853 new facilities and policy innovations were in place that would have enabled the criminal justice system in Great Britain to function without transporting convicted offenders beyond the seas or consigning them to the hulks. It was to be a few years, however, before Her Majesty's officials were finally able to jettison their addiction to these revered practices. In 1855 passage of the Penal Servitude Act effectively ended transportation as a criminal sanction,[†] substituting for it specific terms of imprisonment in English prisons, accompanied by a domestic version of the ticket-of-leave program. The British public had seen no objection to ticket-of-leave men on the farms or in the towns of the Australian colonies, but were unhappy about having such fellows on the loose in England. Needless to say, voices were raised in Parliament about perils being visited on Britain by Jebb's policies. The program needed to be administered conservatively, in order to avoid the risk of having it shut down altogether. The perception in the Home Office was that bed space on the hulks was still needed.

Millbank had become the principal holding station for prisoners awaiting

---

[†] The demand for farm labor in Western Australia resulted in contingents of especially selected convicts being sent there occasionally until 1867.

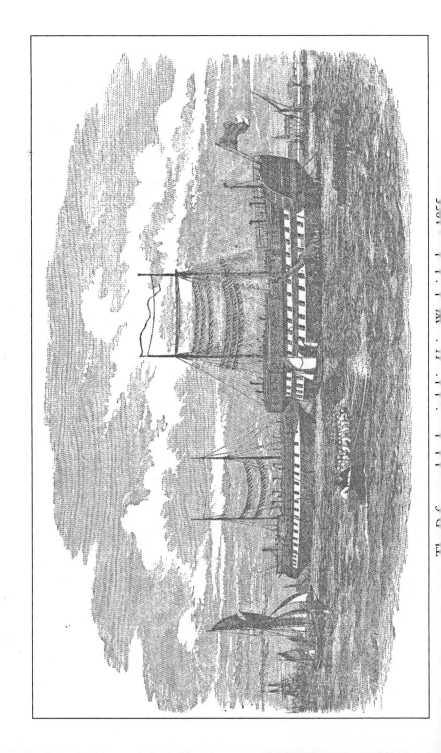

The Defence _____ Wh__ __ 1055

transportation to Australia. The hulks at Woolwich were occupied mostly by "invalids," men too weak, sickly or infirm to make the voyage. But there were a significant number who had been counting on Australia as a place of opportunity for a new life. (The goldrush in Australia was at its height.) These prisoners were outraged by passage of the Penal Servitude Act.[24] Again there were outbreaks of violence. They were quickly put down, but not before the murder of an assistant surgeon to the hulks at Woolwich. Reports described the slain physician, Mr. Hope, as "most kind, attentive, and humane, clever in his profession, and gentle in his treatment of the prisoners."[25]

Now it was the year 1857. Only two hulks remained in England. One of them was the hospital ship, *Unite*, with a dozen or so sick prisoners aboard. She was anchored just a few yards upstream from the *Defense*, off the docks at Woolwich where the story had begun. The *Defense* was a respectable vessel, having been refurbished just seven years before. She housed fewer than 300 prisoners, most of them "invalids," and constant efforts were being made to reduce that number.

On May 7, 1857, the Sepoys of India revolted against their British masters and declared the Mogul prince to be emperor of India. British soldiers, children and women were massacred. In England the public was transfixed by these events.

On July 15, 1857, a one-paragraph story appeared in the *Times of London*:

At 9 o'clock yesterday morning smoke was observed issuing from the hold of the convict hulk Defense, moored off Woolwich Arsenal, which, on closer examination, was discovered to originate in the fore part of the ship, where about 200 or 300 tons of coal were housed for use of the establishment. Every part of the huge vessel was soon filled with smoke and the whole of the inmates were hastily removed to the invalid hulk lying along side, called the Unite. Either from want of ventilation or some other causes the entire body of fuel had become ignited, it is supposed, from spontaneous combustion caused by the confinement of gas. The united fire brigades maintained at the Royal Arsenal and the Dockyard, under the direction of Inspectors Thompson and Budd, were promptly in attendance, and powerful efforts were made to extinguish the fire. It was not, however, extinguished for some hours. There is a probability of the fire having been occasioned from a spark from a pipe of one of the convicts while picking oakum, although the regulations of the establishment strictly forbid the use of tobacco, which regulation, however, it is said, is relaxed in the case of certain invalids.

Before the fateful day, July 14, 1857, the prisoner count aboard the *Defense* had been reduced to 171. All of this sickly remnant, including those who served as nurses and orderlies, were hospital patients. Some of them were "in the last stage of disease." The safe evacuation of such prisoners required prompt, decisive action, and a commendable measure of cooperation between warders and prisoners. Had the fire occurred at an earlier time, when the hulk was near her capacity of 400, a tragedy could hardly have been avoided. The hospital ship, *Unite*, by this time no more of a hospital ship than the *Defense*, had seventy-seven prisoners aboard. According to the *Times* account, all prisoners from the *Defense* were put aboard the *Unite*. It is more likely some of them were rowed ashore. Within hours of the fire, 150 prisoners were taken to Millbank, leaving a total prisoner count on the hulks in England of ninety-eight, all of them on the long-serving and sturdy little frigate, *Unite*. The hulk establishment was to have six more weeks of life, the time required for Jebb to arrange for temporary use of the "war prison" at Lewes. The last of the hulk prisoners were taken off the *Unite*, "and in obedience to the warrant of the . . . [Home Secretary], the whole of the convicts previously forming the 'Defense' hulk establishment were in three drafts removed to Lewes. This event took place on the 1st, 2nd, and 7th September, without any disorder, . irregularity, or casualty occurring."[26]

Thus ended the era of the English prison hulks. It was an event that was neither celebrated nor lamented. There were more important matters. Most prominent among Great Britain's concerns during those days were the valiant efforts of General Havelock's little force of Highlanders and Madras Fusiliers, striving to relieve the garrison at Lucknow. Hardly any notice was taken of there no longer being a need for William Eden's "temporary expedient," on the Thames at Woolwich or elsewhere in England.

# EPILOGUE

The watershed events of 1776 in England's North American colonies temporarily put an end to the British system of prisoner transportation. England had no convict prisons; nothing but the teeming, fetid gaols. And yet, quite suddenly, what they *did* have was a serious prison overcrowding problem. The hulks became the solution.[1]

In the United States the crisis of overcrowded prisons has been brewing for decades. It became a bubbling cauldron in the City of New York during the mid-1980s. In 1986, the city's prisoner census reached 14,000, twice the size it had been six years earlier.[2] An increase in violent, drug-related crime and the public's demand that something be done about it were major causes for New York's prisoner population explosion. One aspect of the solution chosen by that jurisdiction was identical to the British choice 210 years before — prison hulks.

Ironically, among the hordes of new prisoners being shuttled out to Rikers Island every day or jammed into the various other lockups around the city, relatively few were accused of violent crimes. Most were men and women picked up on suspicion of selling drugs. Many of them, perhaps most, were inept, wasted addicts. But the conventional wisdom was, and is, in the City of New York and throughout the country, that drugs are the major cause of violent crime in the cities of America.

Edward Koch, who served as mayor of New York from 1978 to January 1990, was a zealous soldier in the war on drugs. His "TNTs" (Tactical Narcotics Teams) would conduct regular sweeps through the drug-infested streets of the Bronx, Brooklyn, southeast Queens and the pockets of destitution in Manhattan. Along with people suspected of significant trafficking, homeless derelicts who had never before experienced interference with their paltry drug bartering, were gathered up by the hundreds and packed off to Rikers Island. The long-suffering cadre of wardens there packed them in as best they could. Needless to say, disturbances and assaults were daily occurrences. Escapes and inadvertent releases became more frequent. At times staff members were the victims of violence, and, all too often, officers used excessive force against prisoners. There were hundreds of resignations and dismissals for cause. Among those who quit voluntarily were many strong, experienced employees. An increasingly inexperienced work force was having to cope with an increasingly difficult task.

In 1983, United States District Judge Morris Lasker had ruled that the excessive overcrowding in New York City's jails was a violation of the 8th Amendment, which prohibits cruel and unusual punishment. He ordered the release of 611 prisoners.[3] The public was outraged; politicians complained, but no crime wave ensued. Judge Lasker made it clear that the City of New York would not be allowed to overcrowd its prisons to the point of unreasonable suffering on the part of the inmates. His threat to again order the release of inmates was an animating force. Mayor Koch was horrified at the prospect of another court-ordered release of prison inmates, but he was not inclined to relent in his campaign against the city's drug traffic. These circumstances created a desperate need for more jail space.

In the New York City area, land prices have long been astronomical. There is so little land not built upon. There are, on the other hand, spacious stretches of water in the East and Hudson Rivers. Among them, the five boroughs of the City have hundreds of miles of shoreline. Most of the shoreline too has long been taken up. But it occurred to the authorities seeking solutions to the prison overcrowding problem in 1986 that water was more available than land, and that the city had access to piers and moorages around Manhattan Island and on the Brooklyn waterfront. These factors were among those that led to establishment of New York's fleet of prison hulks.

Although space for building new facilities on Rikers Island was all but exhausted, the Koch administration was able to announce in October 1986 a plan to increase the city's jail space by 2,300 beds. The centerpiece of the plan was to be acquisition of two upstate prison facilities, built but not opened by the State of New York. This curious arrangement required spending $2 million a year to fly New York City misdemeanants back and forth between their homes and these jails, three hundred miles away on the banks of the Saint Lawrence River. Prisoners and officers alike called this operation "Air Rikers".

The other measure was for the Department of Correction to take possession of two retired Staten Island ferryboats, and to refurbish them as floating detention facilities.[4] The first of them, the *Joseph F. Merrill*, was to be in service in January. This schedule was not met, but the first ferryboat jail, renamed the *John C. Keane* to honor an esteemed New York City prison worker, was ready to receive prisoners at its Rikers Island moorage on March 27, 1987. By that time the project was $3 million over budget, mainly because of the high cost of constructing a special pier. Department of Correction officials hastened to point out that a second ferryboat jail, to be added in the fall, would be moored at the expensive pier, bringing down the total cost.

These first two vessels of the New York City hulk fleet might have served reasonably well for housing about 320 prisoners, had it not been for the unanticipated U.S. Coast Guard requirement that a licensed mate and engineer be stationed on board twenty-four hours a day. This regulation meant an additional twelve full-time employees on each ferryboat at an annual cost of half a million dollars. The planned staffing pattern was already too high. It became apparent that operation of the ferryboat jails, as had been anticipated, was beyond the Department's financial resources. Plans had to be changed. Regular prisoners, even minimum custody prisoners, could not be housed on the ferryboats. Remodeled at great cost, docked at a specially built $4 million pier, New York City's first prison hulks were limited to housing inmates on *work-release* — inmates away at work in the city most of the day. The ferryboats remained half-empty and thus were of little use in relieving New York City's ongoing overcrowding crisis.[5]

But if there was any significant official disillusionment with the idea of shipboard confinement, it was not apparent. In the summer of 1987 the Department of Correction signed an agreement with Bibby Freighters Ltd. of Liverpool to lease two troop barges that had been built for use by the British army in the Falklands. The first of them, the *Bibby Venture*, had a capacity for about 380 prisoners. The city paid $19 million to lease this craft for five years, after which it would be available for purchase at nominal cost. It was towed over from England, arriving at an East River pier in October 1987.

The *Bibby Venture* was a failed cause from the beginning. Shortly after its arrival it was characterized by the Court's chief compliance officer as an "unsupervisable labyrinth." The Board of Corrections chairman was equally pessimistic. He observed that, its having been designed to give disciplined British soldiers a modicum of privacy and comfort, the barge was unsuitable for people who needed constant visual supervision.

New York City's Board of Correction is an agency of uncertain purpose.

Indeed, it bears an eerie similarity to the unfortunate Committee of Management, formed by the British Parliament in 1816 to oversee the ill-fated Millbank Penitentiary experiment. However accurate, or inaccurate, that comparison might be, the Board chairman's initial comments about the new jail barge from England were on target.

The *Venture* never came close to housing its rated capacity of 380 prisoners and never found a permanent home in the waters around New York City. The vociferous objections of a Lower East Side citizens' group kept it from being placed in use for five months after its arrival, and then for only a few prisoners. Given its hostile reception in Manhattan, the Department of Correction felt constrained to move the *Bibby Venture* to a Brooklyn moorage. Officials of the Department were mistaken, however, if they thought the presumably less sophisticated people of that community would be less vehement in their objections to a jail barge docked on their waterfront. Bay Ridge and Sunset Park citizens' groups promptly organized a vigorous protest. Not long thereafter, the *Venture* was towed back to Manhattan.[†] Meanwhile, the *Bibby Resolution* had arrived, having been towed up from the Falkland Islands. It was moored at the East River pier that had been vacated by the *Bibby Venture*. The *Venture* was taken around to the Hudson River side and tied up at Pier 40, a West Greenwich Village moorage. It was to remain there, never to become significantly useful in alleviating the city's prison overcrowding problem.

To lease the *Bibby Resolution*, a more commodious vessel with a bed-space capacity of 450, the city paid $21 million. The oversight groups did not condemn this more promising barge quite so categorically. With wider corridors, roomier cells and more open vistas, the *Resolution* might have been made to work, if extra staff could be provided.

But there were a number of problems that affected both barges. Plans given to the Bibby firm for refitting did not take into account New York City's fire code or U.S. Coast Guard regulations. The city's fire inspectors and the Coast Guard concluded that *both* agencies had jurisdiction. To the Coast Guard, the barges were ships; to the City of New York Fire Department, they were buildings. The result was a maze of regulations,

---

[†] Two hundred years earlier Brooklyn had a bad experience with a prison hulk. Thousands of American prisoners-of-war are said to have perished from mistreatment and neglect on board the British warship *Jersey*, which lay at anchor in Wallabout Bay during the War of American Independence. These waters have since been enveloped by the Brooklyn Navy Yard complex.

New York City's prison hulk, the *Vernon C. Bain*, Hunt's Point, the Bronx, 1993

which raised doubt as to whether either barge would ever be approved for permanent occupancy.[6]

Opposition on the part of the residents of lower Manhattan was an even more formidable barrier to putting the barges to full use than were the stringent regulations of government agencies. The citizens' groups were given strong support by their local assemblymen. Law suits were filed. A state court temporary restraining order was gained. There were delays of many months, during which the Department was using an inordinately high level of staffing to supervise an insignificant number of prisoners on board the vessels of New York City's hulk fleet.

But now the Department of Correction with the approval of the mayor's office had decided on a new approach to the use of floating detention. The idea was to construct a jail barge that met all code requirements and court-ordered standards, and which conformed to Coast Guard regulations. It would be designed for efficiency and require no higher level of staffing than a dry land jail. It would have permanent moorage at a location to which there could be no possible objection on the part of neighborhood residents. Before moving ahead with this idea, representatives of the Department of Correction fanned out across Europe. They talked to ship builders in Germany, England and Poland, and they explored alternative possibilities. The most promising prospect was a hull laid at Poland's great Gdansk shipyard. It was to have been a floating hotel, but the original client's financial arrangements had not worked out. James Garvey, one of New York City's most respected correctional administrators, accompanied by an architect on the Department's staff, inspected this project. Garvey saw no reason why a workable design could not be installed on the hull. The savings in time and money would have been substantial. Instead, the decision made in the Mayor's office was to have a new jail barge built.

On May 17, 1989, seven months before Mayor Koch left office, a contract was awarded to the shipyard division of Avondale Industries, Avondale, Louisiana. After thirty-two months the barge was completed, towed up from the Gulf of Mexico and tied up at Hunt's Point on the east side of the Bronx. The city had, indeed, found a moorage where objections on the part of citizens in the neighborhood would be unlikely. Six weeks after the new jail barge was made secure at its East Bronx moorage it received the last of the prisoners from the Bibby barges. Those vessels were not used again.

During the twelve-day voyage from Avondale the new jail barge was buffeted by sixty knot winds without suffering significant damage. The

*Vernon C. Bain* was simply too massive to be bothered by an Atlantic storm of routine severity.[7]

New York City's splendid state-of-the-art prison hulk has an overall length of 625 feet, a beam of 125 feet, displacement of 18,000 tons, a five-level superstructure, which accommodates eight-hundred prisoners in fourteen dormitories of fifty beds each, and one-hundred high-security cells.[8] It has a school, a library, a spacious outdoor recreation area on the upper deck and a gymnasium that approaches the dimensions of a university fieldhouse. Errors were made in functional design — too much reliance on elevators, for example, and a central dining room. An arrangement for feeding on separate levels would have been better. Of more concern to Department of Correction personnel, the *Vernon C. Bain* is dependent on an enormously complex set of technical systems. A small staff of technically trained mariners have the task of maintaining an intimidating assortment of high-tech equipment housed in forty separate machine rooms.

Mayor David Dinkins assumed office January 19, 1990. Under the new mayor, activities of the Tactical Narcotics Teams were curtailed. The New York State prison system, meanwhile, had become more accommodating about accepting sentenced prisoners promptly, rather than leaving them in New York City detention facilities indefinitely. The result of these developments was a leveling off of the city's prisoner population at about twenty thousand.

The acknowledged cost of the new jail barge was $180 million, bringing New York City's total expenditure for its hulk fleet to about $230 million. On April 23, 1993, the day of the author's visit, fewer than two hundred of the city's prisoners were confined on the *Vernon C. Bain*. The *Bibby Venture* and the *Bibby Resolution* lay quietly at dock on opposite sides of lower Manhattan Island — no prisoners on board. The ferryboat jails remained tied up to their expensive pier on the island — no prisoners on board them either, new quarters for work releasees having been found a year before. Thus it appears that just over $1 million had been invested in shipboard confinement for each detainee confined aboard a New York City floating facility on that day. The fiscal disaster implied here is mitigated to some extent by a lease of four hundred beds on the *Vernon C. Bain* to the federal government. Moreover, a melancholy certainty is that sooner or later the City of New York will find a way to fill up those empty jail spaces. Meanwhile, a dramatic illustration is again provided as to the prodigious costliness of the imprisonment business. All of the decisions that went toward establishing New York City's indefensibly expensive hulk fleet were rational, made by reasonable, competent men and women.

On that cool and blustery April day, things were obviously under control on the ponderous prison hulk from Louisiana. And all was reported to be peaceful throughout the vast complex of prisons on Rikers Island. The prisoner population had fallen to near nineteen thousand. We can be sure there were occasional acts of violence among New York City's prisoners on that day. Fear, frustration and misery were to be found in every confinement facility in the city. And yet it was a time of blessed respite from the turmoil that had gone before. The Dinkins' administration has made no fundamental changes. The bad times will come again.

What fundamental changes have there been throughout America or in Great Britain, during this, the era of *penal servitude*, now nearing the end of its second century? Those of us who are struck by the repetition of history in the field of imprisonment must first concede that significant improvements in conditions of confinement have been made. Sanitation is profoundly better. Medical care is better. Food for prisoners is more palatable and nutritious. Prisoners have more rights and better access to the courts. The courts have seen to it that prisoners have more space to breathe and marginally better opportunities for self-improvement. Policies condoning sadism are hardly to be found any longer. All sorts of dubious distractions have been devised. Television sets in the dayrooms have become heavily relied upon tools of control.

And yet, misery, fear and despair still stalk the corridors of prisons throughout the English-speaking world. Where the United States is concerned, the politically driven addiction to long-term incarceration as the best and only hope for controlling crime, parallels Britain's tenacity during the 19th-century in holding onto the notion of transportation.

Incarceration is a failed idea if we look on it as anything more than a means of incapacitating criminals for varying periods of time. The American euphemism for the imprisonment business, *corrections*, continues to stand in need of redemption. And now it has become clear that the present measure of America's reliance on imprisonment has become too expensive.

Are there alternatives? Cesare Beccaria's 200-year-old prescription calling for a rejection of severity in favor of swiftness and certainty of appropriate punishment, is rhetorically honored in the highest ranks of government but never implemented.9 And the wearisome idea of getting at the root causes of crime is taken no more seriously in late 20th-century America than it was in Great Britain during the era of the hulks.

# NOTES

CHAPTER I: HOW THE NEED AROSE

1. Abbot Emerson Smith, *Colonists in Bondage* (Chapel Hill: University of North Carolina Press, 1947), 89-91.

2. "The Hypochondriack," The London Magazine's Monthly Intelligencer, vol. LXVII (May 1783.) Reprinted in The *Death Penalty, Selected Materials*, ed. Edward G. McGehee and William H. Hildebrand (Boston: D. C. Heath Co.), 1964.

3. Henry Mayhew & John Binny, *The Criminal Prisons of London* (London: Frank Cass & Co., 1862; Reprint, A.M. Kelly, New York, 1968), 590.

4. John Deane Potter, *The Art of Hanging* (Cranbury, N.J.: A.S Barnes Co., 1965), 169.

5. Smith, *Colonists in Bondage*, 89-91.

6. Katharine Coman & Elizabeth Kendall, *A Short History of England* (New York: Macmillan, 1907), 342.

7. Ibid., 344.

8. Smith, *Colonists in Bondage*, 111.

9. Peter Wilson Coldham, *Bonded Passengers to America, vol. 1 The History of Transportation 1615 to 1775* (Baltimore: Genealogical Publishing Co., 1983), 178-180.

10. Smith, *Colonists in Bondage*, 129-130.

11. Walter Hart Blumenthal, *Brides from Bridewell, Female Felons sent to Colonial America* (Rutland, Vt.: Charles E. Tuttle Co. 1962), 36.

12. G. C. Bolton, "William Eden and the Convicts," *Australian Journal of Politics and History*, vol. 26 No. 1 (1980) 36.

13. Edward Cadogan, *The Roots of Evil* (London: John Murray, 1937), 156.

14. Brigadier O. F. G. Hogg, *The Royal Arsenal* vol. I (London: Oxford University Press, 1963), 36.

15. Bolton, "William Eden and the Convicts," 36-37.

16. Sir Edmund F. DuCane, *The Punishment and Prevention of Crime* (London: Macmillan, 1885), 116.

17. Reg Rigden, *The Floating Prisons of Woolwich and Deptford* (London: A Borough of Greenwich publication, 1976), 6.

18. Bolton, "William Eden and the Convicts," 37.

19. Ibid., 40.

20. Coldham, *Bonded Passengers to America*, 144-145.

21. Ibid.

22. Parliament, Journals, *Sessional Papers* (Commons) 1778, vol. 36, 926.

23. Coldham, *Bonded Passengers to America*, 62-65.

24. Ibid., 75.

25. Ibid., 332-333.

26. Mayhew & Binny, *The Criminal Prisons of London*, 199.

27. Ibid., 149-151.

CHAPTER II: MR. HOWARD'S SCRUTINY

1. Except where otherwise noted, references to John Howard in this chapter are drawn from his writings, primarily *The State of Prisons*, (London, J.M. Dent & Sons, publishers, 1777, 1780 and 1784 editions; reprint 1929 by E.P. Dutton, New York); and from Leona Baumgartner's *John Howard, Hospital and Prison Reformer: a Bibliography*, 1939, Johns Hopkins University Press; from the *Dictionary of National Biography*, and other standard writings on the life and works of John Howard.

2. Parliament, Journals, *Sessional Papers* (Commons), 1778 vol. 36, p. 928.

3. James Neild, *The State of Prisons in England, Scotland and Wales* (London: John Nichols & Son 1812), 619.

4. Rigden, *The Floating Prisons of Woolwich and Deptford*, 4.

5. *Dictionary of National Biography*, (London: Oxford University Press), s.v. "Elizabeth Fry."

CHAPTER III: MR. CAMPBELL'S ENTERPRISE

1. Neil Rhind, "Transportation and the Blackheath Connection," unpublished paper, read before the Greenwich History Society at the Local History Library, Blackheath, London, on October 23, 1991. Also see Dan Byrnes, "Emptying the Hulks, Duncan Campbell and the First Three Fleets to Australia" (*The Push from the Bush: A Bulletin of Social History*, Armidale NSW, April 1987 pp. 2-23). Historians Byrnes of Tamworth, New South Wales; and Rhind, of Blackheath, have done extensive research into the business and social aspects of convict transportation and related activities at Woolwich and Blackheath. A book on this subject by Byrnes is forthcoming.

2. Except where otherwise noted, all information in this chapter on Duncan Campbell's administration of the hulks is drawn from accounts of testimony before the Select Committee on the Punishment of Convicts, chaired by Sir Charles Bunbury in The Journals, *Sessional Papers*, House of Commons, vol. 36, 1778, 926-932, and vol. 37, 1779, 307-314, British Parliamentary papers.

3. Campbell's clerk to Richard Ackerman, March 28, 1777, Duncan Campbell letters vol. 2, Mitchell Library, Sydney.

4. See Chapter IV.

5. Campbell to Captain Erskine, April 17, 1777, Duncan Campbell letters vol. 2, Mitchell Library, Sydney.

6. Rigden, *The Floating Prisons of Woolwich and Deptford*, 14. Also see Hogg, *The Royal Arsenal*, 454.

7. Thomas R. Forbes, "Coroners' Inquisitions on the Death of Prisoners in the Hulks at Portsmouth, England in 1817-1827," *Journal of the History of Medicine and the Allied Sciences*, vol. 33, set 2 (1978.)

8. Pennant, writing in *The Water Companion*, 1802, quotation from Hogg, *The Royal Arsenal*, 453.

9. W. Branch Johnson, *The English Prison Hulks*, (Chichester, Sussex: Phillimore & Co. Ltd., 1957) 134.

CHAPTER IV: NEWGATE

1. Mayhew & Binny, *The Criminal Prisons of London*, 588.

2. Ralph B. Pugh, *Imprisonment in Medieval England* (Cambridge, The University Press, 1968), 330.

3. Mayhew & Binny, *The Criminal Prisons of London*, 589.

4. C.H.B. and M. Quennel, *A History of Everyday Things in England* Vol. III (London, B.T. Batsfort Ltd., 1933), 53.

5. Parliament, The Journals, *Sessional Papers*, (Commons) 1779, vol. 37, 307.

6. Henry Savage, *The Newgate Calendar*, (Hartford, Conn., Edwin Valentine Mitchell Inc., 1926)

7. Mayhew & Binny, *The Criminal Prisons of London*, 592.

8. Henry Savage, *The Newgate Calendar*, 5.

9. Mayhew & Binney, *The Criminal Prisons of London*, 592.

10. John Howard, *The State of Prisons*, (London, J.M. Dent & Sons, publishers of 1777, 1778 and 1784 editions, reprint 1929 by E.P. Dutton, New York), 161.

11. Mayhew & Binny, *The Criminal Prisons of London*, 591-592.

12. D.L. Howard, *The English Prisons, Their Past and Future*, (London, Methuen & Co. Ltd. 1960), 83-84.

13. Mayhew & Binny, *The Criminal Prisons of London*, 363.

14. D.L. Howard, *The English Prisons, Their Past and Future*, 83.

15. Parliament, The Journals, *Sessional Papers* (Commons) 1778, vol. 36, 926-930.

CHAPTER V: ON THE WARREN

1. Information presented in this chapter on the hulks at Woolwich, 1776 through 1779, for which no other source is cited, is drawn from accounts of inquiries conducted by the Select Committee on the Punishment of Convicts, chaired by Sir Charles Bunbury, reported in the Journals of the House of Commons, *Sessional Papers*, 1778 vol. 36, 926-930 and 1779 vol. 37, 307-314.

2. Duncan Campbell's clerk to Captain Hill of the *La Fortunee*, Woolwich, June 8, 1787, Duncan Campbell letters vol. 2, Mitchell Library, Sydney.

3. Ibid., Duncan Campbell to the Duke of Richmond, June 13, 1787.

4. Ibid., Duncan Campbell to Captain Erskine, June 16, 1787.

5. W.T. Vincent, *Records of Woolwich* Vol I, from Hogg, *The Royal Arsenal*, 453.

6. Clipping from Scots Magazine, May 1777, courtesy of Local History Library for the Borough of Greenwich, Blackheath, London.

7. Hogg, *The Royal Arsenal* vol. I, 451.

8. Edward Cadogan, *The Roots of Evil*, (London, John Murray, 1937), 158.

9. J. M. Beattie, *Crime and the Courts of England 1660-1800*, (Oxford, Clarendon Press, 1946), 568.

10. Duncan Campbell to William Eden, August 2, 1777 and December 5, 1777, Duncan Campbell letters vol. 2.


CHAPTER VI: THE AUSTRALIAN CONNECTION

1. See Christina Bewley, *Muir of Huntershill* (Oxford, Oxford University Press, 1981)

2. Douglas Pike, *The Quiet Continent*, (Cambridge, The University Press, 1962), 45-46.

3. Peter Wilson Coldham, *Bonded Passengers to America*, 152.

4. Robert Hughes, *The Fatal Shore* (New York, Alfred A. Knopf, 1987), 68-71.

5. John Fisher, *The Australians, From 1788 to Modern Times* (New York, Taplinger Publishing Co., 1968), 23-24.

6. Dan Byrne, "Emptying the Hulks," 9.

7. Robert Hughes, *The Fatal Shore*, 145.

8. Charles Bateson, *The Convict Ships 1787-1868* (Glasgow, Brown, Son & Ferguson, 1958), 55.

9. Ibid., 142-144.

10. Ibid., 163-166.

11. Parliament, The Journals, *Sessional Papers* (Commons) 1834 vol. XLVIII, 109. Also see accounts and letters concerning wreck of the Amphitrite in *The Times of London*, September 3rd, 4th and 5th, 1833.

12. Jonathan King, *The First Fleet, the Convict Voyage that Founded Australia* (South Melbourne: The Macmillan Co. of Australia, 1982), 22.

13. Manning Clark, *A Short History of Australia* (New York, The New American Library, 1963), 21-29.

14. See Charles Campbell, *Serving Time Together, Men and Women in Prison* (Fort Worth, Texas Christian University Press, 1980.)

15. John Fisher, *The Australians, from 1788 to Modern Times*, 10-42.

16. Hughes, *The Fatal Shore*, 458-474, 498-512, 543-551.

17. Ibid., 461.

18. Douglas Pike, *Australia, the Quiet Continent*, 31.

19. Joseph C. Harvie, *History of the Convict Ship "Success"* second edition, 27-30. Note: According to the author, whose name is not given in the second edition, this booklet

was written and published aboard the *Success* in 1913, long after the ship was deactivated as a prison hulk. 27-30. See Footnote on page 74.

20. Ibid., 5.

21. Ibid., (1895 edition) 14-18.

22. Ibid., (second edition) 31-44.

23. Hughes, *The Fatal Shore*, 543-451.

24. Harvie, *History of the Convict Ship "Success"* (1895 edition) 28.

25. Hughes, *The Fatal Shore*, 549.

26. Harvie, *History of the Convict Ship "Success"* (Second edition) 37-44.

27. Ibid., 51-57.

28. Hughes, *The Fatal Shore*, 543.

29. Harvie, *History of the Convict Ship "Success"* (Second edition) 59-64.

## CHAPTER VII: MR. GRAHAM'S TRIBULATIONS

1. Neil Rhind, "Transportation and the Blackheath Connection" 14-15.

2. Parliament, Report of the Select Committee on Penitentiary Houses, *Sessional Papers* (Commons) 1812 vol. II, 135-136.

3. G.E. Manwaring and Bonamy Dobree, *The Floating Republic* (London, Frank Cass & Co. 1935), 100-105, 112, 188, 237, 249, 250-251, 259.

4. Parliament, Report of the Select Committee, *Sessional Papers* (Commons) 1814-1815 vol. II, 15.

5. Dan Byrnes, "Emptying the Hulks" 3.

6. W. Branch Johnson, *The English Prison Hulks*, 88.

7. Parliament, Report of the Select Committee, *Sessional Papers* (Commons) 1812 vol. II, 136-138.

8. Ibid., 138-165.

9. Robert Hughes, *The Fatal Shore*, 265.

10. Parliament, Report of the Select Committee, *Sessional Papers*, 1812 vol. II, 138-165.

11. James Hardy Vaux, *Memoirs* (London, W. Clowes, 1819), 112.

12. Parliament, Report of the Select Committee, *Sessional Papers* 1812 vol. II, 141-144.

13. James Hardy Vaux, *Memoirs*, 108-112.

## CHAPTER VIII: THE MILLBANK FIASCO

1. Parliament, Report of Hulk Superintendent John H. Capper (chaplain's report) Jan. 20, 1819, *Sessional Papers* (Commons) 1819, vol. 17.

2. *Dictionary of National Biography*, (London: Oxford University Press), s.v. "Jeremy Bentham."

3. Eric R. Delderfield, ed. *Kings and Queens of England*, (New York, Dorset Press, 1988), 107-108.

4. Mayhew & Binny, *The Criminal Prisons of London*, 234-237.

5. Major Arthur Griffith, *Millbank Penitentiary, an Experiment in Reformation* (London, The Grolier Society, 1875), 20.

6. Mayhew & Binny, *The Criminal Prisons of London*, 236.

7. Ibid., 22-32.

8. Giles Playfair, *The Punitive Obsession, an Unvarnished History of the English Prison System*, (London, Victor Gollancz Ltd. 1971), 30-42.

9. Ibid., *The Punitive Obsession*, 30-42.

10. Michael Ignatieff, *A Just Measure of Pain* (New York, Pantheon Books, 1978), 171.

11. Arthur Griffith, *Millbank Penitentiary*, 33-50.

12. Except where otherwise noted, all information in this chapter concerning the evacuation of Millbank is drawn from the following source: Parliament, the report of the Select Committee appointed to inquire into the present State of The Penitentiary, Milbank, June 11, 1824 and the Minutes of Evidence before the Committee, *Sessional Papers* (Commons) 1824, vol. 4.

13. Arthur Griffith, *Millbank Penitentiary*, 63.

14. See testimony of Captain Benjamin Chapman and Captain Robert Kellock before the Select Committee.

15. Arthur Griffith, *Millbank Penitentiary*, 63-72.

16. Mayhew & Binny, *The Criminal Prisons of London*, 236.

17. Arthur Griffith, *Millbank Penitentiary*, 41-46.

18. Ibid., 290-291.

19. Giles Playfair, *The Punitive Obsession*, 60.

20. Mayhew & Binny, *The Criminal Prisons of London*, 49.

21. Ibid., 113-114.

22. Ibid., 135-136.

23. Giles Playfair, *The Punitive Obsession*, 61.

## CHAPTER IX: MR. CAPPER TAKES CHARGE

1. Parliament, Report on Treatment and Conditions of Convicts at Woolwich- Minutes of Evidence pg. 406, *Sessional Papers* (Commons) 1847 vol. 18.

2. Ibid., pg. xxix in vol. 18.

3. Parliament, Papers relating to Convict Hulks in the Rivers Thames and Medway and in Portsmouth, *Sessional Papers* (Commons) 1814-1815 vol. II.

4. Parliament, Appendix to the Report of the Select Committee for the Millbank inquiry, *Sessional Papers* (Commons) 1824 vol. 4.

5. Parliament, John H. Capper's testimony before Select Committee, House of Lords (Die Martis, 19 Maii 1935,) *Sessional Papers* (Lords) 1835 vol. 11.

6. Parliament, Report on Treatment and Conditions of the Convicts at Woolwich, *Ses-*

*sional Papers* (Commons) 1847 vol. 18. See pg. xxix of the report.

7. Parliament, Instructions to John Henry Capper... Superintendent of the Several Ships and Vessels for the Conduct of Offenders under Sentence of Transportation, 10-16, *Sessional Papers* (Commons) 1816 vol. 18. Also see Parliament, Instructions of Aaron Graham to his Captains, 153-158, *Sessional Papers* (Commons) 1812 vol. 2.

8. Parliament, Report of Aaron Graham to Commons, November 18, 1814, *Sessional Papers* (Commons) 1814-1815 vol. 11.

9. See the Dictionary of National Biography articles on Lord Sidmouth and John Russell.

10. Parliament, Report of the Select Committee, and (for the deck plans) Appendix to the Report of the Select Committee, *Sessional Papers* (Commons) 1812 vol. II.

11. Parliament, John H. Capper's report to the Home Secretary dated October 16, 1816, *Sessional Papers* (Commons) 1816 vol.18. This was Capper's first report. Although only three pages long, it was to be perhaps the most informative of the many reports submitted by him during his thirty two years as superintendent of the hulk establishment.

12. Parliament, John H. Capper's report to the Home Secretary dated Aug. 21, 1818, *Sessional Papers* (Commons) 1819 vol. 17.

13. Parliament, Capper report of Oct. 16, 1815, *Sessional Papers* (Commons) 1816 vol. 18.

14. Parliament, Instructions to John Henry Capper, Superintendent of the several Ships and Vessels for the Confinement of Offenders under Sentence of Transportation, Papers Relating to the Hulks, *Sessional Papers* (Commons) 1816 vol. 18.

15. Parliament, Report of John H. Capper dated Jan. 20, 1819, *Sessional Papers* (Commons) 1819 vol. 17.

16. Parliament, Instructions to Capper, Papers Relating to the Hulks, *Sessional Papers* (Commons) 1816 vol. 18.

17. Parliament, Papers Relating to the Convict Hulks in the Rivers Thames and Medway, and in Portsmouth and Langston Harbours, *Sessional Papers* (Commons) 1814-1815 vol. 11.

18. Parliament, Report of John Capper, Jan. 25, 1825, *Sessional Papers* (Commons) 1825 vol. 23.

19. Playfair, *The Punitive Obsession*, 46-49.

20. Parliament, Capper's testimony, Lords' Select Committee (Die Martis, 19 Maii 1835) *Sessional Papers* (Lords) 1835, vol. 11.


CHAPTER X: CHILDREN OF THE HULKS

1. Parliament, Report of John H. Capper dated January 25, 1825, *Sessional Papers* (Commons) 1825 vol. 23.

2. Parliament, Capper report of Jan. 21, 1826, *Sessional Papers* (Commons) 1826 vol. 24.

3. Parliament, Letter from Chaplain Price to Capper dated June 30, 1826 submitted with Capper report of July 26, 1826. Also see Capper report of Jan. 27, 1827, *Sessional Papers* (Commons) 1826-1827 vol. 19.

4. For correspondence from Price to Capper, and comments sent by Mr. Capper to the Home Office concerning Chaplain Price, see Parliament, biannual reports of John H. Capper, *Sessional Papers* (Commons) 1826-1827 vol. 19 and 1828 vol. 20.

5. Parliament, Capper report of Jan. 29, 1829 and letter included from Chaplain Dawes dated Jan. 2 1829, *Sessional Papers* (Commons) 1829 vol. 18.

6. Ibid., Capper report of July 10, 1928.

7. Parliament, Chaplain Dawes' letter to Capper, submitted with Capper report of July 25, 1831, *Sessional Papers* (Commons) 1831-1832 vol. 33.

8. Parliament, Dawes letter to Capper, submitted with Capper report of July 28, *Sessional Papers* (Commons) 1829 vol. 18.

9. Except where otherwise noted, all of the information in this chapter on management of the boy convicts confined on the hulk Euryalus is drawn from Parliament, Minutes of Evidence given before the House of Lords Select Committee appointed to inquire into the State of Gaols and Houses of Correction, *Sessional Papers* (Commons) 1835 vol. 11.

10. Parliament, Dawes' letter to Capper, included with Capper report dated January 29, 1835, *Sessional Papers* (Commons) 1835 vol. 11.

11. Ibid., Minutes of Evidence, Lords' Select Committee.

12. Parliament, Capper report of July 22, 1836, *Sessional Papers* (Commons) 1837 vol. 45.

13. Parliament, Capper report of July 29, 1839, *Sessional Papers* 1840 vol. 38.

14. Parliament, Capper report of Feb. 29, 1844, *Sessional Papers* (Commons) 1844 vol. 39.


CHAPTER XI: BERMUDA

1. Parliament, Report of John Capper, Superintendent of Convicts 27 January 1827, *Sessional Papers* (Commons), 1826-1827 vol. 19.

2. Parliament, Appendix to Evidence before the Select Committee, *Sessional Papers* Commons), 1835 vol. 11.

3. Ferdinand Whittingham, *Bermuda, A Colony, A Fortress, A Prison*, (London, Longman, Brown, Green & Roberts, 1857), 187.

4. Parliament, Report of the Governor General of Bermuda, *Sessional Papers* (Commons), 1849 vol. 43.

5. John Mitchel, *Jail Journal, or Five Years in British Prisons* (Glasgow, 1876), 53.

6. See Whittingham, *Bermuda, A Colony, a Fortress, A Prison*.

7. Hughes, *The Fatal Shore*, 113-119, 402-404.

8. Johnson, *The English Prison Hulks*, 69.

9. Mitchell, *Jail Journal*, 94-96..

10. Johnson, *The English Prison Hulks*, 166.

11. Ibid., 172-173.

CHAPTER XII: MR. DUNCOMBE ACCUSES

1. Parliament, Report on the Treatment and Conditions of the Convicts on the Hulks at

Woolwich, *Sessional Papers* (Commons), 1847 vol.18.

2. *The National Dictionary of Biography*, s.v. "Thomas Slingsby Duncombe."

3. Parliament, Report of Inspector of Prisons William John Williams to Sir George Grey, May 28, 1847, *Sessional Papers* (Commons), 1847 vol. 18.

4. Parliament, Report of Superintendent of Convicts John H. Capper, April 23, 1845, *Sessional Papers* (Commons), 1845 vol. 37. Also see Capper report of February 10, 1847, *Sessional Papers*, 1847 vol. 18.

5. Parliament, Appendix to the Report on the Treatment and Condition of Convicts, (Including extract of article in the Times of London dated January 29, 1847) *Sessional Papers* (Commons), 1847 vol. 18.

6. See "The Hulks at Woolwich", *The Times of London*, Jan. 29, 1847.

7. *Hansard's Parliamentary Debates*, Third series, Vol LXXXIX 19 Jan. 1847 to 15 Feb. 1847, 511-512.

8. Parliament, letter dated January 29, 1847 from S.M.Phillips to John Henry Capper, page one of "Report from Superintendent of Convicts," *Sessional Papers* (Commons), 1847. vol. XLVIII.

9. Parliament, "Report by the Superintendent of Convicts respecting the Treatment of Convicts in the Hulks at Woolwich," 10 February 1847, *Sessional Papers* (Commons) 1847 vol. XLVIII.

10. Parliament, "Minutes of Evidence on an Inquiry into the Treatment and Conditions of Convicts Imprisoned on the Hulks at Woolwich," *Sessional Papers*, 1847 vol. 18, 378.

11. Parliament, Letter from Home Secretary to Captain William John Williams, *Sessional Papers*, 1847 vol. 18.


CHAPTER XIII: CAPTAIN WILLIAMS EXAMINES DILIGENTLY

1. Parliament, William John Williams' Report of Inquiry into the Treatment and Condition of Convicts Imprisoned in the Hulks at Woolwich, Minutes of Evidence, testimony of John George Perry, *Sessional Papers* (Commons), 1847, vol. 18.

2. Ibid., Minutes of Evidence.

3. Parliament, First page of the Report of Inquiry, *Sessional Papers* (Commons), 1847 vol. 18.

4. Parliament, Minutes of Evidence, testimony of Robert Capper, *Sessional Papers* (Commons), 1847 vol. 18.

5. Parliament, John H Capper's testimony before Select Committee, House of Lords (Die Martis, 19 Maii 1835,) *Sessional Papers* (Commons) 1835 vol. 11.

6. See Thomas H. Duncombe, *The Life and Correspondence of Thomas Slingsby Duncombe* in two volumes (London, Hurst and Blackett, 1868).

7. Parliament, Minutes of Evidence, testimony of Robert Capper and William Mawman Brown, *Sessional Papers* (Commons) 1847, vol. 18.

8. Ibid., Testimony of Robert Capper and Report of Inquiry, *Sessional Papers* (Commons) 1847, vol. 18.

9. Ibid., Report of Inquiry.

10. Ibid., Minutes of Evidence, testimony of Robert Capper.

11. Ibid.

12. Parliament, Report of John Henry Capper, 10 May, 1946, *Sessional Papers* (Commons) 1846 vol. 34.

13. Parliament, Minutes of Evidence, testimony of Robert Capper and Report of Inquiry, *Sessional Papers* (Commons) 1847 vol. 18.

14. Parliament, Instructions, Rules and Regulations of the Convict Hulk Establishment in England, Appendix to the Report of Inquiry, *Sessional Papers* (Commons) 1847, vol. 18.

15. Parliament, Minutes of Evidence, testimony of Robert Capper and Peter Bossey, also see the Report of Inquiry, *Sessional Papers* (Commons) 1847, vol. 18.

16. Parliament, Report of Inquiry. Also see Minutes of Evidence, testimony of Henry Masterman, *Sessional Papers* (Commons) 1847, vol. 18.

## CHAPTER XIV: THE END OF A VOYAGE TO NOWHERE

1. *Dictionary of National Biography*, (London: Oxford University Press), s.v. "Sir Joshua Jebb." Also see Ibid. s.v. "William Crawford." With respect to the Pentonville phase plan devised primarily by Joshua Jebb, see Chapter VIII. For a comparative look at the parallel efforts of Joshua Jebb in England and Walter Crofton in Ireland, see W. L. Clay, *Our Convict Systems* and Sir Joshua Jebb, *Reports and Observations on Discipline and Management of Convict Prisons* published in one volume by Garland Publishing Inc. New York & London 1985.

2. Parliament, Report of the Manager of the Convict Hulk Establishment for the Year 1848, *Sessional Papers* (Commons) 1850 vol. 29.

3. Johnson, *The English Prison Hulks*, 189.

4. Parliament, Report of the Manager 1848, *Sessional Papers* (Commons) 1850 vol. 29. With respect to Peter Bossey's tenure as chief medical officer, also see Report of Inquiry, Minutes of Evidence, testimony of Robert Capper, 1847 vol. XVIII.

5. Parliament, Report of the Manager 1848, *Sessional Papers* (Commons) 1850 vol. 29.

6. Ibid. Also see Appendix B.

7. Ibid., Report of the Manager, 1848.

8. Parliament, Report of the Managers, Appendix No. 12, *Sessional Papers* (Commons), 1850, vol. 29.

9. Parliament, *Sessional Papers* (Commons). See John H. Capper's bi-annual reports to the Home Secretary, 1816 to 1846.

10. Parliament, Report of the Managers of the Convict Hulk Establishment for 1849, *Sessional Papers* (Commons) 1850, vol. 29.

11. Parliament, Report of the Manager, 1848, *Sessional Papers* (Commons), 1850, vol. 29.

12. Parliament, Report of the Managers, 1849, *Sessional Papers* (Commons), 1850, vol. 29. See *State of the Hulks*.

13. Parliament, Report of the Managers, 1849, *Sessional Papers* (Commons) 1850, vol. 29.

See *Conclusion.*

14. Parliament, Report of the Directors of Convict Prisons for the year 1854, *Sessional Papers* (Commons) 1854-1855 vol. 25.

15. Parliament, Report of the Managers, *Conduct of the Prisoners*, 1849, *Sessional Papers* (Commons) 1850, vol. 29.

16. Ibid., Report of the Managers, Appendices numbers 1, 2, 6, and 7.

17. Johnson, *The English Prison Hulks*, 190-191.

18. *The Times of London*, quoted in Johnson, 192.

19. Johnson, *The English Prison Hulks*, 197-198.

20. Parliament, Report on the Hulk Establishment, Appendix No. 1, *Sessional Papers* (Commons) 1854, vol. 33.

21. *The Times of London*, January 1, 1852.

22. Parliament, Report of the Directors of Convict Prisons, *Sessional Papers* (Commons), 1954, vol. 33.

23. Clay and Jebb, *Our Convict Systems* and *Reports and Observations* (one volume) xvii.

24. Johnson, *The English Prison Hulks*, 193.

25. Parliament, Report on the Hulk Establishment for the year 1856, *Sessional Papers* (Commons) 1857, vol 23.

26. Parliament, Report of the Chairman and Directors of Convict Prisons, Jan. 1858, *Sessional Papers* (Commons) 1857-1858, vol. 29.

EPILOGUE

1. Except where otherwise noted, the information for this epilogue was gained by way of personal interviews, and tours of the New York City jail barges *Vernon C. Bain* and *Bibby Venture* in April of 1993.

2. "City Plans to Add 2,300 Jail Spaces," *New York Times*, 9 October 1986, A1.

3. "At a Violent Jail, Warden Strives to Ease Tension," Ibid., 4 May 1987, B1.

4. "City Plans to add 2,300 Jail Spaces," Ibid., 9 October 1986, A1. Also see "New York City Wants State To Take Back Two Prisons," Ibid., 3 January 1992, B1.

5. "Facing $3 Million Overrun, Jail Ferry Plan is Modified," Ibid., 3 May, 1987, A40.

6. "Prison Barge Arrives at East River Pier" Ibid., 27 October 1987, B24. Also see "Army Corp Grants One-Year Approval For Prison on Barge," Ibid., 5 August 1989, A29.

7. Gary L. Jayne and Julius A. Laurent, "Design and Construction of an 800 Bed Floating Detention Facility," (Avondale Industries, Avondale, La.) A paper presented before The Chesapeake Section, Society of Naval Architects & Marine Engineers, Curtis Bay, Md., March 23, 1993, 23.

8. Ibid., 3.

9. See Cesare Beccaria, *An Essay on Crimes and Punishment* (Philadelphia: P.H. Nicklin, 1819).

# BIBLIOGRAPHY

American Correctional Association, *The American Prison, From the Beginning, A Pictorial History,* Laurel, Maryland, ACA Publication, 1983.

Bateson, Charles, *The Convict Ships 1787-1868,* Glasgow, Brown, Son & Ferguson, 1958.

Baumgartner, Leona, *John Howard, Hospital and Prison Reformer: a Bibliography,* Baltimore, Johns Hopkins University Press, 1939.

Beattie, J. M., *Crime and the Courts of England 1660-1800,* Oxford, Clarendon Press, 1946.

Beccaria, Cesare, *An Essay on Crimes and Punishment,* Philadelphia: P.H. Nicklin, 1819.

Bewley, Christina, Muir of Huntershill, Oxford University Press, 1981.

Blumenthal, Walter Hart, *Brides from Bridewell, Female Felons sent to Colonial America.* Rutland, Vt., Charles E. Tuttle Co. 1962.

Bolton, G. C., "William Eden and the Convicts," *Australian Journal of Politics and History,* Volume 26 No. 1, 1980.

Byrnes, Dan, "Emptying the Hulks, Duncan Campbell and the First Three Fleets to Australia," *The Push from the Bush, A Bulletin of Social History,* Armidale, New South Wales.

Cadogan, Edward, *The Roots of Evil,* London, John Murray, 1937.

Campbell, Charles, *Serving Time Together, Men and Women in Prison,* Fort Worth, Texas Christian University Press, 1980.

Campbell, Duncan, *Duncan Campbell letterbook* in two volumes (unpublished), Mitchell Library, Sydney.

Chandler, David, *Waterloo, The Hundred Days,* New York, Macmillan, 1981.

Clay, W. L., *Our Convict Systems* and Jebb, Sir Joshua, *Reports and Observations on Discipline and Management of Convict Prisons,* published in one volume by Garland Publishing Inc. New York & London, 1985.

Coldham, Peter Wilson, *Bonded Passengers to America, Volume I, The History of Transportation 1615-1775,* Baltimore, Genealogical Publishing Co., 1983.

Coman, Katharine & Kendall, Elizabeth, *A Short History of England,* New York, MacMillan, 1907.

Delderfield, Eric R., editor, *Kings and Queens of England,* New York, Dorset Press, 1988.

*Dictionary of National Biography,* published by Oxford University Press since 1917.

Duncombe, Thomas H., *The Life and Correspondence of Thomas Slingsby Duncombe* in two volumes, London, Hurst and Blackett, 1868.

Fisher, John, *The Australians, From 1788 to Modern Times,* New York, Taplinger Publishing Co., 1968.

Forbes, Thomas R., "Coroners' Inquisitions on the Death of Prisoners in the Hulks at Portsmouth, England in 1817-1827," *Journal of the History of Medicine and the Allied Sciences,* Volume 33, set 2, 1978.

Griffith, Major Arthur, *Millbank Penitentiary, an Experiment in Reformation,* London, The Grolier Society, 1875.

*Hansard's Parliamentary Debates,* Third series, Volume LXXXIX, 19 Jan. 1847 to 15 Feb. 1847.

Harvie, Joseph C., *History of the Convict Ship "Success",* (According to the author, this booklet was written and published by him aboard the deactivated prison hulk *Success.*) 1895, second edition 1913.

Hogg, Brigader O. F. G., *The Royal Arsenal Volume I,* London, Oxford University Press, 1963.

Howard, D. L., *The English Prisons, Their Past and Future,* London, Methuen & Co. Ltd., 1960.

Howard, John, *The State of Prisons.* London, J.M. Dent & Sons, publishers, 1777, 1780 and 1784 editions; reprint 1929 by E.P. Dutton, New York.

Hughes, Robert, *The Fatal Shore.* New York, Alfred A. Knopf, 1987.

Ignatieff, Michael, *A Just Measure of Pain,* New York, Pantheon Books, 1978.

Johnson, William Branch, *The English Prison Hulks,* Chichester, Sussex, Phillimore & Co. 1957.

King, Jonathan, *The First Fleet, the Convict Voyage that Founded Australia,* South Melbourne, The MacMillan Co. of Australia, 1982.

Manwaring, G.E. and Dobree, Bonamy, *The Floating Republic,* London, Frank Cass & Co. 1935.

Mayhew, Henry & Binny, John, *The Criminal Prisons of London.* London: Frank Cass & Co., 1862; Reprint, A.M. Kelly, New York, 1968.

McGhee, Edward G. and Hildebrand, William H., editors, T*he Death Penalty, a Literary and Historical Approach, Selected Materials,* Boston, D. C. Heath Co., 1964.

Mitchel, John, *Jail Journal, or Five Years in British Prisons,* Glasgow, 1876.

Neild, James, *The State of Prisons in England, Scotland and Wales,* London, John Nichols & Son 1812.

New York Times

Parliamentary Papers—Sessional Papers, House of Commons

    House of Commons Journals: 1778 Volume 36

    House of Commons Journals: 1779 Volume 37

    Report of Select Committee on Penitentiary Houses: 1812 Volume II.

    Instructions of Inspector of Hulks, Aaron Graham to his Captains: 1812 Volume II.

    Papers relating to Convicts on the Rivers Thames and Medway and Portsmouth and Langstone Harbours: 1814-1815 Volume 11.

Report of Aaron Graham to Commons, Nov. 18, 1814 and Report of the Select Committee: 1814-1815 Volume 11.

Instructions to John H. Capper, Superintendent of the Several Ships and Vessels for confinement of Offenders under Sentence of Transportation: 1816
Volume 18.

Biannual reports submitted by Superintendent of the Hulk Establishment, John H. Capper, to the Home Secretary:

October 16, 1816: 1816 Volume 18

January 20, 1819: 1819 Volume 17

August 12, 1818: 1819 Volume 17

January 25, 1825: 1825 Volume 23

January 21, 1826: 1826 Volume 24

July 26, 1826: 1826-1827 Volume 19

January 27, 1827: 1826-1827 Volume 19

January 2, 1829: 1829 Volume 18

July 25, 1831: 1831-1832 Volume 33

January 29, 1835: 1835 Volume 11

July 29, 1839: 1840 Volume 38

February 29, 1844: 1844 Volume 39

April 23, 1845: 1845 Volume 37

Report of the Governor General, Bermuda: 1849 Volume 43.

Correspondence of John H. Capper and Home Secretary, Sir George Grey, January 29 and February 10, 1847: 1847 Volume XLVIII.

Report of Inquiry by William John Williams, the Hulks at Woolwich, May 28, 1847 and Minutes of Evidence: 1847 Volume 18.

Report of the Manager of the Convict Hulk Establishment, Herbert Voules for year 1848: 1850 Volume 29.

Report of the Managers of the Convict Establishment for 1849: 1850
Volume 29.

Report of the Directors of Convict Prisons for 1854: 1854-1855 Volume 25.

Report on the Hulk Establishment: 1857 Volume 23.

Report of the Chairman and Directors of Convict Prisons, January 1858: 1857-1858 Volume 29.

Parliamentary Papers— The House of Lords:

Report of Lords Select Committee for Millbank: 1835 Volume 11.

Testimony of John H. Capper, House of Lords Select Committee, (*Die Martis Maii 1835*): 1835 Volume 11.

Pike, Douglas, *The Quiet Continent*, Cambridge, The University Press, 1962.

Playfair, Giles, *The Punitive Obsession, an Unvarnished History of the English Prison System*, London, Victor Gollancz Ltd. 1971.

Potter, John Deane, *The Art of Hanging*, Cranbury. N.J., A.S Barnes Co., 1965.

Pugh, Ralph B., *Imprisonment in Medieval England*, Cambridge, The University Press, 1968.

Quennel, C.H.B. and M., *A History of Everyday Things in England Volume III*, London, B. T. Batsfort Ltd., 1933.

Rhind, Neil, "Transportation and the Blackheath Connection." Unpublished paper read before the Greenwich History Society at the Local History Library, Blackheath, London, on October 23, 1991.

Rigden, Reg, *The Floating Prisons of Woolwich and Deptford*. London: A Borough of Greenwich publication, 1976.

Savage, Henry, *The Newgate Calendar*, Hartford, Conn., Edwin Valentine Mitchell Inc., 1926.

Smith, Abbot Emerson, *Colonists in Bondage*, Chapel Hill: University of North Carolina Press, 1947.

*The Times of London.*

Vaux, James Hardy, *Memoirs*, London, W. Clowes, 1819.

Whittingham, Ferdinand, *Bermuda, A Colony, A Fortress, A Prison,* London, Longman, Brown, Green & Roberts, 1857.

# APPENDIX A

## The British Prison Hulks

| Ship | Year placed in service | Est. time in service | Typical prisoner count | Station |
|---|---|---|---|---|
| Tayloe | 1777 | 3 months | 100 | Woolwich |
| Justitia (1st) | 1777 | 25 years | 265 | Woolwich |
| Censor | 1777 | 20 years | 250 | Woolwich |
| Reception | 1777 | 5 years | 100 | Woolwich |
| Stanislaus | 1780 | 22 years | 230 | Woolwich |
| Chatham | 1787 | 2 years | 125 | Plymouth |
| Dunkirk | 1788 | 5 years | 375 | Plymouth |
| Lion | 1788 | 12 years | 270 | Gosport |
| La Fortunee | 1788 | 15 years | 330 | Langstone Harbour |
| Ceres | 1787 | 10 years | 220 | Woolwich |
| Prudentia | 1794 | 8 years | 300 | Woolwich, Langstone |
| Captivity | 1802 | 34 years | 450 | Gosport, Devenport |
| Laurel | 1802 | 18 years | 200 | Portsmouth Harbour |
| Portland | 1802 | 13 years | 300 | Langstone |
| Retribution | 1804 | 30 years | 450 | Woolwich, Sheerness |
| Zealand | 1810 | 3 years | 470 | Sheerness |
| Justitia (2nd) | 1814 | 34 years | 475 | Woolwich |
| Leviathan | 1818 | 27 years | 580 | Portsmouth |
| Bellerophon | 1816 | 9 years | 480 | Sheerness |
| Ganymede | 1820 | 19 years | 240 | Chatham, Woolwich |
| York | 1820 | 30 years | 500 | Gosport |

| | | | | |
|---|---|---|---|---|
| Dolphin | 1824 | 8 years | 650 | Chatham |
| Discovery | 1824 | 6 years | 200 | Woolwich, Deptford |
| Hardy | 1825 | 9 years | 100 | Tipnor |
| Euryalus | 1825 | 18 years | 385 | Chatham |
| Dromedary | 1825 | 30 years | 300 | Woolwich, Bermuda |
| Antelope | 1824 | 30 years | 300 | Bermuda |
| Coromandel | 1829 | 25 years | 275 | Bermuda |
| Weymouth | 1829 | 7 years | 230 | Bermuda |
| Fortitude | 1831 | 13 years | 475 | Chatham |
| Leven | 1836 | 4 years | 80 | Deptford |
| Thames | 1840 | 6 years | 150 | Deptford, Bermuda |
| Stirling Castle | 1840 | 15 years | 350 | Portsmouth |
| Warrior | 1840 | 15 years | 400 | Woolwich |
| Owen Glendower | 1842 | 20 years | 485 | Gibraltar |
| Tenedos | 1846 | 16 years | 300 | Bermuda |
| Medway | 1850 | 12 years | 100 | Bermuda |
| Defence | 1850 | 7 years | 300 | Portsmouth, Woolwich |
| Unite | 1847 | 10 years | 200 | Woolwich |
| Briton | 1848 | 8 years | 200 | Portsmouth |
| Sulphur | 1848 | 1 month | 200 | Woolwich |
| Hebe | 1848 | 2 years | 200 | Woolwich |
| Wye | 1847 | 1 year | 200 | Woolwich |
| Morning Star | 1848 | 2 years | 200 | Woolwich |

# APPENDIX B

*Instructions, Rules and Regulations to be followed in governance of the Convict Hulk Establishment, issued by the Home Secretary to the Superintendent John H. Capper on November 22, 1839, filed with the Report of William John Williams, May 28, 1847: House of Commons Sessional Papers: 1847 Volume 18.*

1. You are, by virtue of the Acts of Parliament relative to the transportation of offenders, to take upon yourself the superintendence of every part of the hulk establishment in England, for the proper management of which you are to be responsible. You will, therefore, carry into effect the several orders and directions specified in those Acts, and in these Instructions, which you are to fulfill instead of those issued on 12th March, 1828, and 12th December, 1832.

2. The Overseers acting under you, and all such other officers as are or shall be appointed to any of the ships employed for the confinement of offenders, except Chaplains and Surgeons, shall constantly reside on board the respective ships to which they are appointed; and whenever any Overseer or officer in charge of any such ships has occasion to leave the same, he is to give strict orders to the next officer not to quit her during his absence, so that one or the other may always be the commanding officer on board; and that officer is to obey such orders.

3. The Overseer of each ship, or officer acting as such, is to enter in a book, to be called the "Prisoners' Register Book," the name of every prisoner, and make correct entries respecting the particulars enumerated in the several headings thereof. He is to keep an "Occurrence Book," in which is to be entered all occurrences of importance in each day, noting therein the Surgeon's having visited the ship or any omission thereof, and the times of the Chaplain's attendance on board. He shall be ready at all times to examine into complaints made on the part of a prisoner, and shall proceed immediately to take such steps as may appear to him to be necessary for redressing the same, referring to you for instruction in every case of importance or emergency. Whenever the Overseer or officer acting as such, shall have occasion to inflict any punishment on a prisoner, he shall enter the date in the Occurrence Book, with a full account of the offence for which it was inflicted.

4. The Overseers and other officers are to exercise the powers entrusted to them with strict justice and humanity, but with firmness and decision; and to exemplify in their own persons and deportment that cleanliness, temperance, decency, and orderly behavior, which they are commanded to enforce among all convicts. They are on no account to hold unnecessary discourse with any convict, but must confine themselves to giving their instructions and directions with as little conversation as possible. They are absolutely prohibited from all kind of traffic whatever with the convicts under any

pretext; neither are they to derive any profit or advantage from any provisions or other articles provided for the convicts' use.

5. The Overseers are to be careful that all the officers and guards punctually do their duty; and in the event of any vacancy happening by death, illness, or otherwise, the next officer in seniority is to do the duty, until you shall have had an opportunity of inquiring whether he is a proper person to fill it up; and as an encouragement to all the officers on board the respective ships, the Overseers are from time to time to send you an impartial account of their behavior. And in every case of vacancy of any of the officers, you are to notify the same to me, with the name of the successor whom you, from his good behavior in the service and qualifications, may deem a proper person to fill such vacancy.

6. The Overseer, or officer in command of each ship, is to visit daily every part of the ship, and to see that it is well ventilated, and kept in the most perfect state of cleanliness. The hammocks are to be lashed up and taken down every morning before the convicts go on shore to work, and to be brought upon deck to be aired. The decks above and below are to be washed twice a week at the least, and to be swept fore and aft regularly every morning and afternoon, and oftener if necessary.

7. The Officers and Guards upon duty are to overlook the convicts throughout the whole of he night, and the superior officers upon duty are occasionally to go between decks, and ascertain that the Quarter-masters and Guards are so overlooking and watching the convicts.

8. The Overseers and other officers are to be particularly attentive in watching and making minutes of the behavior of the convicts from time to time, so that they may be able to judge of them properly and form an opinion of their disposition to reform. They are also faithfully to report any departure from the regulations, in order that the same may be entered in a book to be kept for that purpose, to be called the "Offence Book."

9. The following regulation is to be observed with respect to those prisoners who are not intended to be sent abroad. Every prisoner is to serve two years certain, as a period of punishment, without any reserve earnings; and, after that time, to be eligible to commence a period of probation. The period of probation is invariably to commence when the prisoner has mustered eight times (that is, two years) either good or very good. This, and his subsequent character, is to determine the duration of his period of probation. But, in case of misconduct during the period of his punishment, that period is to be continued until he raise himself in the scale by his good conduct, so as to possess eight good musters without blemish. When a prisoner enters his period of probation, his reserve earnings are to commence, and continue until his ultimate liberation; subject, however, to be withheld for misconduct. The cells throughout each hulk are to be numbered consecutively, beginning from the lower deck upwards— and prisoners of the worst character, or during their period of punishment, are to be classed in the lower deck, and rise upwards as they progress in character, from the lower to the middle, and from the middle to the upper deck; so that the highest number shall be on the upper deck, and contain the men of best character.

10. The Overseers and other officers are not to keep any pigs or poultry on board any of the ships.

11. The Chaplains, who are to be in priest's order, are to read the common form of prayers and preach a sermon every Sunday throughout the year, and on Christmas-day and Good Friday, in the chapels on board the respective ships; and in case of the absence of any Chaplain by illness, or for reasons allowed by you, he shall provide a substitute to officiate for him. His absence, and the cause thereof, is to be entered in a book, which he is to keep for that purpose. The Overseers and other officers belonging to the establishment on the duty, are constantly to attend Divine service. The officers are to take care that no convict absents himself from chapel during Divine service, and that every convict be clean in his person and dress, and that no improper behavior be shown during the time of service. In case any prisoner shall declare himself of a religious persuasion dissenting from the Established Church, and shall express a wish to be attended by a minister of the communion to which he belongs, he may apply to the Chaplain for permission for such minister to attend, which permission shall be granted to such minister at reasonable times; but he must confine his ministration to the prisoner requiring his attendance. The Chaplains shall consider it part of their duty to visit any prisoner who may request their attendance; and, for the purpose of obtaining every information as to the moral state of the convicts, a weekly report shall be furnished by the Overseer, or officer in command, to the Chaplain, of all offenses committed in the preceding week, with the names of the offenders and punishments inflicted, with a view to interposition by way of advice when expedient. The Chaplains are to keep a register of all such offenses and punishments; they are to give notice to the Overseers of any misbehavior or improper conduct of any prisoner or inferior officer which may come within their knowledge or observation, and to represent to you whatever may appear to them worthy of notice and suggest whatever they may conceive likely to benefit the prisoners or tend to their reformation. The Chaplains are to have access to the Occurrence, Register, and Offence Books, and are twice in every year, viz, on the 1st of January and 1st of July, to transmit to you a faithful report of the behavior and improvement, or otherwise, of the convicts under their charge, in which reports they are to specify the religious and moral condition of the prisoners.

12. The Chaplain is to visit every prisoner who may request his spiritual aid and assistance, and impart suitable admonition and religious instruction generally to all the prisoners as occasion may require. He is to attend the sick in the hospital, and read prayers therein at least two days in each, and show himself at all times ready and desirous to afford such spiritual advice and consolation to the sick as they may stand in need of, and administer the Sacrament to such persons as, in his judgment, are fit for receiving the same, at least twice in every year; and, according to his discretion, distribute among the prisoners any books or tracts provided for their edification. He shall concert with the Overseer, or officer in command, such arrangements, in respect to the schools, as may be consistent with the convenience of the service, and shall select portions of Scripture to be read to the prisoners in the chapel and respective wards, when they assemble for that purpose, which is not to be less than three evenings in each week. On the death of any convict the Overseer or officer in command is to give the Chaplain timely notice, so as to ensure his attendance at the funeral, which is never to take place without the Burial Service being performed, and one of the officers of the ship, with six at least of the convicts, attending; unless, in any case, it may not be deemed expedient to inter the body of any convict dying on board the hulks in the usual place appropri-

ated for that purpose, and the same is to be minuted in the Occurrence Book. The Chaplain is to visit the school at least once a week, and to read prayers in the chapel one evening in the week, and the Chaplain of the ship appropriated for boys is to visit the school twice or oftener in each week, and two evenings in each week to read prayers in the chapel, and perform Divine service twice on each Sunday.

13. The Surgeons belonging to the establishment are to attend all sick prisoners and Officers and Guards residing in the hulks, and are to visit the respective hospitals and the several ships under your superintendence once a day at the least; and they are to inquire into the mental as well as the bodily state of every sick person and at all times to be ready to render assistance when called upon so to do. In difficult and dangerous cases they are to attend as often as the state of the patient may require. Each Surgeon is occasionally to go over the ship to which he is attached, as well as the hospital, and see that they are properly ventilated; and shall occasionally inspect the quality of the provisions dressed and undressed. The Surgeon or Assistant-surgeon shall examine all prisoners on arrival in the ship; and in case any prisoner be brought on board in a state which he deems improper, he will report the same to you. The Surgeon is occasionally to see every prisoner, for the purpose of paying attention to such as may appear to him out of health, although they may not complain; and he is upon such examination, to see that the prisoners are cleanly and properly clothed, reporting any defect to the Overseer or officer in command of the hulk. Each Surgeon is to keep a Journal for your inspection, containing the names of the convicts in the hospital, the nature of their diseases, and the manner of his treatment of them during their continuance therein; he is from time to time to state to you any article of extra bedding, clothing, food, or liquors which he shall consider necessary for the use of the sick prisoners, in order that you may be enabled to judge of the propriety of furnishing the same; and in cases of great emergency, he is to procure any such extra articles, and report to you his having done so, without delay.

14. Upon complaint being made by any convict of his being too ill to go on shore to labour, the Overseer or officer commanding the ship is to defer sending such convict on shore until he shall have called upon the Surgeon to examine into the convict's complaint; and if the Surgeon shall, after examination, report that he is unfit to work, the officer commanding the ship is to follow the recommendation of such Surgeon, either by detaining such convict on board, or causing him to be removed to the hospital, there to be taken care of until he shall be recovered; and when the Surgeon shall report that such convict is fit for labour again (of which he is to give the Overseer the earliest notice), he is to removed from the hospital back to the ship to which he belongs, and sent to labour as theretofore. The Surgeon is daily to visit every convict punished by solitary confinement, or upon reduced allowance of provisions, and to attend every infliction of corporeal punishment.

15. The Overseer or officer in command of each ship is to make a minute, in his Occurrence Book, of the Surgeon's having visited the ship and hospital as aforesaid, or of any neglect thereof, and a book is to contain the entries of all convicts sent thereto and the discharges therefrom; and during their continuance on that book they are to be checked of their common provisions on the ship's book. The greatest care is to be taken of the hospital bedding, and all furniture and utensils, etc., used therein. The officers in charge

of the respective hospital vessels, and Surgeons belonging thereto, are to see that no abuses or irregularities are suffered therein, and that the wards and every part of the hospital be properly ventilated and kept in the most perfect state of cleanliness. The officer in charge of the hospital is also to keep a book, to be called the "Occurrence Book," in which is to be stated the times of the Surgeon visiting the hospital, and the attendance of the Chaplain upon the sick.

16. The Overseer or officer in charge of each ship is to cause all the healthy adult convicts to be sent daily on shore to labour, when the weather will permit; and none are to be suffered to remain on board during the working hours, except such a number of shoemakers and tailors as it may be necessary to employ in repairing the convicts' clothes, and such other convicts as may be requisite for doing the duty of the ship. The convicts so sent on shore are to be employed only upon the public works carrying on at the several places where the ships may be stationed; and the hours of labour on each day of the week (except Sunday) are not to exceed, in the months of October, November, December, January, February, and March, nine hours, and in the months of April, May, June, July, August, and September, 10 hours. As far as practicable you will cause the most burthensome labour to be allotted to prisoners who are serving the first period of punishment, and on their entering the second portion of their sentences or period of probation, they are to have less laborious work assigned to them. The boy convicts, confined in the ship specially appointed for that purpose, are to be kept on board such ship, and employed in making clothing and other articles exclusively for the convict service; they are not to be sent on shore except for air and exercise, and then at such times only as may be deemed expedient, either upon the suggestion of the Medical Officer or Overseer of the hulk; and they are to be victualled upon the following scheme of diet, via.:—

Daily Allowance to every Boy confined on board the Boy Convict Hulk.

| Day of the week | Bread | Cheese | Beef w/Bone | Oatmeal | Potatoes | Salt |
|---|---|---|---|---|---|---|
| Sunday | 1 lb. | .. | 7 oz. | 6 oz. | 3/4 lb. | .5 oz. |
| Monday | 1 lb. | .. | 7 oz. | 6 oz. | 3/4 lb. | .5 oz. |
| Tuesday | 1 lb. | .. | 7 oz. | 6 oz. | 3/4 lb. | .5 oz. |
| Wednesday | 1 lb. | .. | 7 oz. | 6 oz. | 3/4 lb. | .5 oz. |
| Thursday | 1 lb. | .. | 7 oz. | 6 oz. | 3/4 lb. | .5 oz |
| Friday | 1 lb. | .. | 7 oz. | 6 oz. | 3/4 lb. | .5 oz. |
| Saturday | 1 lb. | 3 ozs. | .. | 6 oz. | .. | .5 oz. |
| Total: | 7 lbs. | 3 ozs. | 42 ozs. | 42 ozs. | 4.5 lbs. | 3.5 oz. |

17. The prisoners are on no account to lie suffered to work for any officer, or any person belonging to the establishment; neither are they to be allowed to work for any person on shore, and they are not to be suffered to work on Sunday.

18. The Overseers or officers in command of the respective hulks are to class all the convicts according to character, in the following manner: —A book is to be kept on board each ship, to be called the "Character Book," in which are to be entered the names of all the convicts; and on the first Sunday in every quarter, in the presence of the Chaplain, officers, and Quarter-masters, they are to be mustered, and the character which each convict may by his conduct during the last quarter have deserved, is to be ;marked against his name, in the manner following, by the Overseer, who is to make known to each convict the character so given him at each quarterly muster.

*Form of Character Book.*

Very Good ................................................................. V.G.

Good ......................................................................... G.

Indifferent ................................................................ In.

Bad ........................................................................... B.

Very Bad ................................................................... V.B.

By this mode of classing the convicts they will be aware of the character given them by their officer which, it is hoped, will be a stimulus to them so to behave themselves as to lead to their removal into the highest class, from which class selections are to be made of those who have served more than one-half of the term of their respective sentences, and certified by the Overseer and Chaplain, in order that you may make further inquiries into their case and prior character previous to your reporting thereon to me, that I may be enabled to judge of the propriety of recommending them to Her Majesty as deserving of a free pardon. The convicts, after they are classed, are to be kept in separate compartments on board the respective ships; and upon no account are they to be allowed to mix with any other class than that to which they belong.

10. One moiety [half-share] of the daily allowance of two-pence, how granted by the Admiralty and Ordnance Boards as a reward for the prisoners' labour, is to be expended for them by the Overseer, in the purchase of white bread and vegetables only: but on no account is a prisoner to be allowed to have any part of the said money in his own possession. The other moiety is to be reserved: and, on their discharge, you are to pay to them such part thereof as they may be deemed entitled to receive, under the ninth clause of these Instructions: but in no case is a prisoner to receive any part of this gratuity, unless his conduct has been such as to render him deserving of their indulgence.

If any convict at labour, or otherwise, should misbehave himself, the officers and guards appointed over him are not to beat him, but in ordinary cases to use mild and persuasive means to induce him to alter his conduct; and if these should fail, the Overseer is to punish him on board the ship, according to the nature of his crime, either by reducing his daily allowance of provisions for a term not exceeding seven days, or by confining him in a dark cell, with no other provisions than bread and water, for a term not exceeding seven days, or by moderate whipping; but in no case is such whipping to take place upon adult prisoners until you are made acquainted with the nature of the offence for which the punishment is proposed to be inflicted, and your approval thereof is obtained. The punishment in any case is not to exceed 24 stripes; and the Overseer is to make a minute in the Occurrence Book of the name of the convict, the name of the complainant, the nature of the crime, and the punishment inflicted. When the punishment is corporeal, it is to be inflicted in the presence of the rest of the convicts, for the sake of example; but it is never to take place unless the Surgeon is present, in order that he may judge how far the state of the prisoner's bodily health will admit of such punishment. The Surgeon is also to visit daily every convict under punishment, and to report to the Overseer if it should appear dangerous to his health.

21. A daily account of the convict's labour is to be kept, and transmitted by every Sunday's post to you in London, with an abstract of every material occurrence that may have taken place during the preceding week, and a weekly account of their labour is to be annexed to the quarterly account.

22. A daily allowance of provisions is to be issued to the convicts, according to the following scheme of diet, a copy of which is to be kept constantly hung up upon each deck, so that the convicts may always know what they are entitled to receive:—

| Day of of week | Oatmeal | Soft Bread | Biscuit | Beef w/bone | Cheese | Salt | Small Beer |
|---|---|---|---|---|---|---|---|
| Sunday | 7 ozs. | 1 lb. | 4 ozs. | 14 ozs. | .. | 1/2 oz. | .. |
| Monday | 7 ozs. | 1 lb. | 4 ozs. | .. | 4 ozs. | 1/2 oz. | 1/2 pint |
| Tuesday | 7 ozs. | 1 lb. | 4 ozs. | 14 ozs. | .. | 1/2 oz. | |
| Wednesday | 7 ozs. | 1 lb. | 4 ozs. | .. | 4 ozs. | 1/2 oz. | 1/2 pint |
| Thursday | 7 ozs. | 1 lb. | 4 ozs. | 14 ozs. | .. | 1/2 oz. | |
| Friday | 7 ozs. | 1 lb. | 4 ozs. | .. | 4 ozs. | 1/2 oz. | 1/2 pint |
| Saturday | 7 ozs. | 1 lb. | 4 ozs. | 14 ozs. | .. | 1/2 oz. | .. |
| | | | | | | | |
| Each Convict per Week | 3 lbs. 1 oz. | 7 lbs. | 1 lb. 12 oz. | 3 lbs. 8 oz. | 12 ozs. | 3 1/2 ozs. | 1 1/2 pints |

Prisoners who may be kept on board the respective hulks for the purpose of making or repairing convict clothing, or preforming the necessary duties of the ship, are to be allowed half a pound of biscuit per diem, on six days in the week, in addition to the foregoing daily allowance of food, in order to place them on the same footing as the prisoners who are sent on shore to daily labour.

You are to use every possible means to prevent convicts from selling any part of their allowance one to another, or to any other person, and you are to be careful that no other than standard weights and measures are used.

23. The officer, having the guard upon deck, when the provisions which are furnished daily by the contractors are brought on board, is to attend with the Purser or Steward,

in order to see them weighed and measured; and if any of the provisions should be damaged, or otherwise unfit for use, or found short of weight or measure, an immediate report thereof is to be made to the Overseer, or in his absence to the First mate, who with the assistance of the Surgeon (if he should be then on board) will inspect the same; and such as they shall find unfit for use, if acknowledged so to be by the contractor, or decided so to be upon the arbitration required by the contracts, are to be returned upon the contractor's hands, and an equal quantity of good provision in lieu thereof is to be demanded immediately; and if bad provisions should again be sent on board on the same day, the overseer or Purser is to cause them to be returned, and purchase an equal quantity of good provisions in the market, and charge the amount to the contractor, making a minute thereof in the Occurrence Book; and you are to take credit for the same in your account at the end of the quarter, when you are to deduct the amount from the contractor's account.

24. When the provisions are issued for the convicts' use, the Overseer is to direct the officer having charge of the deck, with the Steward and two convicts (to be chosen daily from their own body), to see them weighed and measured, and delivered to the cooks to be dressed; and as the presence of two of the convicts is calculated and intended to prevent, on their part, all just cause of complaint respecting the weight and measure of their provisions, the Overseer is carefully to enforce their attendance; and for a neglect of this precaution on the part of the Overseer, no excuse whatever will be admitted. A minute of their names is to be made daily in the Occurrence Book.

25. Upon no account are the convicts to be allowed to have any spirits or strong beer. If any officer, guard, or other person, should be detected supplying them therewith, the Overseer is immediately to report the same to you. No convict is to be permitted to see his friends, unless he has conducted himself in such a manner as to entitle him to that favour. The interview between convicts and their friends is only to take place in the presence of an officer, and then only at reasonable and stated times.

26. The convicts are on no account to be suffered to take up their allowance of meat raw; but the Overseer is to see that every convict belongs to a regular mess; and those employed on board must have their provisions served to them with the rest of the convicts.

27. The following yearly allowance of clothing, if required, may be issued by you to each convict, viz., two jackets, three pair of breeches, three shirts, four pair of stockings, three pair of shoes, two hats, two neckhandkerchiefs, one waistcoat, and one blanket; and a Guernsey frock once in a two years to such prisoners as may stand in need thereof; provided, nevertheless, that if the nature of the work upon which the convicts may be employed shall require a greater consumption of clothing than is stated in the above rate of allowance, you will be at liberty to distribute such extra clothing as may appear absolutely necessary in such cases. And the Overseers are to furnish you, at the end of every quarter, with an account, in the Pay Book, of the several articles which may have been issued; and on no account is any convict to wear any other clothing than the suits provided for them before mentioned.

28. The clothes of bedding of convicts who may be discharged, have made their escape, or died, (except such of the latter as may have died of fever or any contagious disorder, in which case the Surgeon's opinion of the propriety of preserving the same is to be taken,)

are, after having been duly ventilated, to be carefully preserved, and issued by you to such of the others as shall stand most in need of them.

29. Upon every convict being brought to the hulks, he shall be washed, cleansed, and purified, and the clothes in which he shall be then clothed shall be burnt, if necessary; otherwise they are to be carefully preserved, and sold, and the produce thereof brought to the public account; and the money, if he has any, is to be kept in the hands of the Overseer, and accounted for by him in a book to be kept for that purpose, an abstract of which he is to deliver to you at the end of each quarter, in the following Form: —

1st January. A.B. in hand.......................................................................... £

Received since .................................................................. _____

31st March. Expended this quarter ................................. _____

'Remains ................................................................. £_____

But no prisoner is to be allowed upon any pretext whatever to have money in his possession, and any money found on the person of a prisoner, or secreted in or on board the ship, or in the works, by or for him, is to be forfeited and carried to the public account.

If convicts, escaping or dying, leave any money behind them, a memorandum of such money is to be minuted in the Occurrence Book on the day of the escape or death, and the overseer is to sign his name thereto, and to report the same to you in the account before mentioned. Upon the discharge of any convict you are to provide him with such decent clothing as you may deem necessary, a nd and also a sum of money for his immediate subsistence, which sum shall not exceed three pounds, in case his reserved earnings shall not amount to that sum.

30. A book is to be kept in the office, in which every occurrence of the day is to be entered; and every day the following minute is to be inserted in it:—

Total number of convicts victualled, of which
    were on shore at work.
    kept on board for ship's duty.
    sick, in the hospital.
    old and infirm, incapable of labour.
    shoemakers, tailors, and others, employed on board.

31. Whenever a convict effects his escape, the Overseer is to make strict inquiry into the cause thereof, and to leave no means untried to recover him; and if he should find the escape has been occasioned by the negligence of any officer or other person belonging to the ship, he is to make a minute of the circumstances in the Occurrence Book, and transmit a copy thereof to you; and if proof can be had of any officer or other person being concerned in effecting the escape of any convict, you are to suspend the officer, and proceed against him or others concerned as the law directs. The name and description of every convict making his escape, should be sent immediately to the Editor of the "Police Gazette," at the Police Court, Bow Street.

32. The boats and men belonging to the establishment are never to be employed for the purposes of private pleasure; and no convict is to be put into a boat as part of her crew, except upon public duty.

33. The officers are to make seizure of all cards, dice or tokens for gambling, in possession of any convict, and note is to be made in the Occurrence Book of the name of the convict upon whom they were found.

34. No fee or gratuity of any sort is, on any consideration whatever, to be taken by any officer or servant belonging to the establishment, either from the contractor who supplies the provisions and clothing, or from any person having access to the ships on any other account.

35. No convict is allowed to go without an iron upon one or both legs. Those employed on board are to be locked down with the rest of the convicts during the night, and they are to be clothed similar to other prisoners, without distinction.

36. The Overseers or officers in charge of the respective ships are, without delay, to make you acquainted with all extraordinary circumstances that occur on board their ships, or which in any manner relate to the convicts, so that no time may be lost in your repairing on board, whenever your presence is required.

Given at Whitehall, the 22nd day of November 1834.

NORMANBY

# INDEX

Printed in the United Kingdom
by Lightning Source UK Ltd.
9822700001B